❖ ❖ ❖ ❖ ❖ ❖ ❖ ❖ ❖ ❖

Recruiting, Training, and Retaining New Employees

Jack J. Phillips

with the assistance of
Sharon L. Oswald

Recruiting, Training, and Retaining New Employees

Managing the Transition from College to Work

Jossey-Bass Publishers

San Francisco   •   London   •   1987

RECRUITING, TRAINING, AND RETAINING NEW EMPLOYEES:
Managing the Transition from College to Work
by Jack J. Phillips

Copyright © 1987 by: Jossey-Bass Inc., Publishers
433 California Street
San Francisco, California 94104

&

Jossey-Bass Limited
28 Banner Street
London EC1Y 8QE

Library of Congress Cataloging-in-Publication Data

Phillips, Jack J., date.
Recruiting, training, and retaining new employees.

(The Jossey-Bass management series)
Bibliography: p.
Includes index.
1. Recruiting of employees—United States.
2. Employees, Training of—United States. 3. College
graduates—Employment—United States. I. Oswald,
Sharon L. II. Title. III. Series.
HF5549.5.R44P49   1987   658.3'14   86-46332
ISBN 1-55542-042-7 (alk. paper)

Manufactured in the United States of America

JACKET DESIGN BY WILLI BAUM

FIRST EDITION

Code 8720

❖ ❖ ❖ ❖ ❖ ❖ ❖ ❖ ❖ ❖

A joint publication in
The Jossey-Bass Management Series

Consulting Editors
Human Resources

LEONARD NADLER
ZEACE NADLER
College Park, Maryland

Contents

Preface

The scenario is repeated often. After interviewing several companies for potential employment, a new college graduate receives and accepts a job offer. Initially, it appears to be a good match between applicant and company. Having visions of a successful career in a meaningful job with a reputable firm, the new graduate begins work. After a few days, however, the excitement begins to diminish. The warm friendliness co-workers extended during pre-employment visits seems to have cooled. The entry-level job appears to be rather mundane and boring, not nearly the challenging opportunity described by company recruiters and in company literature. After a few months, feeling disappointed and frustrated, the new graduate leaves for what he or she perceives to be a better opportunity.

The problems of college graduates entering the job market can frequently be traced to improper transitions from college to workplace. The transition process can be said to center around programs for entry-level recruiting, orientation, and training and education, as well as job assignment decisions. Too often these programs are so unstructured that they cannot meet the needs of new graduates or the organization. Moreover, misunderstandings are rampant concerning the needs and aspirations of entry-level graduates and about what they expect on the job. Mistaken ideas often get their start in recruiting, where potential employees develop false expectations. Once graduates have joined the organization, other problems surface because of inadequate communication among new employees, transition program coordinators, and management. These problems, however, are not created entirely by the organization. In many cases, graduates' unrealistic perceptions about the "real world of work" are to blame. Nevertheless, the burden is usually on the organization to try to clear up misunderstandings before graduates are employed and to continue to communicate with them after employment so that unrealistic expectations are alleviated.

Realistically, no matter what is done, not all graduate recruits will stay with any organization, and no one should expect them to. However, if the current retention rate can be doubled, a considerable dollar savings can be realized. With today's emphasis on job-related education and training, it is not unusual for a company to spend $30,000 to $50,000 to prepare a college graduate for an entry-level professional, technical, or supervisory position. This is particularly true for management and sales positions. Thus a trained graduate recruit's unexpected departure is not only a tremendous financial loss but also the loss of a potential resource.

For most organizations, in good economic times, the low retention rate of college graduates after a three-year period is horrendous. Yet many organizations return again and again to college campuses in search of new graduates, with the hope that a small percentage will stay with them. Other employers simply "give up": rather than try to recruit college graduates, they wait until after they have gained experience to lure them into their organizations. While this may be a short-range solution to an immediate problem, the long-range consequences may be devastating. There must be continuity in college recruiting programs and, at the same time, effective methods to ease the transition of these new college graduates.

A successful entry process integrates the needs of an individual with the needs of an organization in a formal program. If both sets of needs are satisfied, the organization should have a productive college graduate who will build job tenure and make a contribution. This book presents proven ways to design, implement, and monitor an effective entry-level transition program for new college graduates. Drawing on the experiences of organizations that have implemented successful transition programs in a variety of settings, this book will serve as a useful guide to creating a new program or to improving an existing one. The information it provides will help readers:

- assess and improve the organization's attitude toward new college graduates
- establish work-study programs that minimize or prevent transition problems
- select graduates best suited for the organization's entry-level professional jobs
- design an effective orientation process for new college graduates
- develop and implement a formal education and training program
- structure meaningful and challenging work assignments for new graduates
- evaluate the effectiveness of a formal transition program

This Book's Functional Approach

Several theoretical models have been put forth that focus on the transition process (labeled "employee socialization" in much of the literature). Each of these approaches analyzes the transition process from the point of view of the person hired. Thus, practitioners in organizations have difficulty using such models in deciding how to correct transition problems. The model upon which this book is based is called a functional approach. It consists of seven transitional stages which relate to the organizational functions that address college recruits' experience during organizational entry:

1. *recruiting,* in which organizations identify and select the most appropriate candidates, taking specific steps to minimize transition problems
2. *pre-employment education,* in which organizations begin the adjustment process long before new graduates arrive for employment
3. *orientation,* which occurs in the first few days of employment and is critical in the adjustment period of new graduates

4. *education and training programs,* both formal and informal, which prepare graduates for their jobs or improve the skills they need to succeed
5. *adaptation,* which includes a variety of activities that help graduates adjust to the organization
6. *job assignments,* whether temporary learning projects or permanent duties, in the area or department in which graduates will work in the future
7. *evaluation* of the entire process, which provides for necessary adjustments or improvements

This seven-stage model constitutes a comprehensive framework on which an organization can construct a useful, efficient transition process.

Overview of the Contents

Chapter One begins with a full description of the problems that occur as new graduates try to adjust to full-time work. It examines the differences between the cultural environment of the campus and that of the workplace. The seven steps in the functional approach to building or improving a transition process are illustrated through a series of actions that can be taken to improve the transition process.

Chapter Two examines a variety of work-study programs that can minimize transition problems in the first place. Work-study programs, which allow organizations to interact with students who are still in college, can take the form of cooperative education, internships, summer employment, part-time employment, and college partnerships. All offer fertile opportunities to tackle the transition issue early in order to prevent problems.

Chapter Three focuses on recruiting and selection, the first of the seven stages of transition. Emphasizing the selection of colleges and thorough preparation of recruiters, it outlines how recruiting programs should be developed and implemented. It explains selection systems currently in use that ensure proper matches between organizations and students. Recruitment sources, discussed along with recruiting literature, are very important to the adjustment process.) Much of the material in the chapter focuses on realistic recruitment, which gives new graduates the opportunity to learn much about the organization, the job, and the work environment, thereby diminishing potential problems.

The next two stages of transition—pre-employment education and orientation—are the topic of Chapter Four. Pre-employment education refers to educational activities that occur prior to the first day of employment. Pre-employment education enables organizations to economically tackle the transition problem before putting graduates on the payroll. Orientation—the activities surrounding the first few days of employment—is also discussed in this chapter. Orientation strategy, components, and content are thoroughly examined. Once again, the focus is on realistic communication—that is, on essential information presented in an unbiased manner to adequately prepare graduates for the adjustment process.

Chapter Five presents the most important stage of transition: the formal and informal education and training programs aimed at either preparing graduates for their jobs or strengthening the skills they need to be successful in their assignments. Determining individual interests and needs, developing program content, and communicating program information are fully explored in this chapter. A variety of educational opportunities or training programs are presented that organizations can use to minimize problems during the transition process. The most effective approaches are discussed in detail.

Chapter Six focuses on adaptation activities and job assignments. Adaptation activities that organizations can undertake include conducting effective performance reviews, providing support and recognition for graduates, increasing communications with graduates, and developing high expectations for them. Job assignments are discussed from three angles: the job environment, how jobs for new graduates should be structured, and the supervisors in both temporary and permanent assignments.

Evaluation, the final stage of transition, is the subject of Chapter Seven. Practical and proven evaluation techniques are presented, including instrument design, the use of evaluation data, and how to communicate results to target audiences.

The final chapter, Chapter Eight, discusses the various administrative aspects of ensuring that the transition program functions smoothly and efficiently. It includes such items as staffing requirements, budgets and costs, reporting relationships, compensation practices, the role of the program coordinator, and management support—all important facets of an effective program. An integral part of the chapter focuses on ways to involve management in the transition process, including enlisting them as mentors.

Who Should Read This Book?

This book will be useful to human resource professionals in any organization that recruits new college graduates for entry-level professional, technical, and supervisory positions. Within such organizations, human resources (HR) managers, employment managers, HR planning coordinators, and professional recruiters will find it particularly applicable to the work they do with new college graduates. It will help them to formulate or reform programs for recruiting and selecting new college graduates and for implementing personnel policies and compensation practices to support new graduates. This book will also inform the efforts of professionals who assign jobs to graduates and who monitor their success.

Staff members in the area of human resources development (HRD)—including trainers, training coordinators, HRD managers, and educational directors—will find this book especially applicable to the establishment of education and training programs to prepare college graduates for entry-level jobs. This book is designed to provide assistance in every phase of that process, from identifying training needs and developing programs to monitoring results.

College placement officials—placement directors, job counselors, and career coordinators—who are responsible for providing career and job assistance to new graduates will find this book valuable. It directly addresses issues of helping new graduates select organizations for future employment and providing them with assistance in the transition from campus life to work life.

This book offers insight into the transition process that can help college placement officers give realistic advice to new graduates who are selecting an employer.

Middle and top management—key staff executives, technical managers, administrative managers, and line managers—will be able to use this book to understand the problems of new graduates and the need to support an effective transition program. Managers are ultimately responsible for the success of any formal transition program—and are usually held accountable for a graduate's survival. This book will show them how they can participate in, support, and reinforce the implementation of a formal transition program for new graduates.

Finally, new college graduates in any major designed to lead to professional-level employment in a formal organization need useful insight into what organizations are doing (or should be doing) to ease the transition process and to help new employees succeed. Although this book is not intended to be a handbook for new graduates, quite often such a person's success depends on how he or she can adjust to an employer's current policies. This book should help new graduates develop realistic expectations along with an understanding of management's needs and intentions.

Insofar as this book addresses how to deal with a particular target group's transition into the workplace, it is unique. Most books related to this subject fall into four major categories. First, very good books are available on the topic of education and training. They outline how programs are developed, how the media are selected, how to make programs work, and how to evaluate the results. None that we know of focuses on how to develop an entry-level program for new college graduates.

Second, excellent books have been written on selection procedures and campus recruiting. Focusing on how new graduates are identified and selected, these works stop short of outlining what should be done to ensure that new recruits become viable members of the organization.

Third, there are books on career development that show organizations how to develop careers for all individuals. They offer exercises and techniques to help organizations get the most out of their resources and allow employees to reach their maximum potential. However, to our knowledge, none of these career development books focuses on new graduates and the particular problems and aspirations they bring to an organization.

Fourth, books on survival in organizations provide practical and helpful advice but tend to focus on what the individual should do rather than on what the organization should do. Until now no book has been available that showed employers how to capitalize on the high potential resources in their new college graduates by ensuring that new graduates stay with the organization.

Acknowledgments

No book represents the work of the author alone. Many colleagues have contributed useful insights to the process of refining and developing ideas that ultimately resulted in this book. Also, several organizations have supplied material used in this book; they are given credit in the text.

The individuals who have influenced, supported, or encouraged me in this effort are almost too numerous to mention, but some people deserve special recognition. Sharon Oswald has provided valuable assistance as well as numerous helpful suggestions. Parts of chapters One and Three were supplied by Sharon.

Members of the Human Resources Management faculty of the University of Alabama provided helpful suggestions and were very supportive of this effort. Anson Seers, in particular, provided helpful advice on the initial proposal for this work, and Charles Odewahn encouraged and supported one of the research projects outlined in these chapters.

Perhaps the most important acknowledgment goes to my boss, Carl Register, president of the Southern Division of Vulcan Materials Company. Without his support and encouragement, this project would not have been possible. Carl understands the problems faced by new college graduates as they enter the world of work and plays an important part in making new graduates feel welcome at Vulcan.

Much gratitude goes to Leonard and Zeace Nadler for their meticulous review of the manuscript and very thoughtful suggestions for improvement, the vast majority of which were implemented.

Special appreciation goes to Debra Rousseau, who not only typed the manuscript but also provided valuable suggestions for improving it.

Finally, my warm thanks and appreciation to my wife, Johnnie, and to my daughters, Dawn and Jackie, who provided encouragement, support, and assistance throughout the effort. They made many sacrifices to help this book become a reality.

Birmingham, Alabama   Jack J. Phillips
March 1987

To my parents, Agnes L. Phillips
and the late George W. Phillips,
who prepared me well
for the transitions I've encountered.

The Author

Jack J. Phillips has more than twenty years' experience in human resources, culminating in his present assignment as manager of human resources and administration at Vulcan Materials Company, Southern Division, Birmingham, Alabama. (Vulcan Materials is a Birmingham-based Fortune 500 firm that produces construction materials and chemicals.) Prior to this appointment, Phillips was training and development manager and personnel manager, respectively, at Stockham Valves and Fittings, also in Birmingham. He was training director for America Enka Company, a textile fiber producer in Tennessee, and has served in various capacities in training and production for nine years at the Lockheed-Georgia Company.

A native of Georgia, Phillips received his associate degree in electrical engineering technology from Southern Technical Institute, his bachelor of science degree in physics and mathematics, summa cum laude, from Oglethorpe University, and his master's degree in decision sciences from Georgia State University in Atlanta.

A frequent contributor to management literature, Phillips has authored the *Handbook of Training Evaluation and Measurement Methods* (1983), *Improving Supervisors' Effectiveness* (1985), and *The Fate of Gulf States Steel Corporation* (1985). In addition, he has contributed to *Designing and Delivering Cost-Effective Training and Measuring the Results* (1981), the *Handbook of Human Resource Development* (1984), and *Human Resource Management* (1986). In 1986, *Improving Supervisors' Effectiveness*

(Jossey-Bass, 1985) won an award from the American Society for Personnel Administration. Phillips has written more than sixty articles for professional, business, and trade publications and serves on the editorial advisory board of *Personnel Journal* and the contributing editors board of *Personnel.*

Phillips is an active member of several professional and technical organizations, including the American Society for Training and Development, the American Society for Personnel Administration, the Industrial Relations Research Association, and the Academy of Management. In addition, he has served on the board of directors of the National Management Association and currently serves on the boards of several business and civic organizations.

❖ ❖ ❖ ❖ ❖ ❖ ❖ ❖ ❖ ❖

Recruiting, Training, and Retaining New Employees

1

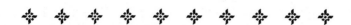

Understanding and Managing the Transition Process: Human Resource Problems and Opportunities

A manufacturing firm regularly recruits engineering graduates for its management education program, which prepares them for first-level production supervisor assignments. The highly structured, two-year program includes internal courses, outside seminars, special projects, department and plant visitations, and rotational assignments. It has been operational for more than thirty years and has produced several top executives. In one fairly typical case, the company recruited the top graduate from a reputable midwestern engineering school. The company courted the candidate for more than a year before graduation and in the recruiting process had boasted about its education program. The new graduate, with his exceptional technical and interpersonal skills, was an ideal participant in the program and should have become a fast-track manager. However, after a year with the company, the new recruit resigned to accept employment elsewhere. In his exit interview, he discussed his rationale for leaving: Although he had developed tremendous respect for the organization and expressed appreciation for the time and expense that had gone into the program, he thought it was much too detailed and too long. Upon graduation he was seeking a challenge and an opportunity to make a

1

contribution. Although impressed by the challenges of first-level supervision, in a year's time he still had not had the opportunity to prove his worth. He had little chance for contribution because most of his time was spent in a structured learning environment with no specific responsibilities. It was not what he had anticipated. After four years of extensive educational experiences, he was unprepared for yet another two years of the same thing, even if it was in a different environment.

A large aerospace firm hired an MBA graduate and assigned him to an administrative engineer position. It was a typical assignment for new MBA graduates, and many of the duties were routine and almost clerical in nature. The new graduate, who had an outstanding academic background, was not challenged and found the work vastly different from what he expected. Few, if any, of the skills acquired in the MBA program were needed on the job. He became disappointed and disillusioned, yet he did not want to change employers until he had gained some "experience." He learned to conform to group norms by finding ways to look busy and by maintaining a low profile. He settled into an unrewarding and unchallenging job. An employee who could have been a significant contributor was allowed to become a mediocre performer in an organization demanding too little from its new recruits.

A human resources management graduate was employed by the human resources department of a Fortune 500 company. Her campus activities had been extensive and she had accumulated several honors and awards. To achieve success in her new position, she had to attain the cooperation, support, and assistance from several secretarial and clerical employees. She became frustrated with her entry-level job and resented having to work with clerical employees. She frequently boasted about her academic achievements and reminded others about her organizational status, which she perceived as far above her support people. She was insensitive to the needs of co-workers and was unprepared to deal with office politics or handle interpersonal relationships. She alienated the support people, lost the respect of managers, and ultimately had to be removed after a year on the job.

These three case studies represent typical scenarios in organizations today. What do they have in common? First, they illustrate the problem of transition experienced by new graduates when they enter organizations for full-time employment. To a certain degree, all graduates face adjustment difficulties and culture shock when moving from a familiar campus environment to an unfamiliar, entry-level assignment. Second, these examples represent the tremendous cost to the organization in terms of recruitment and training. In the first example, the company's investment was estimated at over $50,000, including recruiting expenses, the graduate's salary, travel expenses, staff time, and other educational expenses. Third, the three cases represent a tremendous misuse of resources and lost opportunities for organizations to utilize talent effectively. The outcome of each of these situations could have been prevented if the organization had developed a realistic, effective approach to ease the transition from college to full-time professional work.

Basic Concepts and Definitions

As the above examples illustrate, the adjustment to full-time professional work in an organizational setting can be a traumatic experience for many new college graduates and can create problems and inefficiencies for the organization. This adjustment is sometimes referred to as "reality shock" or "culture shock" because of the vast differences between campus activities, experiences, and expectations and those in an organization. For example, the immediate work environment represents one of the most difficult areas of adjustment. The daily nine-to-five routine of most organizations is difficult for new graduates to grasp; chances are the new graduate's life was never so structured. No matter how dedicated the student or how regimented the student's study habits, the work environment is still a different world. In addition, the work environment frequently lacks exams, grades, and other types of feedback. Graduates are often uninformed about the politics of complex organizations and have little experience working with superiors, subordinates, and peer groups. Gone are the student days of three-month vacations, extended winter breaks, and long weekends; graduates no longer have the flexibility to drop courses they find unappealing or too difficult. Graduates cannot abandon uninteresting assignments, at least not without creating problems. All of these changes can spell trouble for an unprepared new recruit.

The *Random House Dictionary* defines the word *transition* as a movement or passage from one position, state, or stage to another. This definition best describes the process experienced by new college graduates as they secure permanent employment. Although the term *socialization* is often used to describe the adjustment process, it is too broad for this particular setting. Because of this, the term *transition* will be used throughout this book to refer to the movement of new graduates from full-time student to that of professional, full-time employee in an organizational setting.

The *transition process* involves such activities as recruiting, orientation, job training, and performance feedback. Through these various activities, new college graduates learn the skills, behaviors, and attitudes necessary to satisfy the organization and succeed on the job. The *stage of transition* is the specific functional component in the transition process, such as recruiting or training. The specific activities of the transition process vary considerably among organizations, yet the overall goal of transition remains essentially the same: to integrate new college graduates into the organization so as to meld individual goals with organizational goals to the fullest extent possible.

This book discusses new college graduates employed in *professional jobs* in organizations, in positions such as engineer, accountant, sales representative, nurse, social worker, teacher, statistician, or supervisor. Consequently, it is directed to those organizations that recruit and employ graduates in professional occupations. This is not always the case; some college graduates are unable to find employment in their chosen professions and settle for nonprofessional work. In these cases, transition is not as important as survival to the new graduate, and consequently the organization may not emphasize programs to ease the transition.

In this book the term *new graduate* is used to describe a recent college graduate who has little or no professional experience, including a graduate degree holder who is seeking or has secured a professional-level job. Although most of these graduates are in the twenty-one to thirty age group, a small percentage are in an older group who obtained their degrees later in life. Because these older graduates usually have some work experience, their adjustment to professional jobs poses different problems from those who are new to the work force. Some material in this book will highlight the problems of this older group.

The term *organization* refers to an employing entity in which various groups and levels of employees perform tasks to meet goals or objectives. Organizations include businesses, corporations, governmental agencies, hospitals, nonprofit institutions, associations, and virtually all other organized bodies of employees.

The importance of the transition process, as a factor in organizational performance, rests on three assumptions. First, new graduates taking on new jobs are in a state of eagerness. They desire and seek opportunities to learn the requirements of the new job. They want to succeed and make a contribution. Second, the transition process occurs regardless of the management's attention to it, that is, whether it is planned and coordinated carefully by management or whether it occurs informally through trial and error. Efficient and effective management of the transition process, however, can generate significant savings for an organization. Third, the performance of the organization depends upon the collective contributions of those individuals employed for important and responsible jobs. The sooner new graduates are able to perform, the greater the organization's performance. Because of these assumptions, the transition process becomes an important factor that demands significant attention from management (Van Maanen, 1978).

Transition Problems

If every organization would examine the needs of new graduates at every stage of the transition period and address these concerns individually, adjustment difficulties and resulting problems would be minimized. Most organizations, however, do a poor job of managing the transition process. Because of the difficulty of measuring the performance of new graduates, many organizations either do not realize this problem exists or do not realize its magnitude. When they do recognize the problem, they blame the schools or the graduates. Few organizations believe that they contribute to the dilemma, although most graduates can trace adjustment problems to the initial employer after graduation. Poor recruiting practices and selection methods, improperly designed orientation programs, ineffective education and training programs, and inadequate compensation and performance appraisal programs all contribute to the problem.

Transition problems are not new to organizations. Schein (1964, p. 69–70) described a new graduate as seen through the eyes of management.

1. The college graduate is overambitious and unrealistic in his expectations regarding the possibility of advancement and increased responsibility; he tends to think that his education has given him some kind of special privilege to move up fast in the organization.
2. The college graduate is too theoretical, idealistic, and naive to be given an important initial assignment; he must first be "broken in," educated to the practical problems, and shown how the theories taught in college may fail to fit the practical facts in industry.
3. The college graduate is too immature and inexperienced to be given much responsibility; he would not be able to cope with the realities of the job situation and would likely fail.
4. The college graduate is too security-conscious and too unwilling to take risks.
5. The college graduate is unwilling to recognize the difference between having a good idea and the process of selling the implementation of that new idea; he is unskilled in communication and unwilling to work hard to get his ideas across.

6.   The college graduate is potentially a highly useful resource for new ideas, new approaches, and better management, but he must be broken in before this resource becomes available to the organization.

Although the situation has improved, the description is still reasonably accurate. Perhaps not all company managers have these preconceptions about new graduates, but those who do often deal with the issues unsatisfactorily. Criticism, rather than coaching, usually takes precedence. Recent reports have identified some of the problems of today's new graduates as they try to adjust to the business world (Behrman and Levin, 1984; Jenkins, Reizenstein, and Rodgers, 1984). Among the conclusions are:

- Graduates have a short-term orientation instead of a long-term view.
- Graduates are more prepared for data gathering, manipulation of information and personnel, and problem solving than for problem identification, goal determination, and implementation.
- Graduates are more interested in the activities of large organizations than medium-sized, small, and new enterprises.
- Graduates lack preparation in interpersonal relationships, individual development, and the "whole life." They have too much interest in career goals.
- Graduates are unable and/or unwilling to make the difficult decisions enterprises need for survival.
- Graduates are inept and uncomfortable in environments where they must balance corporate and social goals.

Although these studies primarily focused on MBA graduates, the problems also exist at the bachelor degree level. Even Secretary of Commerce Malcolm Baldridge has been critical of the attitude of business school graduates. Speaking at the American Stock Exchange Conference in June 1984, Baldridge stated that "They all want to go up in the ivory tower . . . instead of getting down on the factory floor" (Cheit, 1985).

One recent study of more than 100 organizations in the eastern states provides some insight into the perceived strengths and weaknesses of newly hired college graduates as they enter full-time professional work (Kaplan, 1985). Personnel professionals in the study identified written communication skills, oral communication skills, and a lack of understanding of the business organization as the three most important weaknesses of new graduates. In the same study, 214 seniors in schools of business administration were also asked how they perceived the strengths and weaknesses of college graduates. The results, presented in Table 1, show that the students do not perceive the same weaknesses as employers. Thirty-one percent of the students ranked lack of experience as a perceived weakness, compared to only 9 percent of the personnel professionals. Personnel professionals mentioned technical skills and personal qualities most often as strengths of new graduates, whereas the students perceived personal qualities, academic preparation, and willingness to work hard as their most important strengths.

A typical label placed on the new graduate is "unmotivated." Many managers believe that the new graduate responds to the world differently than they do. Does this make the new graduate unmotivated? In their eyes it does. No two generations are motivated by the same things. In general, today's new graduates had more material items when they were growing up than did those of previous generations. And, unlike earlier generations, many of today's graduates grew up with both parents working and no one at home when they returned from school. Hard work and higher wages might have motivated previous generations, but new graduates of today are seeking satisfaction, recognition, and involvement. While lack of motivation may be what a manager sees in the new graduate, in reality it might be a lack of understanding or differences in perceptions.

Similarly, many managers think that the expression "poor attitude" is often synonymous with new graduates. Attitudes are partially derived from the environment. If the organization has already stereotyped the new graduate as naive and immature, it is likely that the environment is highly frustrating—one which could

Table 1. Perceived Strengths and Weaknesses of
Recent College Graduates.

Strengths	Personnel Groups	Students
Technical skills	26%	10%
Personal qualities	24%	49%
Willingness to work hard	22%	28%
Academic preparation	21%	30%
Computer skills	14%	5%
Weaknesses		
Written communication skills	38%	18%
Oral communication skills	36%	19%
Lack of understanding of business organization	32%	8%
Unrealistic career expectations	21%	4%
Reluctance to work hard	17%	13%
Lack of experience	9%	31%

Source: Kaplan, 1985.

easily breed a poor attitude. In addition, conflicting or unclear expectations of new graduates could create attitude problems.

Still another adjustment problem associated with the transition process is a true lack of preparation on the part of new graduates. Preparation for a new job involves more than just a good education. Many managers have found that graduates might have a good, broad overall perspective of the work but are unable to perform specific job duties without intensive training. This can be frustrating to both the employee and the organization because the organization may expect the graduate to grasp the work immediately, and graduates see this as an unrealistic expectation. While poor preparation in the graduate's field can cause initial transition problems, it is only a fraction of the preparation necessary to succeed on the job. Behrman and Levin (1984) addressed the changes needed to improve graduates' job preparation. This report recommended sweeping changes in business school curricula to develop skills that will help students adapt to and succeed in the organization. Specifically, it called for improvements in teaching communication and negotiation skills and in instilling a personal commitment to continue lifelong education and development.

Another report on business education criticized schools for overlooking important human, organizational, and communication skills (Cheit, 1985) and advocated additional courses aimed at improving these skills. Some schools schedule formal course work to deal with communication, motivation, and the related leadership skills needed in evolving forms of organizations. Professionally active schools address these needs through a variety of joint efforts with executives and business firms.

Most of the above problems can be summarized into two words, "unrealistic expectations"—on the part of both employers and new graduates. The perfect employee for any organization would be one that is made in a factory, is molded to the organization's specifications, and contains all of the "right" qualities. Likewise, the perfect organization would be one where graduates can realize their potential and work in a rewarding, challenging environment.

Adjusting to the Culture

The culture of an organization is the most important contextual variable that affects the adjustment of new graduates to the organization. The organizational culture sets the stage and background within which new graduates must function. Lack of knowledge about the culture can spell disaster for new graduates. Likewise, knowing and understanding the culture is essential to a successful transition.

Culture shock is a result of moving from one setting (college), where the cultural signals are familiar, to a new setting (organization), where the culture is vastly different and unfamiliar. The expectations of new graduates are higher than (or vastly different from) what they actually experience on the job. Students in their last year of undergraduate or graduate work are at the "top" of the organization, having moved "up the ladder" from freshmen. They know the key players (students, professors, administrators), heroes, traditions, rituals, rules, standards, taboos, "must do's," requirements for success, informal groups, powerful factions, dress codes, specific language patterns, special "hangouts," information sources, clubs, and social groups. They have developed many friendships and have several sponsors. They are familiar with campus facilities and services. Contrast this with the culture of a new organization with a completely different environment, mission, and life-style. None of these categories is familiar to students. It is no wonder why new graduates experience adjustment problems.

Sometimes the little things cause problems for new graduates. For example, in some organizations addressing an immediate supervisor on a first-name basis is taboo; in others, *not* addressing the supervisor on a first-name basis is taboo. New graduates must understand the myths, legends, values, taboos, norms, roles, coalitions, and networks that form the organization's culture. Information on these aspects of culture should be provided to the student early, even in the recruiting process. This is particularly true for strong-culture organizations where the culture shock may be a more serious problem. The following represent the major cultural aspects that should be communicated to new graduates in the various stages of transition.

History and Traditions. Every organization has an important history. New graduates should know the organization's beginnings, including the founders and their legacies, the organization's heroes, and the important legends and myths. Information on history and traditions should answer three important questions: Why does the organization exist? How did the organization evolve? and Who were the major characters in its evolution? An understanding of how all of this affects the organization's present work life gives new recruits a decided advantage. Many organizations have colorful pasts, complete with stories about individuals who have developed present cultural norms. In strong-culture firms, such as IBM, Procter & Gamble, and Neiman-Marcus, stories about founders who shaped the organization and developed the culture are plentiful, even today. This information helps new graduates understand the organization's present goals, mission, guiding principles, and philosophy. Although, ignorance in this area may not spell disaster for new graduates, a firm grasp of history and traditions can ease the adjustment. Many organizations have developed a documented history of their past that should be required reading for new recruits, possibly even before they arrive for employment.

Informal Organizational Structures. Along with every formal organizational chart comes an informal structure that affects adjustment. Dominant professional groups, powerful factions, coalitions, and informal networks exist in almost every type of organization. In many organizations, certain functional areas are more powerful or influential than others. For some it is engineering, technology, or research; in others it is marketing or finance. What may be a strength in one organization could be the kiss of death in another. For example, strategic planning is a very powerful function in some organizations but a dead end in others.

Powerful factions and coalitions can boost a career or destroy one. In every organization, several individuals can be identified as powerful and influential. New ideas, suggestions, plans, and policies must have support or they will not work. These factions or coalitions exist at every level, even in small work units, where at least one or two key individuals have influence over work practices and policies. New projects or proposals will not succeed without their support or endorsement. Being unaware of these groups and their influence can spell trouble for new recruits. Knowing these key players and being able to work with them can minimize adjustment difficulties.

Informal networks exist in every organization, and they provide the setting for key employees in a division, department, or plant to meet socially in activities ranging from a friendly poker game to dinner parties. New graduates should be aware of such networks and possibly pursue membership in them. Membership may be particularly difficult for female or minority group graduates because the groups operate informally and sometimes exclude members who do not "fit in." Although new graduates may not be able to enter these networks, they should know about them and at least stay out of their way.

Informal Practices. Every organization has its informal rules, do's and don't's, taboos, norms, and dress codes that are not necessarily spelled out in the personnel policy manual. Yet ignorance of these informal practices can create large problems for new recruits. For example, in some organizations, it is a taboo to criticize top management, while in others critical comments are welcome. It may be taboo to be late for a meeting in some organizations, while in others it is acceptable behavior. Even though the normal workday does not begin until 8:00 A.M., some organizations expect new recruits to be at their desks at 7:30 if they are serious about their careers or staying with the organization. In others, an 8:15 arrival does not cause problems. A few organizations expect new recruits to use lunch hours for business or social contacts. In others, new recruits are sometimes expected to work through the lunch hour. And finally, in some organizations, Saturday or weekend work is "required," even if job demands are not pressing, while in others it is discouraged and taken as a signal that an individual cannot manage the job in five days.

The experiences required to progress in an organization usually have informal elements. In some organizations, it is essential to have a position in operations in order to progress to middle and upper management. In others, a tour of duty in sales and marketing is an absolute requirement for a top job. The sooner new graduates understand these informal rules, the more likely they are to make correct career choices and decisions.

Almost every organization has certain informal physical appearance standards, such as prohibiting beards, moustaches, long hair and certain types of clothes. In some organizations male employees must wear coats and ties, while in others they are not required to do so. The differences relate to culture norms. If dress codes are important, they should be communicated to new graduates before the issue causes problems.

In some organizations there is a preferred family relationship situation. Some want their new graduates to be married so as to be "settled in." Others prefer single graduates who usually have fewer problems with extensive travel or long hours. In almost all cases, being gay is a widespread informal taboo.

Social and Professional Activities. Each organization has a variety of social, professional, and recreational activities that are a part of its culture. A preferred recreational activity is common in many places, possibly even related to the job. For example, in many sales departments, new recruits are expected to play golf regularly with clients and customers. In some organizations, playing tennis after work is popular. In others, racquetball at lunch is the preferred recreation. It is important to know the favorite hangouts where people meet and socialize. It may be a favorite lunch spot, bar, or gymnasium. Membership in certain associations or clubs is sometimes required of new recruits. For example, a few organizations required all new graduates to become members of the Toastmaster's Club, where they learn to develop self-confidence and oral presentation skills. A few larger organizations expect all new professional, technical, and supervisory employees to become members of the organization's chapter of the National Management Association, which develops leadership skills through meetings and other chapter activities. Graduates must know about these opportunities and expectations.

Informal Communication and Language Patterns. Organizations have their own language patterns with their own interpretations, phrases, and meanings of words. This aspect of culture goes beyond the organization's unique terminology related to its processes, services, and products. For example, the names "hard charger," "fast tracker," "superstar," and "competitor" are typical labels given to aggressive employees, but they may have different nuances from one organization to the next. In some, the meaning is positive, referring to a hardworking, outstanding individual who is rapidly advancing. In others, the meaning is negative, referring to an individual who will do anything to get ahead. Examples of other descriptive labels are "bean counter," "bloodsucker," and "mover and shaker." Even the meanings of simple phrases can be different based on the culture. For example, the comment "It won't work here" may mean that the idea is "not appropriate within the context of the situation," or it may mean that "you are embarrassingly naive to even suggest such a stupid idea."

Rumor mills and grapevines are an important part of the informal communication network. Rumors are not always based on fact and can be vicious and can even destroy an early career. New graduates need to know about the dangers of rumor mills and avoid participating in them. Communication grapevines, prevalent in every organization, quickly spread information, often exaggerating the circumstances. Graduates should listen to grapevine information very cautiously, placing little reliance on its accuracy. However, they should also realize that sometimes a basis does exist for the information on grapevines: It just might be an early signal of a more formal announcement.

Dominant Themes and Ideologies. Strong-culture organizations often have major themes or ideologies that they practice and communicate to employees. These may be traced to the organization's traditions and history and may be expressed in slogans, logos, or mottos within the organization. For example, some firms have an obsession for quality. Others have a fundamental belief in complete customer satisfaction. Still others may have a strong sense of need for correct procedures, standards, and policies. High-tech, high-growth firms may have a strong concern for employee autonomy, independence, and entrepreneurship.

Some organizations have a strong concern for political, religious, or life-style beliefs. For example, some firms are extremely conservative in regard to life-style and moral values away from the job, while others have little concern about what employees do away from work. Some firms set very high ethical and moral standards for their employees and expect all of them to strongly adhere to these beliefs, while others may practice a philosophy of "anything goes as long as it is not illegal." Some firms integrate religious beliefs with work practices, providing time off for prayer meetings and religious studies at the worksite.

How does all of this relate to the new graduate? In short, new graduates almost always have a difficult time adjusting to the culture of the organization. Ignorance of the culture makes the adjustment more difficult and can even result in severe culture shock. New graduates must have information on all aspects of the culture outlined above. Organizations have several opportunities for providing this information in the various stages of transition (see Chapters Three through Six). Employers do not ask new graduates to mortgage their souls and operate on the principle of blind obedience, but they do ask new recruits to adopt fundamental beliefs and values perceived to be necessary for success. The culture in an organization is vastly different from that on campus and must be thoroughly understood by new graduates or they will be doomed to fail.

Impact of Transition Problems

The employment of new college graduates may be compared to the implementation of capital improvement projects: They are investments that must be protected—resources for increasing productivity and profitability that ensure the long-term survival of the organization. Top management must ensure that these investments provide adequate returns and are utilized in the most efficient and effective way.

Potential Outcomes. The various activities, actions, and assignments in the transition process can result in several different outcomes. Schein (1978) discusses two basic eventual outcomes—the new employee stays with the organization or leaves—but the matter is actually more complex. Four distinct eventual outcomes may be identified, three of which are unsatisfactory from an organization's viewpoint:

1. New graduates adjust to the organization, conform with the culture, and perform in a satisfactory or above-satisfactory manner. They become permanent members of the organization, committed to its goals and values. They successfully make the transition to become productive members of the organization—the ultimate goal of transition programs.
2. New graduates become frustrated, disappointed, and lose interest in the organization. They seek employment elsewhere once they realize that the organization does not match their interests, values, or abilities. They become voluntary turnover statistics, representing a tremendous loss to the organization.

This is probably the most undesirable outcome and, in many cases, can be prevented with a comprehensive, functional approach to the transition problem.

3. New graduates have difficulty adjusting to the nature and scope of the job, which is not perceived as a challenge. They seek a comfortable state of low activity and at a performance level below their capabilities. They "get lost" in the organization, conforming with certain informal groups that encourage average or below-average performance, or they remain alone. They maintain a low profile, trying to look busy and devoting energies to outside activities. Ego, self-esteem, and motivational needs are met through team sports, recreational activities, hobbies, church groups, or social clubs. Their primary concern at work is "existing."

4. One of the most unpleasant and expensive outcomes is the discharge of new graduates. As distasteful and inappropriate as it seems, this outcome still happens quite frequently in organizations. New graduates cannot adjust to the culture, conform to the organization's rules, or adapt to the job. Their performance is not what the organization expects, and they must be removed from the job. They are not motivated to seek other job prospects or cannot find other opportunities, and discharge is the only course of action. Most organizations are reluctant to take this step, relying on the individuals to correct the problems or find another job. When this does not occur, the organization takes action, usually much later than it should. Although discharge can be a positive action from the organization's viewpoint, it can hamper future recruitment efforts. Potential employees may perceive that new graduates are not given an opportunity to perform properly or were not in an environment conducive to acquiring skills and improving performance and thus lose interest in the organization as a potential employer.

These undesirable outcomes can be prevented with a properly designed and implemented transition program. Numerous research studies have shown that an effective transition program can enhance organizational performance and the well-being of new employees in several ways.

Turnover. A properly designed transition program can have a tremendous bottom line impact by reducing turnover. For example, a redesigned system for introducing professional personnel to Corning Glass Works resulted in a 69 percent decrease in the number of voluntary separations among those with three years or less service. Also, the time required for new employees to reach a desired level of performance decreased from six months to five months. On these two items alone, Corning calculated an eight to one benefit/cost ratio for the first year and a fourteen to one benefit/cost ratio annually thereafter. Texas Instruments reported similar improvements in turnover with its implementation of a program of this type (McGarrell, 1984).

Under normal conditions, voluntary turnover is greater than involuntary, and voluntary is more often studied by management due to its desire to reduce or maintain it on an acceptable level. In terms of transition programs, the most important issue is the turnover of new graduates in the early months and years of employment or "early turnover." Because early turnover is not a standard calculation among organizations, it is imperative for the organization to develop some measure of it to determine the impact of transition programs. In some organizations, early turnover can be as high as 50 percent in the first year of employment of new college graduates (McGarrell, 1984). Several research studies have demonstrated that an effective transition program can reduce early turnover. For more information, see Gomersall and Myers (1966), Kotter (1972), Mobley (1982), Jones (1986), and Fisher (1986).

Organizations must identify the reasons for turnover to help prevent it in the future. The causes of turnover can be traced to some of the stages of the transition program. A summary of selected variables from three reviews of the turnover literature shows several important relationships (Mobley, 1982). The conclusions from these reviews, which apply to all employees, are:

1.   Younger employees are more likely to leave the organization.

2.   Short-tenure employees are more likely to leave than those with more tenure.
3.   Employees dissatisfied with their jobs are more likely to leave the organization than those who are satisfied.
4.   The supervisor's style affects the employee's decision to leave.
5.   Other job factors, such as role clarity, job autonomy and responsibility, task repetitiveness, and overall reaction to the job, appear to be correlated with turnover.

All of these variables are linked to the transition process, so improvements in the transition process should affect them in a positive manner. A recent meta-analysis on turnover confirmed some of the above findings plus additional relationships; Cotton and Tuttle (1986) reported significant relationships between turnover and several work-related and personal variables. Table 2 shows several of these variables, all of which have important ramifications for transition programs. For further discussion of turnover, see Price (1977) and Mobley (1982).

Turnover Costs. The impact of turnover of new college graduates is further amplified when the cost of turnover is calculated. Although detailed dollar amounts are difficult to calculate, estimates of turnover costs, at least in major categories, can be obtained with little difficulty.

The timing of the turnover significantly affects turnover cost. For example, if the new graduate leaves after only one week on the job, the total costs may not be excessive, depending on the costs involved in recruiting, orientation, and the initial week of training or education. On the other side of the spectrum, a graduate who remains on the job for over five years has probably made a contribution that offsets the cost of recruiting, training, and other transition activities. The greatest turnover cost occurs when the new graduate leaves the organization just prior to beginning a full-time assignment. This time period varies considerably among organizations and may range from one week to two years, depending on the organization, the specific job, and the transition program. Turnover costs can be grouped into three major categories, ranging from the subjective and intangible to the

Table 2. Relationship of Turnover to Selected Variables
Based on the Results of a Meta-Analysis.

Work-Related	
Pay	Negative
Performance	Negative
Role clarity	Negative
Task repetitiveness	Positive
Overall satisfaction	Negative
Pay satisfaction	Negative
Satisfaction with work itself	Negative
Satisfaction with supervision	Negative
Satisfaction with co-workers	Negative
Satisfaction with promotion	Negative
Organizational commitment	Negative
Personal	
Age	Negative
Tenure	Negative
Education	Positive
Marital status	Married negative
Intelligence	Positive
Behavioral intentions	Positive
Met expectations	Negative

Source: Cotton and Tuttle, 1986.

objective and tangible. (These costs are based on the turnover of graduates while involved in a formal transition program preparing for full-time, permanent assignment.)

One important cost of turnover is the *loss of morale* and the *tarnished image* the organization may suffer as a result of excessive turnover statistics. A new graduate who leaves the organization unexpectedly affects the morale of other recent graduates. Questions surrounding the departure are often unanswered, leaving other graduates to wonder if they should seek other job opportunities. Excessive turnover affects the functioning of the transition program and, in some cases, the performance of other graduates in the program. The organization's image in the recruiting community may be tarnished when students hear about turnover problems; this can significantly hamper the organization's ability to recruit outstanding new graduates. Additionally, excessive turnover can cause management to lose respect and enthusiasm for the transition program, resulting in a loss of assistance and support. Managers may perceive it as a waste of their time and of the organization's resources. Full support and cooperation from various levels of management are essential to a program's success.

Another important cost of turnover is *lost productivity or contribution* when graduates leave, assuming they have remained with the organization long enough to be productive or make a contribution. After a few months a new graduate usually has the opportunity to contribute through special assignments, tasks, or projects, an effort that would be missed if a turnover occurs. Ordinarily, these contributions represent necessary and meaningful assignments that are important to the organization. Because of the subjective nature of the lost productivity or contribution, it is difficult, if not impossible, to calculate the actual dollar cost. It varies greatly with the organization, specific job duties, the ability of the individual, and the length of time the individual has been with the organization. Consequently, this cost of turnover for recent college graduates is usually not tabulated and reported with much accuracy.

Probably the most significant turnover costs are the *administrative costs* connected with the various phases of the transition program. These are more objective and tangible than the other categories and can usually be calculated. For recent graduates, administrative costs can usually be grouped into the following categories:

- *Direct recruiting costs* are the direct expenses associated with recruiting graduates, including the recruiters' travel, the graduates' travel, entertainment, relocation, management's interviewing time, and other miscellaneous direct expenses.
- *Indirect employment costs* represent the indirect expenses of recruiting, including the cost of advertising, brochures, recruiters' salaries, and office and clerical expenses, as well as the expenses involved in planning and evaluating the recruiting process. This also includes the cost of recruiting and interviewing candidates who do not come to work for the organization.

- *Pre-employment education costs* are the expenses of educational activities conducted prior to the actual date of employment, including such items as meeting expenses, written materials, and travel associated with pre-employment meetings.
- *Orientation costs* include the cost of the time, materials, equipment, and facilities required in conducting the orientation program for new graduates.
- *Education/training costs* are probably the most significant expenditures for new graduates. These costs include the graduate's salary (plus the cost of employee benefits), costs for developing the education/training program and materials, the instructor's or facilitator's time and expenses, travel and lodging related to education and training, and the facilities used for conducting the programs. For outside education and training it includes the cost of seminar fees, as well as travel to the meeting sites.
- *Management/staff support costs* represent the time and expenses of management and staff activity involved in the transition program. It includes the program coordinator, mentors, and other staff members involved in planning, conducting, or evaluating various phases of the transition program.
- *Accounting, payroll, and other overhead costs* cover the costs associated with placing new graduates on the payroll system and removing graduates when they leave. Included in the overhead costs are such items as an office, desk, secretarial services, telephone, and office supplies.

This list of administrative expenses omits other employment-related expenses that are not normally associated with entry-level, professional positions staffed with new college graduates, such as agency and search fees, employment bonuses, and home purchase arrangements.

Total administrative costs can be quite significant when new graduates are employed for almost a year. Exhibit 1 presents calculations of the turnover costs for a graduate who left a firm after eleven months in a formal transition program. The graduate

Exhibit 1. The Administrative Cost of a Turnover Statistic (New Graduate Leaving After Eleven Months in a Management Education Program).

Direct Recruiting Expenses		
Prorated expenses for campus recruiting visit	210	
Travel to headquarters and to major plant	852	
Relocation costs/temporary lodging	2,054	
Subtotal		3,116
Indirect Employment Costs		
Total annual professional employment costs minus direct costs divided by the total number of new graduates employed during the year		3,109
Pre-Employment Education		
Written material mailed directly to candidate prior to employment		48
Orientation Costs		
Total costs of providing a two-day professional orientation divided by the total number participating		350
Education/Training Program		
Graduate's salary for 11 months at $1950 per month	21,450	
Employee benefits at 35 percent of base	7,507	
Direct travel and lodging for education/ training	5,259	
Prorated program development costs	2,850	
Prorated instructor/facilitator's time	3,000	
Prorated facilities/equipment expense	1,250	
Seminar/workshop registration fees	775	
Subtotal		42,091
Management/Staff Support		
Prorated program coordinator's time	3,350	
Adviser time (estimated)	750	
Other management time (estimated)	500	
Subtotal		4,600
Accounting, Payroll, Other Overhead		
Prorated payroll costs	110	
Office/work station costs	2,950	
Direct support expenses (estimated)	1,890	
Subtotal		4,950
Total Costs Invested in the New Graduate		$58,264

left voluntarily for other employment when the program failed to meet his needs. The program was designed to prepare new college graduates for first-level management positions in a manufacturing firm. This example excludes the cost of lost productivity and the intangible costs of potential morale problems and image deterioration. It shows only the administrative costs invested in the new graduate. In this example, pre-employment education costs are almost nil and orientation costs are low, but education/training costs are quite high. The estimates for the education/training costs are difficult to pinpoint in some organizations, depending on the sophistication of cost-tracking systems. The estimates for the costs of management and staff support time are almost arbitrary, leaving a possibility for some error. For a detailed presentation on developing and implementing a system to calculate and monitor education and training costs, see Phillips (1983a, Ch. 7).

These costs represent the organization's investment in the new graduate at the time of departure. They are partially offset by the positive contributions of the individual during the eleven months, but these contributions are very difficult to quantify. The contribution was estimated to be very low in this example because the new recruit was in a learning mode for most of his employment time. In other programs where new recruits are producing soon after employment, this offset can be significant. These costs are similar to the results of an MIT study, which revealed that turnover costs for information systems managers in a large manufacturing company totaled 116 percent of the annual salaries of those who terminated (Barocci and Cournoyer, 1982). For additional information on calculating turnover costs, see Hall (1981), Cascio (1982), and Blakeslee, Suntrup, and Kernaghan (1985). Even taking into account the subjective nature of the data, this example shows that the total costs are very significant and illustrates the tremendous impact of turnover on the bottom line, leaving little doubt as to the importance of designing a transition program to minimize turnover.

Performance. The second major impact of a transition program is on the performance of new college graduates, and practically every component of a transition program can affect performance. Research studies have linked transition programs to faster learning time, a greater sense of competence, and a clearer understanding of organizational goals—all of which affect performance (Gomersall and Myers, 1966; Kotter, 1972; Feldman, 1976a; Hall, 1976; Schein, 1978; Fisher, 1986).

Of the common measures that can illustrate the impact of a transition program on performance, probably the most important is the time required for a new graduate to achieve the desired or acceptable performance level. Rather than wait for new college graduates to learn their jobs through trial and error, most formal transition programs teach them to perform satisfactorily as soon as possible. The Corning Glass Works example, mentioned earlier, provides an excellent illustration of this process. When faced with an unusually high turnover rate for new professional employees, Corning redesigned its orientation system and on-the-job training program. The new training program consisted of nine seminars conducted at various intervals during the first six months of employment, coupled with the development of self-guided workbooks designed to teach employees important aspects about their jobs. Corning set up control groups for comparison with experimental groups to measure the impact of their improved transition process, and the results were outstanding. The time required to reach a predetermined performance level was reduced significantly—from six months to five months. This reduced period saved the company almost $500,000 per year (McGarrell, 1984). Employee time is very expensive for organizations, not only in terms of the salaries and benefits of new graduates but also in terms of the salaries of those who are supporting, assisting, and training these graduates. Any reduction in training time will affect organizational performance.

Another measure of the impact of a transition program is the actual level of performance an individual achieves. In general, above-average and exceptional performances are desired from college-trained talent. A properly designed transition program should enable new candidates to reach higher performance levels than new graduates who are not given the benefit of such a process. Numerous studies using data on performance levels drawn from organizations' performance appraisal programs have pinpointed measurable improvements as a result of various components of transition programs (see the studies cited above and, for additional information on measuring performance, see Flamholtz, 1985; Spencer, 1985; Phillips, 1983a; Fitz-enz, 1984; and Kearsley, 1982).

Job Satisfaction. An important outcome of a formal transition program is satisfaction. An efficient, well-organized, and well-executed transition program prepares the new graduate to tackle problems and tasks, feeling secure and confident and holding a favorable attitude toward the organization and the assignment. Numerous studies have linked transition programs to higher job satisfaction and a less stressful adjustment to the new job and organization (Berlew and Hall, 1966; Gomersall and Myers, 1966; Kotter, 1972; Feldman, 1976a, 1981; Louis, 1980; Wanous, 1980; Pearson, 1982; Fisher, 1986; Jones, 1986). Also, several studies have linked job satisfaction with job performance. One of the most significant reviews of the literature in this area was reported by Petty, McGee, and Cavender (1984). Their meta-analysis of the available studies clearly showed that individual job satisfaction and job performance are positively correlated. These results indicate that increases in job satisfaction, through an improved transition program, should have a resulting increase in individual job performance.

Organizational Commitment. One important reason for implementing a formal transition program is to strengthen the new employee's attachment to the organization. Organizational commitment has been defined as the relative strength of an individual's identification with and involvement in a particular organization. Further, according to Mobley (1982), it has been characterized by at least three factors:

1. a strong belief in and acceptance of the organization's goals and values
2. a willingness to exert considerable effort on behalf of the organization
3. a strong desire to maintain membership in that organization.

This identification can be enhanced by a formal transition program that clearly specifies the organization's goals and values, provides information on the organization in a timely manner, encourages new graduates to learn as much as possible, helps new graduates to learn as much as possible, helps new graduates become contributing members in the organization, and rewards them for their efforts. Several research studies have linked effective transition programs to stronger employee loyalty to the organization and a greater commitment to organizational values and goals (Schein, 1968; Porter, Lawler and Hackman, 1975; Wanous, 1980; Mowday, Porter, and Steers, 1982; Fisher, 1986; Jones, 1986). The important aspect of organizational commitment is that there is strong evidence that commitment is related to turnover (Mowday, Porter, and Steers, 1982; Mobley, 1982; Cotton and Tuttle, 1986). There is also evidence that commitment is a better predictor of turnover than is satisfaction (Mowday, Porter, and Steers, 1982). Therefore, both conceptually and empirically it is evident that organizational commitment is an important variable affected by transition programs. Lack of organizational commitment or loyalty is a common complaint leveled at new college graduates. Top executives want graduates to identify with their values, beliefs, and goals as soon as possible. This can only be accomplished through an effective, efficiently managed transition program.

Other Outcome Variables. New graduates are often employed in organizations with the expectation that they will be able to tackle challenging problems in the future. The skills acquired in a transition program can be applied to solving problems. Also, the infusion of bright, young talent with fresh ideas can spark many innovations. This is sometimes a rationale for hiring new graduates. A formal transition program can enhance the new graduate's ability and desire to develop innovative ideas and suggestions that can in turn improve the performance of the organization. Other variables such as stress, role conflict, and role clarity may be important outcomes of effective transition, but few studies have focused on them to date. More studies are available that tie certain parts of a transition program to one or more variables. For example, studies link orientation, training, and performance appraisal programs with performance. However, there are few studies assessing the impact of the overall transition program on individual and organizational performance.

Developing a Philosophy and Strategy for Transition

As a first step in addressing the issue of transition, an organization should examine its philosophy and strategy toward transition problems. These philosophies and strategies, which vary widely among organizations, have evolved over several years and are based on the value systems in the organization. Some organizations ignore the issue altogether, while others develop specific strategies to face the problem. Still others invest in a variety of college work-study programs aimed at preventing most transition problems prior to actual employment.

Let Others Do It. One basic approach to the problem of transition is to avoid the issue altogether by not hiring new college graduates until they have accumulated experience at another organization, usually at least two to three years after graduation. This approach is usually anchored on the belief that new graduates will change jobs after a short period of time regardless of where they work. (At some colleges, students are even encouraged by their professors to "try out" several organizations before developing a career with one.) An organization choosing this approach is avoiding the expense of training new graduates for employment elsewhere. These organizations actively recruit experienced graduates and sometimes raid other companies, particularly those with effective training programs. They feed off other organizations to satisfy their needs for new talent.

Economically, this may be the best short-term approach to the transition problem. The major advantage is that initial training costs are reduced significantly. The initial orientation and adjustment time, as well as the time for learning the new job, are significantly reduced. Also, the organization may reduce turnover costs, as experienced graduates may be less likely to leave than new, inexperienced graduates. However, letting others train and educate new graduates is a shortsighted philosophy that can have devastating effects in the long run. Imagine what would happen if all organizations took this philosophy. It would be difficult, if not impossible, for new graduates to find meaningful employment. Supply and demand forces would be out of balance, at least in the short run. In addition, many argue that organizations have a social responsibility to share the costs of developing human resources, and that refusing to recruit new college graduates is sidestepping this obligation. However, organizations facing high turnover and excessive training costs may not be too concerned with social obligations.

This approach fails to capitalize on the fact that some very capable individuals never leave an organization from the time they enter the organization after graduation. A few employees, when treated fairly and given adequate career opportunities, may stay with the organization for a long period of time, even until retirement. Thus, an organization may miss an opportunity to recruit talented and dedicated employees straight from college.

Another drawback to this approach is the reputation an organization may develop. An organization choosing to ignore recent graduates may develop an image as a pirate that preys upon others who have developed and implemented excellent training programs.

Investing in College Work-Study Programs. Another approach to minimize the problems of transition is to invest in one or more pre-employment programs for students before they graduate. These programs allow an organization to indoctrinate, train, and/or educate employees while they are still in college; the idea of these programs is that they ultimately minimize transition problems after graduation. There are five basic approaches to work-study.

1. *Cooperative education* programs give students the opportunity to alternate semesters of work and study after their freshman year. Work assignments, often with progressive responsibilities or rotation to different parts of the organization, allow students to work on specific assignments while learning the

organization and enhancing their knowledge of their field of study.

2. *Internships* allow students to work on predetermined projects or regular jobs in the organization, sometimes without pay. They are usually related to the field in which they are studying, and students may receive course credit.

3. *Partnerships with schools* involve organizations and local institutions developing a cooperative relationship. Students may visit facilities, work on projects for the organization, or attend regular courses taught by representatives from the organization.

4. *Summer employment* programs give students jobs ranging from routine, menial tasks to those specifically related to their field of study. This can be helpful in organizations with peak employment needs during the summer.

5. *Part-time employment* involves hiring students while they are attending college full time. Part-time employment allows students to learn the organization, be productive, and gain experience in their field while attending college. Two part-time students are sometimes used to replace one permanent employee, resulting in cost savings while preparing students for the reality of work life.

Some or all of these approaches can be feasible for an organization. Properly structured, they can reduce transition problems because graduates can usually move into regular professional jobs with little or no formal transition program. They are viable solutions to minimize the transition problem, important enough to warrant more attention than they now receive. Chapter Two is devoted to these preventive programs.

Strategies for Transition. When an organization decides to recruit new college graduates for professional jobs, it may adopt one or more of several basic, traditional strategies for dealing with transition.

One strategy is to *do nothing.* New graduates are placed on the job and learn through trial and error. The outcome of this approach is a function of the graduate's own discipline, initiative, and ability, as well as the cooperativeness of peer groups. This could result in an unusually high failure rate as new graduates give up, leave, or are terminated due to their failure to perform in a satisfactory manner. Although this approach is not recommended, it is still used by some organizations today, especially smaller ones. New graduates are recruited and placed on the job with little or no direction. They must sink or swim and survival becomes the most important issue.

Another strategy, although infrequently used, is the use of *debasement experiences.* This technique is designed to change value systems, lower self-confidence, and shock the new graduate into the reality of the chosen profession, career, or organization. It may involve assigning the new graduate to menial or degrading tasks in order to change values or beliefs. Gradually, new graduates "earn" the right to move to other, more productive assignments or tasks. Although this approach to transition can have some value, it can be devastating to new graduates, often leading to morale or performance problems. Ultimately it may cause graduates to seek employment where they are treated with more dignity and respect.

A third strategy is to develop and implement a *structured training program* aimed at improving job-related skills for new graduates. For example, new sales representatives go through a variety of sales training programs before being placed in the field.

A fourth strategy is to *educate* new graduates by preparing them for future jobs. This usually involves extensive internal learning experiences, outside seminars, self-study programs, special projects or assignments, and other job-related experiences. The focus is on future jobs new graduates will assume when they are fully prepared. An example is the typical management trainee program where new graduates are recruited and prepared for the job of supervisor or manager in a department, section, or plant.

A final strategy is to assign new graduates as *understudies or apprentices* to learn new jobs. New graduates work under the immediate supervision of experienced professionals performing the same job. They learn the necessary skills on the job through a one-on-one interaction. This strategy involves a combination of education and training to prepare new graduates for target jobs.

For example, a new electrical engineering graduate may be assigned with a senior engineer to learn the firm's engineering practices and to enhance the transfer of skills learned in college. In this situation, the new graduate prepares for the job of engineer but performs limited engineering functions during this transition period.

These are five basic, traditional strategies. An organization may deviate slightly from any of these five or use a combination of them to tackle the transition issue. More discussion of these strategies is presented in Chapter Five. Progressive organizations that have recognized the seriousness of transition problems use a combination of education, training, and on-the-job teachers, as well as techniques to address the problem prior to employment. This approach, called the *functional approach* to transition, is the fundamental premise of this book.

Stages of Transition

The transition process can best be described by a model having several components or stages. Numerous models have been proposed to describe this process, varying in the number of stages and the activities within each stage according to the perspective of the creator. Transition stages also vary with the organizational setting and the type of work the new employee performs. A comprehensive approach involves separate and distinct activities at each stage of transition, while in condensed programs one or more of the stages of transition may occur at the same time.

Current Models. Table 3 compares the stages of seven popular models for the transition process (or socialization, as it is called in most of these models). Although these approaches vary considerably, they do contain common elements. Generally, the early transition stages involve confrontations with organizational reality and the anxiety that accompanies culture shock. Subsequent stages are concerned with the resolution of role conflicts, clarifications of expectations and perceptions, and ultimately a commitment to contribute to the organization.

Table 3. Stages of Organization Transition (Socialization).

Feldman (1976a, 1976b) Three-Stage Model	Buchanan (1974) Three-Stage Early Career Model	Porter, Lawler & Hackman (1975) Three-Stage Entry Model	Schein (1978) Three-Stage Socialization Model	Wanous (1980) Integrative Approach to States of Socialization	Van Maanen (1976) Four-Stage Model	Pascale (1985) Socialization Steps for Strong-Culture Firms
Stage 1: Anticipatory socialization—"getting in"		Stage 1: Pre-arrival			Stage 1: Self-Selection	Step 1: Careful Selection
Stage 2: Accommodation—"breaking in"	Stage 1: First year—basic training and initiation	Stage 2: Encounter	Stage 1: Entry	Stage 1: Confronting and accepting organizational reality	Stage 2: Introduction	Step 2: Humility inducting experiences
		Stage 3: Change and acquisition	Stage 2: Socialization	Stage 2: Achieving role clarity		Step 3: In-the-trenches training
Stage 3: Role management—"setting in"	Stage 2: Performance years two, three, and four				Stage 3: Encounter	Step 4: Rewards and control systems
						Step 5: Adherence to values
				Stage 3: Locating oneself in the organizational context		
					Stage 4: Metamorphosis	Step 6: Reinforcing folklore
			Stage 3: Mutual acceptance			
				Stage 4: Detecting signposts of successful socialization		Step 7: Consistent role models
	Stage 3: Organizational dependability in the fifth year and beyond					

From a practitioner's standpoint, these models are difficult to use for several reasons:

1. Most of the models, particularly Buchanan (1974), Schein (1978), and Wanous (1980), do not sufficiently address the activities prior to the new employee's entry into the organization. The quality and effectiveness of the recruiting process, as well as the educational activities prior to arrival, can have an important impact on the success of the remaining stages of the transition process. Thus, recruitment and pre-employment education must be considered an integral part of transition.

2. These models focus on individual behavior and reactions rather than the organizational activities designed to ease the transition process. This is strictly a matter of researcher orientation. Although it is essential to understand the difficulties that new graduates encounter, it is more practical to examine transition from an organizational viewpoint in terms of typical functions that focus on transition problems, such as recruiting, orientation, education, and training.

3. These models do not facilitate adjustments in the transition process. Which organizational function must improve or change when a problem is detected? For example, a new graduate may have difficulty in adapting to the culture of the organization. This problem may very well be traced back to the recruitment process; the interests and value systems of the individual conflict with those of the organization. Examining problems by functional components makes it easier for management to pinpoint and correct problems.

4. These models attempt to describe the transition process for virtually all types of jobs and job levels. The transition process for a new employee hired to operate a drill press, however, is vastly different from that of an MBA graduate recruited to enter a fast-track development program to become a general manager. Therefore, the stages of the transition process and the activities in each stage should be specific to the type of work involved.

5. These models do not sufficiently address the evaluation of the transition process. Organizations need to evaluate the success

of the transition program during its various stages. Evaluation should include the individuals in transition as well as other organizational staff and should be considered an integral stage of the process.

Proposed Model. The model shown in Figure 1 focuses on the transition process for new college graduates. It has a practitioner's orientation, addresses the problems outlined above, and presents the transition process in the context of traditional organizational functions that focus on transition problems. These include recruitment, pre-employment education, orientation, education/training, adaptation, promotion/assignment, and evaluation.

Organizational Actions with the Proposed Model

Once an organization recognizes the extent of problems caused by an improperly designed transition program, there are a variety of options available. A few suggestions are presented below, organized around the transition model in Figure 1, and are further elaborated throughout this book. Although individually they are not necessarily innovative, collectively they provide a comprehensive approach to tackle the transition problem.

Recruitment. The transition process begins with the recruitment of the new graduate, an important component in which both the organization and the graduate make decisions to enter a partnership arrangement. Failures in this initial stage of transition cause serious problems in later stages. Recruitment can range from a lengthy, time-consuming process to a brief series of interviews with a decision a few days prior to beginning employment.

Organizations can usually improve the selection of new graduates to ensure a good match between the job and the individual. This requires organizations to evaluate schools and curricula and to focus recruiting efforts on target campuses. Recruiting procedures must be examined periodically for cost-effectiveness and timeliness. Selection methods should be reevalu-

Figure 1. Stages of Transition for New College Graduates.

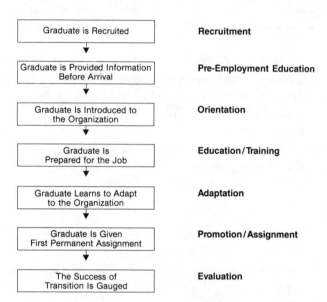

ated to ensure they are based on proper criteria that are not only valid and legal but produce the best job match. Finally, employers should make sure their procedures give new graduates a realistic preview of the type of work they will be performing. Chapter Three presents detailed actions necessary to improve the effectiveness of the campus recruiting process.

The importance of designing a recruiting program to minimize transition problems is best illustrated with an example. An applicant for an entry-level position in brand management at Procter & Gamble experiences an exhaustive application and screening process. The interviewer is part of an elite cadre that has been selected and trained extensively via lectures, videotapes, films, practice interviews, and role plays. P&G regards the selection and training of its recruiters as a crucial task. The applicant is interviewed in depth for such qualities as ability to "turn out high volumes of excellent work," "identify and understand problems," and "reach thoroughly substantiated and well-reasoned conclusions that lead to action." The applicant participates in two interviews and a general knowledge test and then goes to Cincinnati for three more one-on-one interviews and a group interview over lunch. Each encounter seeks corroborating evidence of the traits that P&G believes correlate highly with "what counts" for employee excellence. Notwithstanding the intensity of this screening process, the recruiting team strives diligently to avoid overselling P&G, revealing the company's plusses and minuses. P&G actually facilitates an applicant's "de-selection," believing that no one knows better than the candidate whether the organization meshes with his or her own objectives and values (Kaible, 1984).

Pre-Employment Education. An often overlooked opportunity to minimize transition problems is available soon after a new graduate is recruited. This stage refers to all educational activities directed to graduates from the time an employment decision is made until they report to full-time work. This period, which can extend to almost nine months for those graduates who have accepted offers in the fall to report to work the following June, represents fertile ground for pre-employment education. The climate is right for a variety of educational activities, including sending organizational publications, communicating directly with students, providing self-study materials, and conducting meetings with new graduates.

This approach has several advantages. First, it is inexpensive when compared to other stages of the transition process. Typically, prospective employees are not paid for these pre-employment activities. Second, this process enables new graduates to begin learning the culture of the organization and aligning their values with those of the organization. Third, it allows more managers and executives in the organization to be involved in the transition process. During meetings, through special communications, or in visits, key executives have an opportunity to meet new recruits and learn more about them. Pre-employment education is discussed in more detail in Chapter Four.

Orientation. The orientation period begins when new graduates arrive on the job. It provides essential information needed to enter a formal education/training program or proceed directly to the job assignment. It covers policies, procedures, benefits, compensation, and other important issues necessary for success, and, in some cases, survival in the organization. Orientation programs should be periodically analyzed to ensure they still meet the needs of new graduates. The objectives, format, media, timing, and length, as well as other design features, should be examined for appropriateness and effectiveness. The content should be examined to ensure that appropriate information is presented, including sensitive items such as pay, advancement opportunities, expectations, and basic survival techniques. Few orientations are frank with new graduates about what is expected of them in their early months of employment. Chapter Four contains additional information on the orientation stage of transition.

Education/Training. This stage includes formal and informal programs to educate and train new graduates. For those moving directly to their jobs, *training* that enhances new graduates' skills needed for the job is usually provided either on the job or in the classroom. Training programs are aimed at improving skills to an acceptable level in a brief time period. Other graduates enter formal *education* programs where they are prepared for their new jobs. In this situation it is assumed that new graduates do not possess the ability, knowledge, or skills needed to handle their new job duties; they must have additional education to prepare for their assignment.

Education and training programs should be reviewed to ensure they are effective in addressing transition issues. They must meet the specific needs of new graduates while lifting them to an acceptable performance level as soon as possible. This often requires a formal approach to training as opposed to informal practices where training may be left to chance. The program must be structured enough to meet established goals and timetables, yet flexible enough to adjust to organizational changes and the time constraints of the individuals involved. Although program content varies considerably with the target job, it probably should include training or education on interpersonal, communication, and leadership skills to help new graduates adjust to the organization and quickly become contributors. Organizations use a variety of approaches to education and training for new graduates, including internal classroom programs, outside seminars, self-study programs, job rotations, on-the-job coaching, mentors, special projects and assignments, professional societies and associations, and additional formal education. See Chapter Five for detailed discussion.

At J. I. Case Company, a division of Tenneco, new MBA graduates (called "project specialists") are assigned specific projects as the major part of their training program. The projects last three to five months and are meaningful, not "make work" assignments. The department submitting a project assigns a project manager as supervisor of the MBA graduate until it is completed. Since the initiation of the program, the program has never had a shortage of projects. In fact, there usually have been three to four times more projects than project specialists in the program.

Adaptation. Although the adaptation stage is sometimes considered a part of education and training, it should be a separate and distinct process. Adaptation describes the activities, processes, and experiences that help new graduates to adjust to the organization's culture. Ideally, new graduates will adjust to the culture of the organization, learn to live by its rules, and succeed in making a contribution. Realistically, however, adaptation does not come easily. Some graduates cannot adapt and leave the organization, becoming turnover statistics.

Much of the adaptation problem can be solved with effective performance feedback, which is more difficult to do during formal education or training programs lasting several months. In this setting, performance is sometimes not carefully evaluated because new graduates may not have an immediate supervisor, even though it is a time when more frequent, candid, and specific performance feedback is needed. Undesirable habits, poor attitudes, and unsatisfactory performance must be corrected early in the program before the new graduate becomes a turnover statistic. Ideally, performance discussions require input from both graduates and key managers, particularly supervisors in departments where the new graduates will be placed for permanent assignments. Also, the involvement of the transition program coordinator is essential since this individual may have a better vantage point from which to evaluate initial performance.

Virtually all of the initially planned assignments and activities should focus on areas that are necessary for success in the organization. MBAs joining Bain and Company, a management consulting firm, are surprised by the incredible number of meetings they must attend—company meetings, recruiting meetings, officer meetings, office meetings, case team meetings, and near-mandatory participation on sports teams and attendance at social events. The objective is to build cohesiveness, participation, and close identification with the firm. There are a set of imperatives for working at Bain: "Don't compete directly with peers," "Make major conceptual contributions without being a prima donna," "Demonstrate an ability to build on others' ideas." In aggregate, these features of Bain's culture are viewed as the underpinnings of success—both internally and with clients ("Those Who Can't, Consult," 1982). For additional discussion of the adaptation stage of transition see Chapter Six.

Promotion/Assignment. Planning and executing job assignments and promotions deserve careful thought and deliberation. In most cases graduates are selected for specific jobs, such as an accountant, engineeer, or registered nurse. In some organizations, however, graduates are recruited for a variety of potential jobs with the assignment finalized during the transition program. Even those graduates with predetermined assignments sometimes have a variety of choices within their chosen occupation. For example, an accountant may be recruited for the finance and accounting area but could ultimately be assigned to cost accounting, general accounting, budgets, credit and collection, taxes, or internal audit.

An important factor in assigning new graduates is to ensure that they are given productive, challenging, and meaningful tasks as soon as possible, but only if the graduates are adequately prepared. Although this seems a logical and obvious function, some organizations place candidates in jobs far below their capabilities, while others assign them work for which they are not prepared. Another key issue is the authority and responsibility provided to new graduates, particularly those destined for supervisory or managerial jobs. The extent of authority and responsibility should be based on the graduates' capability to make proper decisions. Graduates must have enough authority to function effectively, particularly in temporary assignments that may be part of an education or training program.

Job assignments for new graduates are straightforward at Macy's, which has an outstanding reputation for attracting and keeping top-notch college graduates. Those who enter the prestigious training program (dubbed the "training squad") have some very tough acts to follow. Both chairman of the board Edward Finkelstein and chief executive officer Mark Handler began their careers in the training squad, as did the chief executive officers of three of Macy's four merchandising divisions. Once the eleven-week program is completed, trainees begin their careers as sales managers, each in charge of a selling area. At this junior executive level, they have across-the-board responsibilities, including the analysis of sales statistics, supervision of sales personnel, merchandise presentation, inventory control, and customer relations. This high-level responsibility is considered part of the competitive advantage that Macy's offers new graduates (Koeth, 1985). Job assignments and promotions are explored in more detail in Chapter Six.

Evaluation. The final stage of transition is the evaluation of the entire transition process. Program evaluation is too often neglected, not only in the transition process but in other human resource programs. Even when evaluation is planned, it is often haphazard and incomplete. An effective evaluation process requires activities at various stages of the transition model, including:

- evaluating the effectiveness of the learning process
- monitoring the success of new graduates as they move through the various stages of transition

- measuring the overall results of the program
- calculating cost/benefit analyses
- tracking the long-term performance of graduates.

Evaluation data can be used to make program improvements as well as justify future investment in transition programs. The results should be communicated to the management group who are actively involved in the process or who must support it in the future. Chapter Seven is devoted to the evaluation stage of transition.

Coordination and Support of Transition Programs

All activities in the different stages of transition should be fully coordinated. Coordination should include a thorough analysis of reporting relationships and staffing requirements and careful control of program costs and pay considerations, both when establishing starting salaries as well as in keeping salaries competitive and linked to performance. The simple question of which department pays the salaries of new graduates in a formal transition program can affect program operation and even the program's success. The selection and training of the program coordinator is an important issue that must receive serious consideration. These and other questions must be carefully considered and appropriately answered to meet the needs of the organization.

The influence of the management group cannot be taken lightly since they can make the difference in the program's success or failure. The members of the group must have a positive attitude toward the program, be willing to support it enthusiastically, and participate in the program in a variety of ways. The most visible involvement role is that of mentors. Other types of participation range from serving on advisory committees to evaluating the success of the overall transition program. Detailed discussion on program coordination, administration, and control is presented in Chapter Eight.

Responsibilities of Colleges and Graduates

To a certain extent, every new graduate suffers from culture shock and transition problems. This book tackles the issue from the organizational viewpoint, but the problem can also be viewed from two other angles: the viewpoint of the colleges and the viewpoint of the individuals.

Colleges. Colleges and universities, and particularly the professional schools, have been criticized for creating much of the transition problem. Even the top-ranked schools face criticism (see, for example, Hacker, 1981; Brief, 1982; Cheit, 1985; and Miles, 1985). As a result, they are evaluating their curricula to improve its job-relatedness and are tying learning experiences more closely to job realities. Professional schools are constantly reevaluating their curricula to ensure that they relate to the demands and needs of the profession and the needs of employers. Accreditation standards for colleges are sometimes based on the timeliness and relevancy of the curricula as they relate to what employers need. Business schools are increasing their efforts to improve business education (Swartz, 1985), but a great deal still needs to be done.

Graduates. Students share some of the responsibility for their transition problems. Career education appears in the school system at early stages; even elementary school students are provided information about careers to stimulate interest and help them begin focusing on a career choice. However, far too many graduates obtain degrees as a result of a career choice based on faulty assumptions or misinformation.

College graduates need to select employers more carefully. Information to help graduates select an employer is scarce. The literature is flooded with materials on writing resumes, conducting an employment search, or preparing for job interviews, but little has been written on ways to identify the type of employers that provide the best match with the interests and needs of students. In tough economic times, most graduates do not have the luxury of choosing from a wide range of employers, but multiple employment opportunities are common in good economic times or when certain degrees are in high demand. In these situations students still select them for the wrong reasons, often letting location, salaries, and perceived advancement be the driving forces behind their decision when other factors, just as important, should be considered in selecting the future employer. One organization identified sixteen such factors to consider when selecting an employer, assuming that the new graduate has several employers from which to consider permanent employment.

Summary

This chapter outlined the basic problems created when new college graduates enter organizations for full-time professional employment. The adjustment problems caused by this transition affect organizational performance and represent a significant expense. The starting point in examining this issue is the organization's philosophy and strategy toward transitional problems, and a variety of possible strategies were discussed in this chapter. All new graduates experience adjustment problems. Organizations interested in minimizing these problems should examine the functions that relate to the transition process. A model focusing on this functional orientation was presented. It includes the transition stages of recruiting, pre-employment education, orientation, education and training, adaptation, promotions/assignment, and evaluation. Proper planning and attention to these basic stages of transition provide the organization with a comprehensive approach to resolve transition problems and minimize their impact on organizational performance.

2

Building a Bridge
Between College and Work:
Work-Study Programs

Before discussing how the organization can effectively manage the transition process, it is prudent to examine ways in which adjustment problems can be prevented at earlier stages. Several types of programs, designed for students while they are still in college, are available that integrate employment-related activities with academic preparation. These programs allow students to adjust to the realities of work life and to preview their future professional jobs. The payoff: Culture shock is reduced and poor performers are screened out with little investment.

This chapter describes five programs representing standard approaches used by organizations to prevent or minimize transition problems. The list includes cooperative education, internships, college partnerships, summer employment, and part-time employment. The variety inherent in these programs provides flexibility for organizations to satisfy their own needs while helping students adjust to real work problems. One or more of these programs can work for practically any organization, and a healthy strategy for transition should include the utilization of at least one of these approaches.

Although work-study is not a stage of transition as depicted in our model, this type of program can have a tremendous impact on the transition process. Discussion is included here to encourage organizations to consider their implementation as a way of subsequently reducing the resources needed for a formal transition effort.

Cooperative Education

One of the most common types of work-study arrangements is the cooperative education program. This plan originated in 1906 at the University of Cincinnati, where it was developed to improve the education of engineering students through alternate periods of work and study (Wilson and Lyons, 1977). The idea has developed and spread to all types of degree programs. According to the National Commission for Cooperative Education based in Boston, nearly 200,000 students participate in cooperative education at more than 900 colleges and universities and are paid more than $1 billion in wages (Kleinman, 1986). Organizations develop and implement cooperative education programs for a variety of purposes, and they have tremendous potential for easing the transition from campus life to full-time professional work. Culture shock is minimized, if not completely eliminated, as students learn to adjust to full-time work while they are still in college.

How Cooperative Education Works. Cooperative education is defined as an educational plan that integrates classroom experiences and practical work experiences in industrial, business, government, and service workplaces. Work experiences constitute a regular and essential element in the educational process, and some minimum amount of work experience and minimum standards of performance are included in the requirements for a degree. In addition, the program must include a liaison between the college administration and the employing firm (Wilson and Lyons, 1977).

Cooperative education works in virtually any type of setting and usually adopts one of two basic forms. The first, and most popular, consists of alternating periods of work and study. Traditionally, cooperative education students attend college for a minimum time period, usually a year, and then begin alternating quarters or semesters of work and college until their senior year, at which time they devote their full attention to completing their degree. These alternating schedules vary and in some cases students even alternate a full year of work and study. The other basic form is a part-time arrangement in which students attend college full time and work part time with an employer.

From an organization's viewpoint, the essential requirements for a successful cooperative education program are relatively straightforward. First, the college must be willing to work with the employer in a cooperative arrangement. (Theoretically, an organization could establish a co-op program with an individual student without the assistance or cooperation of the institution, but this would not be optimum, as the co-op program works best when responsibilities for both the employer and the institution are spelled out in a formal agreement). The institution's degree programs must be related in some way to the organization's needs. The college must have an adequate supply of students with career objectives that coincide with the concerns and goals of the organization. The organization must develop work assignments that are related to the institutions' degree programs and can provide practical experiences for the students. A program coordinator must be designated whose duties are to develop and administer the program and ensure that it meets the organization's needs. Depending on the extent of the program, this could be a part-time or full-time arrangement. In large organizations a full staff of professionals may be involved in administering a cooperative education program. Finally, adequate on-the-job supervision must be available to ensure that students have meaningful, challenging assignments and receive the proper feedback on their progress. These are essential ingredients. Other elements can enhance the success of programs (see Mason, Haines, and Furtado, 1981; Mitchell, 1977; and Bennett, 1977).

Benefits of Cooperative Education. From an employer's viewpoint, cooperative education results in many significant benefits. Cooperative education enables students to gain experience in the real world of work and thus to avoid some culture shock. These programs give students a chance to form good work habits early and develop a serious attitude toward job performance and expectations of the job. Students can use the work experience to build and apply their skills, receive feedback on their performance, and perform meaningful work and make a contribution. This positive reinforcement enhances their overall ability and improves self-confidence.

A cooperative education program provides students with realistic views of a career and helps them determine if their chosen field of study is suitable to their interests and needs. Without this experience, students could complete their degrees, go to work in their chosen fields, and then find out (sometimes too late) that they are in the wrong occupation. This is expensive, not only for themselves but also for the organization that provides them with their initial job. Ultimately, this results in lower performance or a turnover statistic when they decide to leave to pursue other interests. Cooperative education allows students to work with professionals and learn from them on the job. It gives them an opportunity to see the relationship between theory and practice— to see what is actually practiced versus what is taught in college.

Cooperative education provides a steady flow of talent into the organization, which in turn enhances the future recruitment of college graduates; for some organizations co-op programs serve as the primary source of new college graduates employed in professional jobs. Some organizations feel it is less expensive to train students in a co-op program than to train new graduates without experience after they are hired and risk the excessive turnover that is sometimes characteristic of new college recruits. Much of the training and education provided for inexperienced college graduates can be provided to co-op students at lower wage rates and usually while they are performing essential duties for the organization. Cooperative education students can be used as a source of semiskilled and semiprofessional labor who can relieve higher-paid professional employees from detail duties and routine tasks, allowing them to devote their energy to more productive assignments. This kind of program works best when the organization has developed permanent slots with specific duties for co-op students in a section or department.

Finally, a cooperative education program can help an organization develop minority employees. Most organizations have affirmative action plans through which they recruit and retain professional, technical, and supervisory employees from various minority groups. Co-op programs allow the employer to select outstanding minority students, help them adjust, and ensure their success in the organization. The results can significantly improve affirmative action statistics.

Although many organizations enter cooperative education arrangements, few appear to undertake these programs for the purpose of easing the transition from campus life to full-time work. Numerous studies have shown that co-op graduates can perform and make a contribution in the organization faster than those without cooperative experience. One study, involving a major co-op employer, compared the success of co-op graduates with nonco-op graduates. The graduates' progress in the company, as measured by salary increases and promotions, was significantly different for the two groups. Based on twenty years of data, salary increases and promotions were much greater for co-op graduates than nonco-op graduates (Phillips, 1978a). These findings imply that the cooperative education experiences allow graduates to adjust to new jobs and make a contribution sooner than their counterparts without cooperative training. In another study involving over 600 engineers, co-op graduates were found to reach certain job levels faster than graduates without cooperative experience (Jarrell, 1974). When considering these studies, coupled with the benefits outlined above, it makes good business sense for employers to pursue cooperative education vigorously.

Developing Work Assignments. Much of the success of a cooperative education program lies in the nature, scope, and type of work assignments developed for co-op students. This responsibility should not be taken lightly. Unplanned and haphazard approaches to developing work assignments can cause problems for the co-op program and eventually turn it into a liability rather than an asset. Assignments should be developed around organizational needs and program objectives.

Organizations that merely provide jobs for college students to help with educational expenses can utilize any type of routine, menial task. However, this may be a shortsighted approach representing a misuse of resources and will usually result in few co-op graduates returning for full-time work. Students may develop a poor image of the organization if they have not been provided opportunities to utilize their abilities. Co-op students have many ideas and want to use their minds and make a contribution. They must feel needed and respected by the organization. Assignments for co-op students should be appropriate for the students' majors and the organizations' needs. It makes little sense to require a student to perform laborious tasks for long periods unless the exposure will be helpful or meaningful to the student's chosen career. For example, accountants would probably not need extensive assignments performing manual labor, whereas a production supervisor might benefit from the experience.

Ideally, the more routine assignments should be restricted to co-op students who are beginning their program. Similar to basic training in the military, this approach provides the toughest, least-liked assignments early. Then, the student progresses to more responsible and mentally challenging assignments. Ultimately, near the end of the program, students should be performing work similar to that contained in full-time assignments. For engineering graduates, engineering technician or junior engineer are typical jobs for the latter assignments. For marketing graduates, the job of junior marketing research analyst may be appropriate. This progressive responsibility approach leaves students with the full appreciation for the scope of the responsibilities inherent in the career occupation. An improper match between the individual student and job assignment can lead to poor performance, which in turn can hurt the success of the program. Assigning co-op students to the same job each work period can also be disastrous. Some firms do this as part of a debasement exercise to foster real world adjustment. Although this tactic has some value, it can lead to an unusually high drop-out rate and inhibit the program's effectiveness.

An important part of the assignment is the preparation and attitude of the supervisors and managers in the sections or departments where co-op students work. Unprepared and unenthusiastic supervisors who do not fully support the co-op concept can destroy what would ordinarily be an excellent program. Supervisors and managers involved in the co-op program must understand the purposes of the program and their role in making the process work. In some organizations, they receive training in how to supervise co-op students, provide counseling, and render assistance in performance problems.

Co-op assignments can be made for virtually all types of majors. Although started initially for technical professions such as engineering, this concept has rapidly spread to other fields in business, social sciences, and even liberal arts. The federal government is the largest employer of co-op students, employing about 15,000 students in thirty-six departments and agencies at 2,000 work sites. In the private sector, General Motors employs 3,314 co-op students and IBM, 3,609 (Kleinman, 1986).

Follow-Up. A potential problem area with co-op programs is the lack of follow-up after students have completed their last assignment with the organization. Some organizations rely on students to pursue full-time employment with them, but some students, particularly those in occupations in high demand, will have several employers pursuing them for permanent employment. In addition, their co-op experience makes them more attractive to recruiters. Although students usually appreciate the co-op experience and are grateful that the organization has provided the opportunity, if the firm does not keep in contact after the last assignment, students may interpret this as a lack of interest in them for permanent employment and may therefore pursue other possibilities. Frequent contact is best and job offers should be extended as soon as possible. This follow-up can help ensure that a co-op program is successful and meets the goals of the organization as well as the needs of the students. Ultimately, a successful program can minimize or, in some cases, virtually eliminate the transition problems of new graduates as they move from full-time campus life to full-time career positions.

Internships

Another way to minimize or prevent transition problems is to participate in some form of internship program with a college. Internships are very similar to cooperative education programs, although they are usually not as structured. Because of the flexibility of the internship almost any organization can develop this type of program.

How Internship Works. An internship program is an employment relationship with college students on a flexible schedule that meets both the interests of students and the needs of the organization. Some interns work for the summer only, others work on a part-time basis, and still others work one or more semesters or quarters. The primary purpose of the internship program is to provide students with insight into the real world of work, preferably in their major field of study. Students may or may not be provided compensation but usually receive academic credit for the work assignment, which is designed to contribute to their development.

The concept has been applied in a variety of organizations, including retail, manufacturing, banking, human services, government, insurance, communication, and general services. This approach typically provides more flexibility than a formal cooperative education program, which may involve a long-term employment relationship.

Internship programs are not limited to undergraduate students; they work well for graduate students, particularly in professional schools such as business administration. Projects for graduate students should require advanced skills. The MBA Internship Program at Congoleum Corporation's Resilient Flooring Division is a good example. The program was launched in 1979 to attract top talent to assist on research projects. The program has worked so well that it has become an important part of the company's recruiting effort. The process begins by asking company directors and managers for projects that are substantial enough to bring out the best in the interns. Managers are asked what academic preparation is needed for the projects (such as accounting, finance, or marketing) and how the interns will be used. Then they develop a project statement describing the desired end result and the time requirement. The most challenging projects are sent to local university coordinators for posting. The university provides prospects and the company makes the ultimate selections. Most projects last about ten weeks to coincide with the length of the school semester and require eight to ten hours a week. Students earn three graduate credits from the university and are provided a small stipend. Overall, the company has been extremely pleased with the results of the program, and several former interns are now in middle-management positions ("MBA Interns," 1985).

Benefits of Internship. As with cooperative education, internship participation has several benefits for organizations (Hite, 1986):

- Management observes potential employees with little or no risk.
- Permanent employees have more time to devote to other duties.
- The organization learns about current academic developments.
- Students bring an influx of creative energy.
- The organization receives favorable publicity.

Another study provided insight into the perceived benefits of an internship program (Dobandi and Schattle, 1984). Organizations in the New York area were surveyed for their reaction to internship programs. Only organizations that had participated in a formal internship program were considered. A total of 142 organizations responded, with 134 providing usable data. The top five positive attributes of an internship program, along with the five most negative attributes, are presented in Table 4. The mean score is based on a 1 to 5 Likert scale, where 1 represents a "strongly disagree" response and 5 indicates "strongly agree." The results reveal some very strong positive feelings about internships, and the low mean scores for the negative attributes tend to dispel many of the perceived problems with internships. Additionally, this study attempted to compare differences in responses in large versus small organizations, unionized versus nonunionized, tenured versus nontenured respondents, and organizations currently participating in an internship program versus nonparticipating respondents. Although these groups differed significantly on a few

Table 4. Positive and Negative Attributes of Internships.

Factor Statement	Mean Value
Positive Attributes	
Internships contribute to the development of better qualified college graduates.	4.49
Internships provide firsthand opportunity to evaluate the student's aptitudes and abilities for future employment possibilities.	4.13
Internships promote favorable company/student relations, which aid recruitment.	3.88
Internships promote company image and goodwill.	3.84
Students are conscientious about the quality of their work.	3.80
Negative Attributes	
Time involved in orientation and supervision of an intern is too costly.	2.52
Students are not sufficiently prepared to assume the responsibilities of an internship position.	2.32
The decline in business activity eliminates the need for interns.	2.31
The time involved for the internship does not allow a meaningful work experience for the students.	2.20
Students are not dependable.	2.00

Source: Dobandi and Schattle, 1984.

statements, overall there were very few differences in the responses. This suggests that internships work in a variety of settings.

Disadvantages. A few disadvantages of internship programs keep some organizations from utilizing this type of program. The first is the amount of time necessary to develop and maintain an internship program. Management time is expensive and someone must keep the program coordinated. Supervisors must work with students to get them to the point where they can adequately perform assignments. The second disadvantage, closely linked with time, is the training expense, which includes all expenses required for students to learn their jobs. For a brief internship assignment, it makes little sense for an organization to invest heavily in a training activity. The third drawback is that the program can be a liability if not executed properly. Students experiencing serious difficulty in the program may leave the organization with a bad impression, deciding not to return for full-time employment. This negativity can spread, saddling the company with a poor reputation, possibly one that is not justified. Therefore, an organization should not attempt to implement an internship program unless it is willing to invest the time necessary to prepare students properly and keep them motivated.

Two other areas can create problems for an internship program. The first occurs when management perceives the internship program as a source of cheap labor. Although the wages may be low (and in some cases nil), students do expect some reward for their efforts. Menial tasks are acceptable when the student learns important lessons by performing those tasks, but even then the student is due an explanation of the importance of that assignment. Second, interns should not be considered as temporary clerical help. Most projects will require clerical duties and this is expected. However, assignments that involve only clerical work—unless it is related directly to the students' career needs—can demotivate students and ultimately cause the program to fail.

Developing Projects/Assignments. The most important aspect of an internship program is the student's project or job assignment. Several guidelines can ensure that the project is developed appropriately and under conditions that lead to success. First, the time required to prepare students for the assignment or project should be minimized. Excessive time to prepare students may lower the potential return on the investment, giving some managers reason to question the worth of the program.

Second, students should be matched with the assignments to the extent possible. Students bring certain strengths and weaknesses to an organization and projects require a variety of skills. Greater success can be achieved when the student's strengths and interests are appropriately matched to the scope of the project. For example, it makes little sense to assign students to projects involving the use of computers if they have no computer training or have a fear of working with computer systems.

Third, managers must be convinced that they should be involved in the program. This is best accomplished by explaining the benefits of the internship and discussing what can be accomplished with the program. Success stories taken from previous internship projects make convincing evidence.

Fourth, students should not be over-challenged. Some managers, in their eagerness to impress students and to secure answers to difficult problems at the same time, may assign very challenging projects, far beyond the abilities of the student. This can demotivate and frustrate students and guarantee failure for the project. Quite often, interns are involved in their first work experience, and it is not very difficult to baffle a nineteen-year-old when it comes to sophisticated organizational systems. Simple, manageable tasks may work best unless there is evidence that the student possesses exceptional skills or the experience needed in a particular assignment.

Fifth, projects should be perceived as important and useful by both the employer and the student. "Make-work" assignments or projects with little meaning to the organization may leave the students with an unfavorable image of the program. It is difficult to fool most students about the importance of an assignment. In a month or two they usually know whether the organization will use the information from the project.

These guidelines should help organizations develop meaningful, challenging projects while providing useful information for the organization. A wide variety of assignments can be developed, as illustrated by the internships at Pan Am. One required an intern to research competing airline route authority, flight schedules, and services in a certain region to help Pan Am develop its case for obtaining new route authority from a foreign government. In another project, an intern, after taking several computer courses, compiled and developed a computer program to provide a set of indices that would allow appropriate cost-of-living allowances for expatriates in foreign locations. In a third example, an intern was allowed to code and analyze consumer correspondence and prepare a brief report on the analysis for the company's chairman (Solomon, 1985).

The Salary Issue. The decision whether to pay interns for their efforts is an important one. Some schools require employers to pay their student interns. Others recommend it, while still others suggest no salary. There are advantages to each approach. If the student is doing work that would normally be performed by someone else, they should probably be paid. Some union contracts and some state or federal laws may actually require pay. However, projects strictly for training purposes usually do not have this requirement. Providing a salary for a service is "morally appropriate" in the eyes of some organizations. Also, providing a salary may provide more control over the students, allowing organizations to demand certain levels of performance.

Arguments against a salary are just as convincing. Students interested in real work experiences, with the goals of understanding how an organization functions and making a contribution related to their major, will not consider compensation an issue, although it may be desired. Students willing to undertake assignments without pay and successfully complete them to satisfy the organization have their hearts in the right place. That alone will impress management. In the Pan Am program, the interns are not compensated with salary but are provided lunch and transportation costs to and from work. As a bonus for completing their assignments, the interns are given a round-trip ticket to any location where Pan Am flies.

Although there is no clear-cut answer to the payment question, a few questions can help develop the answer.

1. Is the project something the company would like to have completed but would not devote its current resources to pursue? In this case, the organization probably should not offer pay. The organization would be paying for something it does not need.

2. Will the student benefit much more than the organization? If so, perhaps no salary should be offered.
3. Is the organization devoting a considerable amount of time preparing the student for the assignment and making the program work? If so, the organization's contribution of time may be enough expense, and the student should not receive a salary.
4. Is the student performing work that would normally be preformed by a salaried employee? If the answer is "yes," the student should probably be paid for the work, even though the student does gain other benefits from the work experience.
5. Are there any legal or contractual issues related to pay for the job? If so, those restrictions would probably determine the best course of action.

The concept of working without pay to learn a job is not necessarily new, nor is it restricted to programs for college graduates. For example, in the Nissan plant in Smyrna, Tennessee, individuals who are interested in a job at the plant must attend classes on their own time to learn the skills required for the job. This serves as a screening device for the employer and is an inexpensive way to develop a steady supply of employees who are attracted to this offer because of the higher pay than is typical for the market area (Buss, 1985).

General Guidelines. In addition to the information on developing a meaningful and productive job assignment, other guidelines can help ensure success for internships. First, a competent, professional employee should coordinate the program. In most organizations the human resources department provides a coordinator. Depending on the scope of the program and the size of the organization, this could be a part-time responsibility or a full-time effort. The capability of the coordinator, in large measure, determines the success of the program. A professional, results-oriented individual will make the program work as long as sufficient management support is present; a weak, ineffective coordinator will be detrimental to the program's success.

In addition to a program coordinator, other professionals should be available to counsel interns. Ideally, students should be counseled by their supervisors when job-related personal problems arise. However, students may feel closer to the program coordinator or some other employee who is assigned this specific role. Students must be kept motivated and enthused. This may be difficult to do, particularly with unpaid interns. Positive attitudes are important for students and others involved in the program. A variety of activities, together with appropriate feedback and recognition for their efforts, may be necessary to stimulate performance from students.

Comprehensive orientation should be provided for new students. One important benefit of an internship program is developing a favorable image for the organization. Therefore, it is important for the student to know as much as possible about the organization. A thorough orientation, coupled with follow-up discussions, provides detailed information about the company and the opportunities available in the future.

If feasible, supervisors of interns should be trained for their assignment. Just as the students need preparation to tackle projects, supervisors need preparation to work effectively with students. Brief meetings before the internship assignment might suffice. (In most cases, the supervisor is involved in developing the initial project and is aware of what needs to be done.) In addition, the supervisor should be briefed on potential problems that might occur and how they should be handled. Most important, the supervisor should enthusiastically support the process and understand the long-range impact of his or her actions, both positive and negative.

If possible, students should be provided samples of the organization's products or services. In a consumer products company this is very easy and should be considered an integral part of the program. After all, the organization is attempting to build a long-term relationship with the student, and product or service identification helps. In some cases, products or services could supplement compensation or act as the sole form of compensation. In the Pan Am example discussed earlier, the primary compensation of a free round-trip ticket underscored the importance of the interns' assignments and provided them tangible evidence of the ultimate service provided by the airline.

College Partnerships

A flexible and creative approach to exposing students to work situations is through some type of partnership arrangement between the organization and the college. Although a partnership usually does not involve direct employment of students, it combines a variety of activities designed to assist the organization, college, and students. The U.S. Department of Education defines this type of partnership as a voluntary formal agreement between a private sector entity and a school, in which the partners match educational needs with available private sector resources in order to improve the quality of education within a community. Four types of partnerships are described below.

Applied Research. Some colleges are joining with organizations to conduct applied research at the employer's facilities. This type of agreement benefits both parties: The university benefits by having its faculty and students exposed to the latest technology and practices in real work settings; the employer gains by tapping the knowledge and ideas of the faculty, graduate students, and undergraduate students and usually at a lower cost than using outside consultants. The employer also benefits from the good public relations and the opportunity to recruit students for potential employment after graduation.

An effective example of such a partnership is the applied research facility located at the General Motors Rochester plant in Tuscaloosa, Alabama. In 1983, the University of Alabama formed a partnership with General Motors and the United Auto Workers to provide resources and assistance to keep the Rochester plant open. This carburetor assembly plant employs about 250 employees and was scheduled to be closed by General Motors to cut costs. As part of the partnership agreement, the plant was designated an "Applied Research Facility" where professors and students from a variety of disciplines studied ways to reduce costs and make the plant more efficient. The team from the university promised to find $470,000 in annual savings within three years but achieved that target in eight months.

Although this partnership was created to save a doomed plant, it was also an important project for students. They collected data and conducted cost analyses, and in some cases employee teams used students as staff specialists to address potential cost-cutting items. Over 150 students have participated to date and have gained valuable experience and insight into an industrial operation. Students work on projects for academic credit, on an independent study or clinic basis, or even as part-time university employees assigned to the project. They are welcome on the shop floor to watch and talk with employees about their jobs but may not take any job on the assembly line. With this partnership, the plant has become a 300,000-square-foot classroom for the university (Campbell and others, 1985).

Teaching. In some cases organizations enter into a partnership agreement to teach a course or series of courses for a college. Courses are selected in which a local employer has expertise not readily available within the faculty. The "visiting faculty" from the organization provide instruction on the latest practices and techniques of their profession, explaining actual work situations and problems students will face on the job. Sometimes these courses are supplemented by visits to and tours of the employer's facilities.

One successful use of this approach is conducted by a worldwide engineering/contracting firm, which provides engineering faculty for a nearby university's school of engineering. Under the agreement, the firm's engineers teach the latest engineering practices and the students see how their studies relate to the engineering field. Teaching assignments rotate among several engineers, and the experience provides them with exposure to the talent available in the colleges and allows them to gain valuable instructional and public speaking experience. Overall, students gain a favorable impression of what they can expect on the job when they graduate.

Visitations. A third possibility for a partnership approach is an agreement between an employer and a local college whereby the employer conducts regular visits or field trips for students. This approach provides an excellent opportunity for students to observe the work setting and learn what·is expected of graduates in that particular field.

In one example, a large producer of crushed stone regularly invites geology students from a nearby university to visit its quarry operations and its research and development facilities. Students observe geological formations, and the company explains what geologists do for their organization. In the laboratory they observe the typical activities and duties a geologist performs.

Special Projects. Special projects of mutual interest and benefit offer a wide range of possibilities for colleges and employers and provide students exposure to real world job situations. One project involved the B. F. Goodrich Company and a student-run advertising agency, Laws, Hall & Associates, based at Miami University in Ohio. Organized in the 1960s, the agency is staffed with senior students who are doing practical course work. Each year the students take on a product development and marketing project for a major firm. During the 1984–85 academic year, the students worked on a new collection of wall coverings to be made by B. F. Goodrich. Divided into three teams, seventy-two students involved in market research developed and named wall covering patterns and designed an advertising campaign with sales aids. A Goodrich team characterized the students' work as innovative and of high quality. The company was impressed enough that it copyrighted some of the results ("Practical College Relations," 1985).

These different types of partnership agreements offer a wide range of possibilities for employers and colleges. In terms of addressing the transition issue, they are not as effective as actual work experience, but they do provide opportunities to expose students to the work environment and practical experiences. This can help minimize adjustment problems of graduates as they enter full-time work. This approach usually limits participation to schools in close proximity with the employer. It may require considerable time from the employer, but the effort frequently pays off in long-term benefits for the students, faculty, and employer.

Summer Employment

Employing college students in summer jobs can be an efficient way to familiarize future full-time professional employees with the organization. As with the other student employment arrangements, this approach can reduce adjustment problems for graduates. In some respects, summer employment is no different from cooperative education programs or internships; the benefits and disadvantages are very similar.

How Summer Employment Works. Summer employment programs can take on three basic approaches. The first approach involves placing students in meaningful, full-time jobs where they have the opportunity to learn about work realities. Placements may include existing jobs created by a peak demand, special projects, or seasonal assignments. Examples include a retail store chain conducting an annual inventory; a federal agency conducting a survey on the quality of its services; and a manufacturing firm providing annual maintenance and clean-up services for its plants. In all three cases, summer employees perform these important and necessary tasks. In departments with several relatively inexperienced and/or low-skilled employees, summer employees can be used to fill in for vacationing permanent employees or to handle a peak seasonal demand. This approach is cost-effective because students are performing necessary work, usually at a lower wage.

The second, more expensive alternative maximizes student learning while helping to minimize future transition problems. This approach involves a structured program in which students rotate to different parts of the organization to learn how each functions within the unit. Summer employees have little opportunity to make a contribution, since they are principally involved in learning activities, and merely have an opportunity to be exposed to the people, products, services, and structure of the organization. They learn about different career opportunities and jobs, as well as observe the problems, frustrations, and challenges employees face in the organization. It provides a good dose of organizational reality and helps the student make career decisions about that particular organization or the industry. More important, it provides future employees insight into the organization—insight that can help ease the shock when full-time, permanent employment is secured.

With the third approach (which is not primarily aimed at avoiding transition problems) college students are employed primarily to meet peak labor demands during summer months. These jobs must be filled and summer students are the most economical candidates. The emphasis is not on preparing the student for potential full-time employment but on satisfying immediate employment needs. In this situation it is important to select students who can perform the work and at the same time consider their potential for later full-time employment.

Variations between the first and second approaches can maximize the potential benefits of summer employment. If the organization is willing to invest time and money in these approaches, it will have well-rounded students who can adapt to organizational life if and when they return for permanent employment.

Objectives. Summer employment programs have several objectives, which vary with program emphasis. Typical objectives for programs that focus on minimizing transition problems are:

- to familiarize each student with the people, products, and operations of the organization
- to provide exposure to as many aspects of the industry as possible
- to make participants aware of the various job opportunities available in the organization after graduation
- to develop an understanding of how all the functions, or at least a group of functions, coordinate to create an effective department, division, plant, or segment of the organization
- to handle special projects and meet seasonal labor demands

- to evaluate each participant for potential permanent employment after graduation.

A program following the second approach described above
may include all of the above objectives, whereas a program
designed along the lines of the first approach may have only some
of the objectives.

Selecting Students. The success of any summer employment
program depends on the quality of its students. Three major
factors should be considered in selecting students for summer
employment: academic major, career interests, and educational
level.

Majors should be compatible with the organization's
general field or industry. In government agencies it may be public
administration; for financial institutions, finance; for hospitals,
hospital administration. However, the organization might also
consider less-related majors: Students are not always clear about
their career plans when they declare their majors, and summer
employment activities could easily influence the decision to
change majors.

Ideally, summer employees should have a strong interest in
the organization, the type of work they are pursuing, and the
organization's industry. Although not all students have decided on
their career or vocational interests, many of them do have interests
and desires which they need to satisfy. A structured summer
employment program provides exposure to help develop and
refine their career interests.

A final area of consideration is the educational level
attained by the student. Some organizations restrict summer
employment programs to seniors; others consider freshmen,
sophomores, and juniors as well. If permanent full-time employment is one of the purposes of the summer employment program,
the student should be hired as near as possible to the graduation
date. As a trade-off, some organizations offer sophomores or
juniors employment opportunities for both years, so they will have
a chance to learn more about the organization.

Work Assignments. The work assignment developed for summer employees depends on which of the above approaches the organization adopts. Assignments should be carefully developed to maximize learning while allowing students to make a contribution. It is also important for students to be fully challenged and not assigned obvious "make work" projects, which tend to lower the students' morale and raise serious doubts as to whether the organization should be included in their future plans. Too often summer employees are placed on the payroll to help them with their personal finances, and consequently the student is given only menial work or sometimes little work at all. Although this may help the student, it does not expose him or her to the realities of professional employment.

In more elaborate and sophisticated programs, students are required to complete research and writing projects in which the student submits a completed package at the end of the summer. Still others require summer employees to develop a critical review of the program as a final assignment. In one organization this final assignment covers the following areas:

- a reaction to the program
- a recap of what the participant gained from the program
- an assessment of career opportunities in the organization
- recommendations for changes in the program.

This approach can be beneficial to the student and at the same time provide valuable information about the success of the program.

Follow-up. Follow-up is very critical to the ultimate success of summer employment programs, and it is essential during the actual work assignment. An organization employee must be assigned the responsibility of periodically checking the status of summer employees to assure that (1) the students are functioning in the planned work assignment, (2) they are fully challenged, and (3) the work assignment is helping to meet the objectives of the program. An end-of-summer follow-up for seniors may include a discussion of the program and of future opportunities for permanent employment or, in the case of juniors or below, an assessment of future summer employment activity. Part of this follow-up should include a twofold evaluation: (1) the students' evaluation of the program, which provides their reactions to the program and assesses its effectiveness and (2) the organization's evaluation, which focuses on the student's performance and behavior during the program. The second part of the evaluation helps determine if summer employees are prospects for future permanent employment. If the decision is made to continue to cultivate the relationship with the student, it is important to maintain contact with the student while on campus through additional summer employment or by inviting the student to a campus interview. Follow-up letters from the program coordinator can be useful. Without this follow-up, the long-range success of the program may be in jeopardy.

Part-Time Employment

A fifth and final approach to help prevent transition problems is to consider employing college students on a part-time basis in progressively responsible assignments, with the goal of employing them in full-time, professional positions after graduation. Although this approach has a wide range of possibilities, it does have limitations based on scheduling, the nature of part-time work, and the organization's geographical location in relation to the college.

How Part-Time Employment Works. Part-time employment designed to prevent transition problems and to provide a steady source of professional employees differs from other types of part-time employment. More is at stake than just getting the job done; the organization is recruiting and preparing for the future. The part-time work, or at least some portion of it, must be similar to that which the graduate can assume after graduation; in this way, it becomes an important part of the learning process for the permanent assignment.

An example can best illustrate the differences in these two types of part-time work experiences. Consider an organization that employs a college student part time to sort the mail for a large office. Although it is a necessary job, the person performing it may learn little else than names and locations of employees and so would probably not be prepared for future, full-time assignments. Suppose the same organization employed an accounting major on a part-time basis in the accounts payable department, eventually rotating the student to accounts receivable and finally to the credit and collections area. The second part-time employee, although performing a job that is clerical in nature, is learning the accounting and control system of the organization and preparing for a future job as an accountant.

Part-time employment has an added advantage of reducing costs. In some cases two employees work twenty hours each to perform a job normally handled by a full-time employee. This process (sometimes called "job sharing") can be cost-effective because the organization's full benefits package is not usually available to part-time employees. Also, it may be easier for employees to maintain high levels of job motivation in routine jobs in a twenty-hour week than in a forty-hour work week. Therefore, more work can sometimes be accomplished by two employees than by one full-time person. This approach has become so attractive to some organizations that they have eliminated some permanent jobs and have replaced them with part-time employees.

Selecting Candidates and Tracking Progress. As with the other approaches for preventing transition problems, candidates for part-time employment must be carefully selected, using some or all of the selection criteria for new college graduates. Many organizations that employ part-time employees use the same instruments, tests, and selection procedures. Although failures or poor performance in a part-time employment arrangement may not be as costly as in other work-study programs, they still represent an unnecessary expense. Candidates who cannot succeed in their jobs should be replaced with other candidates who are more likely to succeed. This requires a performance review process that will spot potential problems early. This additional effort in the part-time employment process can reap dividends in the future.

Ensuring Success with Work-Study Programs

Although the five basic approaches used to prevent or minimize transition problems differ in format and scope, their success can be enhanced by following standard principles in their design and administration. The following principles can serve as guidelines for developing and evaluating work-study programs.

- *Monitor the quality of student selection.* Except for the partnership arrangement, the selection of students is an important issue. These programs serve as a recruiting tool for organizations, and candidates should be selected with almost as much care as in the formal recruiting and selection process for new college graduates.

- *Make the program relevant to job needs.* Assignments and activities in each program should relate to the jobs new graduates would likely assume after graduation. Work assignments should be carefully selected and developed to ensure a proper balance between routine and challenging work. To the extent possible the focus should be on learning.

- *Ensure that students make a contribution.* Work-study students need to see the results of their work and feel they are making a contribution, particularly in their chosen field of study. Most assignments and activities can be developed so that the end result of their efforts is tangible, meaningful, and rewarding.

- *Minimize the investment in the program.* Work-study programs are costly because the organization is absorbing an expense as a trade-off for future employment relationships with reduced transition problems. If the investment in these programs is too costly, it overshadows the benefits derived from them.

- *Follow-up with students.* Probably the most important step is to follow up with students after they have completed the program. Otherwise, most of the students may be lost to aggressive competitors who recognize the value of experience and make attractive offers. In too many cases, organizations have prepared college students for future jobs, only to have them recruited by another organization. This can be avoided through a carefully designed and controlled follow-up procedure.

Summary

This chapter described work-study programs designed to minimize or prevent transition problems. These programs include cooperative education, internships, college partnerships, summer employment, and part-time employment. These options provide a strategy to tackle transition problems early, usually with less expense than trying to solve them after they occur. Though preventing transition problems is the major goal of these programs, they also have other objectives, such as developing an important recruiting source.

Each organization should examine its needs and review these approaches for potential implementation. A large, aggressive organization may use all five approaches, whereas others may tap only one of them. Some arrangements may not work for some organizations because of their specific requirements and environment, while others may fit neatly into the organizational setting.

3

Finding and Selecting
Future Employees:
Campus Recruiting Programs

It happens all too often. The newly recruited college graduate, once on the job, turns out to be vastly different from the promising individual who emerged as the best prospect from the recruiting and selection process. The problem often lies in the inadequacies of the selection process, particularly relying too much on the interview to make the selection decision.

Effective recruitment practices are important to the organization's long-term survival. The quality of new employees is essential to the organization's success in providing its products or services. In addition, recruiting mistakes can be very costly—for all parties. Because of this, more organizations are reviewing their recruitment practices to see if improvements are necessary.

Although recruitment can be accomplished through several advertising sources, such as trade journals, newspapers, and other publications, the major focus of a good recruitment program aimed at college graduates is campus recruiting. One report showed that college campus recruitment programs account for more than 50 percent of the college-educated talent hired each year (Bergmann and Taylor, 1984). Still, no secret formula can ensure that an organization secures its share of "the best and the brightest" graduates available. And with the vast number of colleges from which to choose, an organization's campus recruit-

71

ment program provides a narrow view, at best, of the available candidates graduating each year.

Much criticism has been expressed about the traditional method of campus recruiting. First, the organization has limited time to get to know the students or to "sell" them on the organization. Second, the organization may be missing the "super" students who either have been directly contacted by a firm or choose not to work through the job placement office. Third, a great deal of time (and money) is wasted interviewing uninterested or underqualified applicants (Seidel and Powell, 1983). Some firms are beginning to question the effectiveness of their campus recruitment procedures, citing as major concerns higher costs and average or unfavorable results. One study found that employees recruited from college campuses were poor performers and had more negative job attitudes than those recruited from such sources as direct applications or professional journals (Bergmann and Taylor, 1984).

Even with these problems, campus recruiting remains a viable alternative, and the challenge to organizations is to get the most out of the process. Although there is no one best approach to campus recruiting, Stoops (1985) presents some practical advice:

1. *Develop comprehensive plans to serve as program road maps.*
2. *Focus recruitment activities on a specific, handpicked group of schools.*
3. *Provide sustained communications with students at the selected colleges.*

This practical advice is amplified further in this chapter. The recruiting process, which is the first stage of transition, is reviewed with a focus on improving results and minimizing culture shock. The chapter examines recruiting from determining needs to conducting follow-up with candidates and contains many helpful suggestions that an organization can use to revitalize the process. It is not intended to present a thorough analysis of college recruiting. Excellent coverage of recruitment and selection can be found in Thain, Yoxall, and Stewart (1979), McBurney (1982), Babbush and Bormann (1982), and Arthur (1986).

Determining Recruiting Needs

Conducting an effective college recruitment program requires a great deal of planning. A major step in the planning process is an assessment of recruitment needs—in terms of both numbers and types of graduates. The exact number to be recruited can be critical. An oversupply will probably result in increased turnover, as many of the new graduates will be unchallenged and underutilized; an undersupply of new graduates will tax the existing resources and leave new graduates frustrated, overworked, and inadequately prepared for their assignment. The type of graduate is just as important as the number. Many organizations have found they prefer generalists or even liberal arts majors because of the opportunity to mold these new employees to fit the organization. Others find specialized training imperative to a smooth transition period.

The numbers are usually derived from organizational requirements and are shaped by five major influences that are developed from the organization's planning process: planned employee growth, need for technical personnel, new market growth, management succession, and affirmative action.

Employee Growth. One of the most important determinants for recruiting new graduates is the projected employee growth. An organization facing steady employee growth, particularly at the professional level, needs a constant supply of new graduates to fill future job openings. Even an organization with relatively stable employment needs new graduates to replace others through normal attrition. For example, a firm with 1,000 professional, technical, and supervisory employees, experiencing a 10 percent annual employee population growth and realizing a 20 percent annual turnover, would need approximately 300 new employees each year for those job categories. In this example, the majority of these recruits would probably be new college graduates and this translates into transition opportunities and issues.

Technical Requirements. Organizations with large numbers of technical employees need a steady supply of professional and technical personnel, usually with engineering or science degrees, ready to assume new positions in the organization. High-tech firms and organizations with a large investment in research and development typically have considerable need for new technical and scientific employees to fulfill future growth projections. For example, a high-growth computer manufacturer could easily project a need of 500 technical and scientific personnel per year. The firm faces a tremendous task to recruit, train, and educate that many employees, particularly in periods when some technical specialties produce few qualified prospects.

The need for technical specialists must be addressed early because of supply and demand cycles. Technical graduates tend to enjoy feast or famine in the job market because of the mismatch in supply and demand. A high demand for a certain type of technical graduate attracts new students to that discipline, but this additional supply soon outsteps the demand, leading to an abundance in the field. As a result, large numbers of people enter and leave the technical specialty. With careful planning, organizations can monitor supply and demand forces for graduates, forecast their needs, and try to plan appropriately. During periods of shortages the organization may focus on educating current nondegree employees and preparing them for future professional jobs.

Market Growth. Another important reason for securing additional graduates is the increase in market growth as a result of acquisitions, expansions, new product introductions, and planned market share increases. Major developments in any of these areas will increase the need for new employees, particularly those with professional and technical backgrounds. Market growth plans should include preparations to recruit and train new graduates necessary to assume the professional, technical, and supervisory positions created by the growth. For example, a life insurance firm decides to expand into the health care insurance field, marketing individual and group policies. The new product line represents an important departure from existing lines and almost instantly creates a substantial need for professional employees, particularly in the sales area.

Management Succession. Another important reason for recruiting graduates is to fill supervisory and managerial openings created through normal management succession. A progressive organization must plan appropriately for replacement of its key people. Qualified candidates must be prepared and available to fill key technical, administrative, supervisory, and managerial positions. An approach used by many companies is to recruit college graduates and prepare them for managerial and supervisory careers through extensive education and training programs. The number required each year is based on potential management succession needs, as well as the additional jobs created through normal growth of the organization or growth stimulated by one of the influences above. For example, a government agency fills all of its first-level supervisory jobs through a formal training program, which is staffed by new recruits from college campuses. The number of graduates sought and the types of degrees depend on the particular vacancies or anticipated vacancies in the supervisory ranks. Supervisors eventually are promoted to middle-management positions and then to top management positions. This normal succession leaves vacancies at the entry-level supervisory positions and ultimately creates needs for the supervisory training program.

Affirmative Action. A final important reason for recruiting graduates is the organization's affirmative action plan. Most organizations have affirmative action goals to recruit minority group employees for key professional, technical, and supervisory jobs. Goals and timetables translate into specific recruiting targets for graduates to enter education/training programs. For example, a large metropolitan city actively recruits minority graduates for its police force. Law enforcement majors are selected to enter the police academy. The city has a goal of recruiting one minority officer for every nonminority officer.

Types of Majors and Degrees. The question of which degree is appropriate for which job is an important and often misunderstood issue. In some cases the job analysis identifies a particular degree or major. For example, an accountant position would usually require an accounting major; a nurse position should require a nursing degree; a computer programmer position requires a computer science degree.

For other positions the match-up is not as obvious. Consider a first-level supervisor position. Is a business administration degree appropriate or is a management major better? Or would a technical degree in an area related to the work performed be still a better choice? Some even argue that a liberal arts education provides a more appropriate background for a supervisory position. Sometimes the decision boils down to a choice between technical and managerial skills.

The process of selecting graduates who will eventually become technical managers has long been both elusive and problematical. Typically, the graduating scientist or engineer does not have any immediate interest in assuming a managerial role. Although many students express a rather vague interest in management in the distant future, most see the management route as a means of advancing as their technical skills become obsolete; they do not understand what the job of a manager really involves.

Recruiters have a difficult time wrestling with this problem. Most find the specification of critical selection criteria and methodology either haphazard or lacking altogether. It is fashionable these days, for example to recruit MBAs who have an undergraduate science or engineering degree. Many recruiters feel this set of credentials ensures technically oriented graduates with the ability to manage. What is forgotten, however, is the fact that schools of management do not teach students *how* to manage— they teach them only *about* management. Consequently, MBAs are not always the "best buy," and recruiters must learn to assess the trade-offs between the immediate availability of technical skills, the cost of training, and the salary necessary to attract candidates with good management credentials. This is an important issue that cannot be ignored. The tremendous surge of technological transfer and innovation into many countries around the world is forcing industry to realize that increased productivity and leadership can be attributed to better management of human resources. This trend makes it even more imperative that organizations select technical graduates who can also manage effectively (Brush, 1979).

Similar confusion swirls around graduates recruited to become sales representatives. Is a marketing degree best? Or does a business administration degree with a sales concentration provide the most appropriate background? Some organizations require specific technical knowledge related to the product, service, or process and thus recruit technical graduates. A large chemical company, for example, requires their sales representatives to be chemistry or chemical engineering graduates. A construction firm requires its sales representatives to have a civil engineering degree, and a pharmaceutical company requires its sales representatives to have a degree in pharmacy.

For graduates interested in achieving executive-level positions in large companies, the type of degree does not seem to make a great deal of difference. Odiorne (1984) has identified six major routes to the top in an organization. Four of these paths, outlined below, focus on academic preparation and cloud the issue of appropriate degree or major even further.

1. *Obtaining an MBA degree.* Regardless of the criticism of MBAs, they have an impressive track record of advancing into upper management. Executives with MBAs usually turn to younger MBAs when they choose their successors. And when compared to other degrees, none comes as close to focusing on the specific responsibilities that top managers perform in their daily work.

2. *Studying engineering or other technical curricula.* Many large corporations deeply committed to technical innovation and managerial excellence have turned to engineering and science graduates as a major source of quality management. Technical schools frequently supplement their curricula with internally developed management and executive programs, which are aimed at developing the needed skills to move up the organizational ladder.

3. *Applying a liberal arts education.* Many corporations have come to recognize that a liberal arts education can be admirable preparation for leadership responsibility in many areas of life, business included. A quality liberal arts education covers a

wide range of accumulated knowledge of our civilization, which is exactly what the executive of the future will need. Business and government leaders recognize that the ability to write, speak, listen, and read with insight and understanding is of the highest value for the executive of the future. Recent research by a team of psychologists indicates that the liberal arts experience prepares graduates more effectively than career-oriented programs to (1) adapt to new environments, (2) think critically and conceptually, (3) integrate broad ranges of experiences, (4) set goals and develop independence of thought, and (5) seek leadership roles. In the more responsible managerial positions reached later in a career, these skills have proven vital for advancement and excellence (Winter, McClelland, and Stewart, 1982).

An in-depth study of educational competence by American Telephone and Telegraph (AT&T) traced the careers of corporate employees for twenty-seven years. The study showed that nearly half (46 percent) of its humanities and social science graduates reach mid- to higher levels of management after twenty years with AT&T, but only 25 percent of its engineers and 31 percent of its business majors rise that high. Within the Bell system, liberal arts majors are especially strong in interpersonal skills—leadership, oral communications, and personal forcefulness. In administrative skills—organizing, planning, decision making, and creative thinking—they rank about even with business majors but are superior to the technical majors, such as math/science and engineers (Goddard, 1986).

Much of the criticism of recruiting liberal arts majors for managerial positions is founded on their apparent lack of motivation for a career in business. Liberal arts graduates have not always had a favorable attitude toward business, and few firms were wise enough to deliberately seek out and cultivate these graduates. Faced with declining job opportunities and the changing culture in the 1970s and 1980s, liberal arts graduates today are much more friendly toward business. And from the employer's viewpoint, it makes good business sense to pursue them.

4. *Possessing special education or experience.* A relatively small but significant number of executives follow none of the usual paths to the top. They find direct routes to top management positions without ever slugging it out in the lower ranks of marketing, manufacturing, finance, or engineering. Lawyers and accountants are two examples of specialized talents. They are commanding more respect and wielding more clout in corporations today than ever before. Also, family members of corporation owners, top managers, and major stockholders have a unique opportunity to move up within an organization, sometimes ahead of more capable and deserving individuals.

Determining the desired major is a difficult issue that must be addressed early in the recruitment process. The following guidelines may help an organization confront this issue:

1. Examine the success of previous graduates by degree and college major. This effort should yield insight into the degrees and majors that correlate with success. Monitor studies on the success of liberal arts majors in various professional settings. In recent years evidence has accumulated to compare the success of liberal arts graduates with other more vocationally defined majors. An excellent work on this topic is Johnston and associates (1986).

2. Reexamine job requirements focusing on the skills necessary for the job rather than on the degree or college major required.

3. Redesign the selection process to detect the level of skills necessary for job success that are possessed by the individual.

4. Avoid inflexibility in the requirement of specific majors and degrees.

Evaluating and Selecting Colleges

The focus of the recruitment effort requires organizations to limit carefully their recruiting to a certain number of campuses and consistently maintain a presence there. Thus, every organization should develop criteria for determining the colleges at which it will recruit.

Previous Successes. A first step in this process is to review the experience of recent graduates in the organization. Adjustment problems may be traced to the curriculum of the college they attended. For example, the college's accounting department may prepare graduates for public accounting instead of management accounting. Or the college's pharmacy school may focus on retail pharmacy instead of hospital pharmacy. If the organization has been extremely pleased with recent graduates, a logical course of action may be to focus energies on the colleges of these graduates. Thus, present employees are a good starting point for determining where to recruit, but it is risky to generalize from only a few cases.

One Dallas-based bank that uses previous successes as its primary criterion focuses recruitment efforts on those colleges where the "perceived" profile of the students fits the norm of the bank's employees. The bank recruits heavily in local colleges, such as the University of Texas, to ensure they have some home-based employees, but they also recruit at such midwestern colleges as Indiana, where the average student seems to fit well into the bank's environment. Ivy League colleges are not on the bank's recruitment list because the "perceived" profile of these students (upper-middle-class, northern/eastern background) does not seem to mesh with the bank's employee profile.

Past success is a very common factor in selection of colleges for campus recruitment, which seems logical since organizations want to repeat past successes, whether determined by the retention rate of graduates, their track record after recruitment, or some other method. In the 1985 Northwestern Endicott Report (Lindquist, 1985), which surveyed 250 organizations on the subject of campus recruiting, respondents ranked previous successes very highly on their list of criteria for selecting colleges for campus interviewing: 94 percent ranked "past success in recruiting" either important or very important, and 75 percent listed "success of employed graduates in company" as important or very important. In a survey the author conducted with organizations recruiting MBAs, forty organizations out of fifty responded that the success of previous graduates was their first, second, or third criterion in their selection of colleges.

Overall Curriculum. Traditionally, organizations recruit at colleges that graduate a significant number of students in the field. This method can have both positive and negative considerations. With a large number of graduates from which to select, organizations may be more selective, but quality is not always equated with quantity—a large graduation class can often mean a less stringent curriculum. Thus, organizations should evaluate the curriculum at the college to determine if students are being prepared adequately for future jobs. The curriculum, not just a large program, should be the primary consideration. In the Northwestern Endicott Report, mentioned above, the actual disciplines offered was the most important criterion in selecting a college. Ninety-five percent of the 250 organizations responded with an important or very important ranking on this item. In the survey of MBA-recruiting organizations, thirty-eight of fifty organizations responded that overall curriculum was their first, second, or third criterion in selecting a college. These results highlight the importance of curriculum in recruitment decisions.

Reputation of College and Faculty. Opinions differ on the factors that should be considered in determining a school's reputation. According to a survey conducted by Jenkins, Reizenstein, and Rodgers (1984), high admission standards, strong leadership by the dean, and a large number of graduates in key industry positions within ten years are the primary determinants of an MBA program's reputation. Such qualifications probably closely parallel other college programs aimed at preparing graduates for business. Some organizations believe the quality of a program is closely associated with how well the school's faculty focuses on practice rather than on theory. Others feel the only way to judge the reputation of a school is to see how well its graduates succeed in the work world. In the author's MBA recruiting survey referred to earlier, the reputation of the school was clearly the most important criterion for selecting campuses for recruiting. Nineteen out of fifty organizations selected it as their number one choice and forty organizations ranked it as one of their top three choices.

The reputation of the faculty deserves further comment. A faculty member, well known for research or teaching in a field closely related to the organization's, may attract the attention of some organizations. If possible, recruiters should try to gain some insight into the background and research experience of key faculty members. This practice was supported by respondents in the Northwestern Endicott Report (Lindquist, 1985): 91 percent rated the reputation of the faculty/program as important or very important in selecting colleges for campus interviewing. However, in the survey of organizations concentrating on MBA graduates, the reputation of the faculty was not as important: Although thirty-three respondents did consider the reputation of the faculty as one criterion, only two considered it important enough to rank it as first choice and only eighteen ranked it in the top three choices.

Content/Quality of Courses. The content and quality of the courses offered is also important in evaluating schools for recruitment potential. In the survey of organizations recruiting MBAs, thirty-three organizations reported that they evaluate the content and quality of courses in their decision-making process to determine recruiting locations. Twelve of these companies ranked it as their number one choice and twenty-three ranked it in their top three factors. This seems logical since a recruitment trip to a college may be fruitless without knowledge of the content and quality of courses offered (though this information is not always available).

Location. The location of colleges is another factor to consider in determining where to direct recruitment efforts. The size of the recruitment budget may dictate whether location is a primary consideration. Usually, the greater the distance, the greater the costs. This philosophy is supported by the Northwestern Endicott Report, in which 79 percent of the 250 organizations surveyed ranked nearby geographic location either important or very important. Whether this finding was based on the cost of travel or the likelihood of attracting students to the organization was not clear. In the aforementioned survey of organizations recruiting MBAs, location did not seem to be a major consideration for selecting colleges to recruit. Only two companies considered it number one and only eight ranked it in their top three choices.

There is no one method of selecting colleges that is right for all organizations. With an adequate budget and staff, some organizations have the luxury of selecting colleges in all parts of the United States or adding another location each year. Others must contain recruitment efforts to regional colleges. When the number of recruits is relatively small and the organization is located near several colleges, it is likely that recruitment needs can be met by working with those colleges. However, as job opportunities increase, the geographical scope of recruitment usually expands.

Regardless of which criteria are used, it is important to know as much as possible about the colleges, curricula, faculty, and if possible, the course content, prior to investing in campus recruitment. A little extra time on the front end to plan recruitment location adequately should reduce costs and enhance results. Tables 5A and 5B summarize the results of the two surveys presented in this section. These results are consistent with another detailed study of the recruiting practices of twenty-five organizations (McBurney, 1982), which identified the following factors as most important in deciding whether to visit a college: (1) the curriculum, (2) the general reputation of the college, and (3) the productivity of the college, chiefly measured in terms of hires. Other factors mentioned as important were relationship with colleges, past experience in hiring, and geographic location.

Preparing for College Recruiting

College recruiting, and in particular recruiting on campus, is an efficient means of meeting bright young people. Even with its pitfalls, recruiting talent directly on campus generally costs less than hiring by any other means, even allowing for travel and recruiting time. Some organizations are consistently successful in recruiting the quantity and quality of college graduates they need, regardless of the level of competition, while others rarely fulfill their recruiting requirements. The difference in success could be their approach to the issue. Although there is no blueprint for

Table 5A. Factors Used in the Selection of Colleges for Campus Recruiting.

Factor	Rating Important or Very Important
1. Disciplines offered	95%
2. Past success in recruiting	94%
3. Reputation of faculty/program	91%
4. Recruiting effectiveness	90%
5. Geographic location	79%
6. Success of employed graduates in company	75%
7. Cooperation and effectiveness of placement office	74%
8. Company-faculty relationships	65%
9. Preparation of students for interviewing	62%
10. Retention rate of college's graduates	60%
11. Allows pre-screening/closed schedules	49%
12. Number of alumni now with company	45%
13. Published ratings or ranking (Gourman Report)	39%
14. Availability of resume books	30%
15. Institutional size	23%
16. Pressure from alumni executives in company	22%
17. Physical facilities of placement office	18%
18. Solicitation by placement office	9%

Source: Lindquist, 1985.

Table 5B. Curricula/Program Evaluation for Organizations Recruiting MBA Graduates.

Criteria	First Choice	Second Choice	Third Choice	Total Respondents
Reputation of school	19	13	8	45
Success of previous graduates	7	12	14	40
Content/quality of courses in the concentration	12	9	2	33
Overall curriculum	10	5	6	38
Reputation of faculty	2	7	9	33
Location	2	1	5	35

success in college recruiting, five major characteristics of successful programs were identified by Thain, Yoxall, and Stewart (1979):

- strong top management support
- a well-organized college relations program
- administration by well-trained and experienced professionals
- continuity from year to year
- continuous evaluation and improvement.

Presenting detailed discussion of these areas is beyond the scope of this book, but each is briefly examined below.

Gaining Top Management Support. A prerequisite for any successful human resources program is the strong support of top management. Without this support, cooperation from middle management, which is also crucial to successful recruitment programs, may be difficult to achieve.

The most effective approach to elicit top management support is to seek their input and involvement while apprising them of plans, policies, and problems in college recruitment. Most recruiting goals for new professional talent are usually a direct result of the strategic planning conducted by top executives. As a logical extension of this process, top executives should have an opportunity to help determine annual college recruiting goals, discuss the anticipated cost of recruiting, and review previous recruiting successes and problem areas, such as noncompetitive starting salaries, excessive turnover of new graduates, or lower than expected hire rates.

Direct top management involvement in recruitment activity can be an added benefit. A few executives have enough interest in the process to visit campuses and interview students. Others can be helpful by speaking on campus or by utilizing faculty contacts to strengthen the relationship with the college. Still others can be involved in receptions, dinners, or other social events when prospective candidates are brought to the organization for a site visit. A variety of creative methods can be used to secure top management's involvement and support in the college recruiting activity. A word of caution is needed here. Managers may opt for the "old school tie" and support their alma mater at the expense of other colleges

Assigning Responsibilities. The structure of the college recruiting function is important to its success. As with other functions in the organization, clear lines of authority and responsibility are necessary to avoid confusion and duplication of activities. The human resources department is the likely place in the organization to find the responsibility for college recruiting. Depending on the scope of the department, the function may range from a part-time responsibility for the employment manager to a joint responsibility of a complete staff of professionals under the direction of a college relations manager.

In some organizations the college recruiting function is centralized; in others it is decentralized. Both approaches have advantages. Centralized recruiting provides an opportunity to economize by organizing the specialists and recruiting activities in one area under the direction of a single executive. Centralized recruiting can avoid omissions, duplications, and communication problems connected with recruiting visits. In addition, a centralized function provides for more control over the quality of different steps in the recruiting effort and ensures that it is staffed with professionals.

An increasing number of large companies are managed on a decentralized basis, and subsequently the college recruiting function is decentralized, usually under the direction of a local human resources manager. The principal advantage of decentralization is that it brings the recruiting process closer to the target jobs, allowing recruiters to monitor the success of their efforts, a task difficult to accomplish in a remote, centralized, headquarters office. A decentralized approach also allows divisional or regional locations to develop recruiting practices and programs consistent with their specific needs.

When minimizing transition problems is a high priority, college recruiting should be decentralized to the extent possible. In this arrangement, recruiters are more likely to know more about the jobs the graduates will perform and to be held accountable for their results. Recruiters in a corporate office, removed from the outlying operations, may lose touch with the needs of those facilities. Unless administered carefully, however, a decentralized approach can be confusing to students and to college placement officers, particularly in situations where two or more divisions of an organization are recruiting on the same campus.

The advantages of both centralized and decentralized recruiting can be realized in an integrated approach. Under this arrangement a centralized coordinator provides overall direction and coordination of the college recruiting effort, while at each major location an individual is assigned the duties for local college recruiting. A dotted-line reporting relationship usually connects the local representative with the centralized coordinator, keeping the responsibility for results at the lowest possible level while ensuring organization-wide coordination and communication.

During periods of peak demand, most organizations select part-time recruiters from within the organization to assist. Line managers searching for first-level supervisory candidates, engineering managers seeking new technical graduates, or an accounting manager needing a new cost accountant are three examples of potential part-time recruiters. Human resources staff professionals, not usually involved in recruiting, may be temporarily assigned to recruiting to help with peak demands.

The quality of college recruiting programs is no better than the quality of the employees assigned to the recruiting task. Therefore, the individuals selected as recruiters must be knowledgeable about the organization as well as the target jobs. They must be excellent communicators, high achievers, and self-starters. They should enjoy working with students and representing the organization with outside groups. Although some of the skills needed for the assignment can be taught in preparation sessions, a minimum level of skills and abilities should be required in the selection process. Most organizations rotate recruiters so they do not get stale or bored with the assignment, although this approach requires an additional investment in recruiter preparation. However, part-time recruiters are not as likely to become bored as full-time recruiters.

Preparing Recruiters. Few activities in the recruiting process are as important as recruiter preparation. Recruiters must have a thorough knowledge of the college recruiting function and be effective interviewers. Training sessions or workshops, in which recruiters devote one or more days to preparing for their assignments, are common. Also, through meetings, correspondence, policy manuals, and guides they can be kept informed about the status, plans, and policies of recruiting. Some organizations develop detailed policy and procedures manuals that outline how the recruiting process works and the recruiters' responsibility in the process. Manuals can help ensure recruiting consistency and serve as an excellent training tool to prepare recruiters for their campus visits.

As a minimum, recruiters need to have an understanding of the following topics:

• recruiting needs
• target jobs for the graduates
• recruiting schedules
• recruiting results from last year and expected results this year
• how the recruiting process will work
• compensation plans
• benefit packages
• fair employment requirements and restrictions
• how the formal education/training (or transition) program operates
• how candidates will be evaluated
• principles and practices of interviewing
• career opportunities
• how to handle communication and correspondence
• follow-up with candidates.

One report has identified over fifty questions to which recruiters must have answers before visiting campuses (Edwards, 1986). Training for interviewing skills is probably the most critical part of preparation. Recruiters should be provided with interview guides and have ample time to understand and practice interviews. Ideally, they should observe positive role models of effective interviews, have their practice interviews videotaped, and receive appropriate constructive criticism.

Other Recruitment Sources for College Graduates

Although campus visits may be the primary source of the new college graduate, other important sources are available that should not be overlooked.

Internal Referrals. Current employees or recent retirees are an excellent source for recent college graduates through an internal referral process. These individuals, who are knowledgeable about the organization and sometimes the particular job in question, can present a realistic description of the job and thus help ensure that the graduate selected can adjust to the job. This is a low-cost recruiting source, although some organizations pay referral fees, particularly for jobs in shortage occupations. A referral plan usually has two stipulations: The referring employee must be a full-time employee at the time of the award and the new recruit must remain employed for six full months before an award will be made. Two problems can arise with the internal referral process. First, employees tend to recommend relatives and close associates, and hiring relatives is a controversial issue and is sometimes even prohibited. However, it does work in some organizations, particularly in those where a flexible policy is developed to avoid sensitive situations. The second problem occurs when this recruitment source is used excessively, resulting in an inbreeding of employees who think, act, and look alike. This may cause problems when new and "different" talent is not regularly brought into the organization.

Walk-In Applicants. Walk-in applicants are plentiful for most organizations, and some of these applicants become excellent professional employees. Generally, unsolicited candidates are attracted to the organization because of its reputation or its visibility. At other times they may apply in response to advertisements, particularly ones announcing career opportunities. One potential drawback is that accepting walk-in applicants affects applicant flow data necessary for affirmative action practices. Changing guidelines from the Equal Employment Opportunity Commission make it wise to treat such applicants carefully and to file information in an orderly fashion for possible audits.

Job Fairs. A popular recruitment source is the job fair, an event often sponsored by an association, student group, or professional society. The job fair, or "career day" as it is often called, may focus on a particular type or class of student, such as female accountants, minority engineers, or Hispanic school teachers, or it can be broadly based for all students in a particular school or local area. Some job fairs limit attendance to junior and senior classes, while others allow students at all levels to attend.

At the job fair, organizations usually set up displays in a large auditorium. Students are provided ample time to visit booths and informally discuss career opportunities. From the organization's standpoint, the most important requirement is to keep good records of students who visit the booth so that follow-up contacts can be made. Some organizations compile this data by asking students to enter drawings for door prizes. Some even go a step further and have recruiters standing by to interview the most promising. Still others provide toll-free numbers for students to call and schedule a time to visit the organization.

Although a job fair does not allow the organization the luxury of in-depth conversations, it does provide an opportunity to contact many students, which may be extremely important when college graduates are in peak demand. Job fairs are usually inexpensive for the organization and can be an effective recruiting tool for new college graduates.

Open House. Broadly defined, an open house is any employer-sponsored gathering open to the public. In the recruitment process, it serves as a useful tool for attracting employees in nearly all classifications, from such professionals as engineers and programmers to administrative assistants and secretaries. It focuses primarily on entry-level, professional jobs. Hospitals, manufacturers, and banks all have had success with open houses. According to one report, the open house is the most cost-effective means of recruiting while still maintaining high quality of recruits. It is the best way to get maximum utilization out of each recruiting dollar (Kenney, 1982).

A well-orchestrated open house attracts many people from diverse backgrounds. Some are new graduates while others may be interested in changing jobs. Still others may be simply satisfying their curiosity about the organization. The open house reaches one of the most desirable yet usually unreachable employee types—the person genuinely undecided about changing positions.

In most cases, holding the open house on-site provides a distinct advantage, for it can include tours, demonstrations, and special talks about the type of work performed. In some situations, however, an on-site location is not the most effective because some employees may not want to visit or be seen visiting another organization's facilities. In this case the neutrality of a hotel, motel, or restaurant provides a relaxed, comfortable atmosphere for all participants. Also, it may allow the organization to hold the open house closer to the concentration of population. Newspaper ads and other media publicize the event, and if the announcements are effective, the facility or hotel suite will be bulging.

Trade and Professional Associations. Other important resources are industry trade groups, professional associations, or technical societies that may have a placement service for their members. In addition, they frequently publish membership directories, which provide an excellent source for recruiting specialized college-educated talent. Contacts can be made through the group's placement service or directly with members by telephone or direct mail solicitation.

Alumni Associations. Major alumni associations sometimes offer a placement service for their members. The quality and extent of this service vary considerably depending on the association and the college's budget. Frequently, when recent college graduates are considering job changes, they return to their alma mater for help in making a move. This is an excellent source to recruit recent graduates who are experiencing adjustment difficulties in other organizations. They are interested in cutting their attachments quickly, making a move as gracefully as possible, and preparing for a second try in a new organization. Also, this is a very inexpensive source because fees are not usually charged.

Employment Agencies. Private employment agencies sometimes place new college graduates. A few agencies even target new graduates who for some reason prefer not to use the college's placement office. (Some colleges, particularly small liberal arts colleges, do not have a formal placement activity and thus graduates are on their own to seek employment.) Private agencies place candidates for a fee that is paid by either the candidate or the employer. Some organizations refuse to pay agency fees, particularly for new college graduates. Others will pay as long as the agency has done its homework and accurately represents the candidate. Use of this source hinges on the policy of the organization and its past experiences with agencies, whether good or bad.

Pre-Employment Programs. As discussed in Chapter Two, formal programs that combine work and study for students before they graduate can serve as an excellent recruiting source for future full-time, professional employees. Cooperative education programs, internship programs, summer employment programs, and part-time employees (who usually attend school full time) are four excellent sources of new professional employees. It is extremely important for organizations with work-study programs to consider participants for full-time employment when they graduate.

Components of the Selection System. At the heart of every selection system are the key components used to evaluate skills and abilities. Although it may be easy to identify graduates who appear to have the potential for professional employment, it is more difficult to establish the selection criteria necessary to make a final decision.

A variety of techniques are available for gathering data and making the final selection decision. The interview is the most common technique, and it can be designed to gather different types of data. Other data-gathering instruments are resumes, tests, job simulations, background/reference checks, security clearances, recommendations, assessment centers, and physical examinations. These selection system components must be integrated to establish a formal selection system, such as the one shown in Figure 2, which is used to select candidates for commercial banking account officers. A formal selection system accomplishes several goals essential to a successful recruiting program: (1) it presents the components in an efficient sequence and helps ensure that the selection process is standardized; (2) it provides clearly defined decision points to reject new graduates early in the process when sufficient data justifies this action; and (3) it prevents unplanned overlap in coverage of background information and in providing information about the job and organization. Although systems vary with the organization, most use the following components.

Resumes. Resumes are necessary but not critical as a selection tool. They are necessary because they furnish valuable information needed early in the process, usually at the first contact. Resumes are used to identify individuals with the appropriate backgrounds, and in this regard they serve as a useful screening device. This does not mean, however, that resumes should not be prepared professionally. Graduates will be ignored when their resumes are sloppy, inadequate, and poorly organized.

Background or Reference Checks and Security Clearances. Every selection system should include reference checks and a review of past performance. Reference checks provide useful insight about preparation and work habits and usually include a confirmation of education and training background. Degree verification is becoming more important, particularly with the growing number of fraudulent degrees and fake transcripts being used by applicants. Transcripts should be secured even when applicants produce copies of diplomas. If the organization is unfamiliar with the institution, it might be helpful to check the credentials and accreditation of the institution. Diploma mills are plentiful, granting degrees to individuals for a price. Fraudulent degrees should not be a problem wih graduates interviewed through the college placement office, as academic records are usually furnished to prospective employers.

Figure 2. Selection System for Commercial Banking Account Officer.

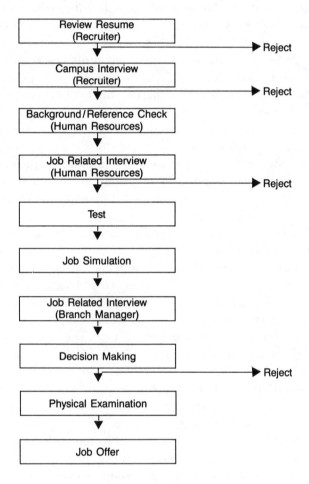

Source: Taken in part from Byham, 1985.

For experienced new graduates, checks of previous work experience should center on job-related requirements. Work habits, skills, abilities, and characteristics necessary for the job should be thoroughly checked with previous employers. If possible, reference checks should be made directly to the former supervisors or to fellow employees if supervisors are not available. Personnel departments are very cautious in what they say and may limit their comments to job classification, pay, and date of termination. It is important to stick to job-related questions, keeping both the reference checker and the former employer within the limits of the law. Reference checks should be conducted in the same way as interviews and should seek specific examples of on-the-job behavior related to target jobs. For the latest material on reference checking, see Byham (1985).

Recommendations: Faculty and Others. Although a few organizations consider recommendations supplied by the candidate, most ignore them because of the small substantive value they bring to the selection decision. New graduates are likely to give references that are extremely favorable, and few letters of recommendation from faculty members or close associates are objective in presenting qualifications. Although they may be useful in obtaining input on the candidate's character, most professional jobs require more than good character for success. Because of this, recommendations are rarely used, and in most studies regarding selection criteria, letters of recommendation are usually at the bottom of the list.

Physical Examinations. Organizations usually require physical examinations for all new employees, and college graduates are no exception. This practice is reasonable and justifiable because an organization must hire employees at all levels who can function effectively on the job. Some jobs can be very stressful and demanding, requiring high levels of physical energy. Unhealthy individuals may not be able to withstand the tremendous physical pressures involved. In an office setting, of course, the physical requirements are not so stringent.

Physical examinations should focus on job requirements. Applicants should not be disqualified unless physical impairments or deficiencies prohibit them from functioning in the job. The examining physician must understand the physical requirements for the job and establish a dialogue with the company's medical coordinator. These requirements vary with the type of job and the environment in which the work is performed, as well as the organization's policies and procedures. For additional information on the use of the physical examination in the selection process, see Byham (1985).

Drug Testing. In addition to physical examinations, pre-employment testing for drugs is becoming a common practice, not only in large companies but in local, state, and federal governments. Drug-testing procedures usually detect six categories of drugs: stimulants, depressants, narcotics, hallucinogens, synthetic drugs, and marijuana. Employers have dual concerns when considering a drug-testing policy—the implications of drug use for the employee's safe and acceptable job performance and the implications for the organization if such activity is allowed. Thus, an employee's unlawful use of drugs on the organization's premises or during working time is often treated more severely than similar conduct during nonworking hours. In the latter situation, work performance may not be affected directly, but the organization may still consider such activity contrary to its interests.

Generally, employers have the right to require an applicant to submit to a pre-employment blood or urinalysis test to detect drugs in the applicant's system. An applicant's practices or past record regarding drug use can also be a part of the employment decision. In addition, employers have the right to disqualify an applicant for employment if the applicant refuses to submit to a test or if the test results are unsatisfactory. Though these rights apply to employees generally, they have been limited to some degree by state legislatures, judicial developments, and collective bargaining relationships. It is extremely important for new college graduates to understand the organization's drug-testing policy, possibly even before job offers are extended; in this way, drug users can withdraw from consideration, avoiding misunderstandings and the potential embarrassment of a rejection.

Interviews. Probably the most important component of a selection system is the interview. Structured interviews, often referred to as "pattern interviews" because they contain a predetermined list of interview questions, are very common. However, more organizations are beginning to use unstructured interviews that allow the interviewer to ask additional questions as information is uncovered. Unstructured interviews are developed around specific job-related objectives. For convenience, selection interviews have been grouped into three categories: preliminary or screening interviews, campus recruiting interviews, and detailed job-related interviews.

Preliminary or screening interviews are brief interviews used to eliminate casual applicants. Their purpose is to determine if candidates meet basic qualifications and have genuine career interest in available job opportunities. They are usually reserved for candidates who have applied to the organization through such informal recruiting sources as referrals or for walk-in candidates. Few job-related questions are asked; instead, the interviewer explains the job and the selection process and discusses the candidate's potential.

Perhaps the interview requiring the greatest skill is the *college campus interview.* The initial interview is conducted usually within a thirty-minute or one-hour time frame. Although initial screening is usually performed by the college placement office, it usually schedules only those students who have certain majors and an interest in the position to be filled. In some cases employers screen applicants through resumes. The backgrounds of the students vary, and most of them do not have job experience. The age, language, or appearance of the student may create a barrier between the student and the interviewer. At best, the campus interview serves as a screening device to check the interest in, and basic qualifications for, professional employment. This interview is important because the decision to move to the next step in the selection system often includes the expense of a visit to the employer's facilities.

The most important interviews in selection systems are the *detailed job-related interviews.* Typically conducted at the employer's facilities by professionally trained interviewers, they include questions relating to the characteristics, skills, and abilities (usually called "dimensions") required for successful performance on the job. An interviewer will ask for specific examples of behavior, both good and bad, related to each job dimension. For example, on the dimension of initiative, a potential candidate might be asked the following questions:

- How was your education financed?
- How did you go about finding your first job?
- What were your most important accomplishments while at your first job?

In another example on the dimension of judgment, a candidate may be asked the following questions:

- Why did you select the University of Michigan?
- Why did you select finance as a major?
- What is the most difficult decision you have made in the last six months?

In these two examples, responses provide evidence of a candidate's skills on these two dimensions. Interviewers then rate candidates on a sliding scale for each dimension, providing a basis for comparison among candidates being considered for the same job. Usually more than one person conducts job-related interviews: a representative from the human resources department and the manager of the department with the job vacancy make an ideal pair for conducting them.

The interview process has come under fire as a valid selection tool because of discrimination suits. Much of the attention has been on the types of questions asked, and thus some organizations have developed interviewing guides listing questions to avoid. Because of these legal concerns, organizations have placed increased emphasis on other methods of arriving at the final selection decision. The interview then becomes just another component of the total selection system. Limiting questions to those specifically related to the job can prevent many problems in the interview process. However, there are no hard and fast rules for conducting interviews that will ensure infallibility in selecting the best candidate. Interviewing is not a science and does have significant weaknesses as a selection tool.

Testing. Many organizations abandoned selection tests when they were challenged by discrimination suits in the 1960s and 1970s. The majority of the tests in use could not be validated while others were of questionable validity. The safest course of action appeared to be the elimination of testing altogether. Today, however, psychologists, lawyers, and personnel specialists are increasingly being asked to provide opinions as to whether testing programs will be acceptable to the EEOC and/or the Office of Federal Contract Compliance (OFCC). Both of these federal agencies have published guidelines and other documents in an effort to reduce uncertainty and to assist employers in complying with legislation and executive orders affecting testing. Yet nothing has been published to date that would provide a sure guide to employer action; many uncertainties and ambiguities remain. Faced with the prospects of terminated federal contracts and sizable awards for damages, some organizations have decided to eliminate further testing until the situation is clarified. Such a strategy may require a long wait. For more information on the status of testing, see Walsh and Betz (1985).

On the positive side, there has been a general improvement in the quality and quantity of validated tests available for employee selection. The difficult task is to find reliable criteria to relate the results of the selection test to future job performance. Considering the variable nature of people, performance, and tests, it is easy to see the problems organizations have faced in test validation. For a comprehensive listing of tests, see Yoder and Heneman (1979).

Job Simulations. Job simulations (sometimes called "work samples") are another effective technique to evaluate ability to handle a professional job. These simulations are usually behaviorally oriented, since most of the actions and behavior of professional employees correlated with job success can easily be observed and documented. By definition, a behavioral simulation is a controlled situation in which candidates display behavior related to success on the job. For example, sales representatives must frequently make presentations about new products or services. A sales job simulation can be developed by giving candidates the appropriate product features and information and asking them to make a sample presentation. Each candidate's behavior is observed by a trained representative, who might even play the role of the customer. In other cases it might be a third-party observation. The candidate's behavior in the presentation would then be placed in categories or dimensions and rated.

Job simulations are particularly appropriate in situations where it is difficult to evaluate the ability of graduates when they had little or no opportunity to demonstrate the job-related skills in previous work assignments. For example, it might be difficult, if not impossible, to observe a graduate's planning and organizing skills in a previous job. A simulated exercise in which the graduate has an opportunity to demonstrate planning and organizing abilities can provide additional important information. Several types of job simulations are commonly used to supplement other components of the overall selection system, including the four discussed below.

In-basket exercises require new graduates to handle the accumulated memos, notes, letters, and other written items found in a simulated in-basket. They must make decisions, ask for cooperation, write letters and reports, and plan, organize, and schedule activities based on the information supplied in the in-basket. This type of job simulation is well-suited for supervisory and managerial jobs. It measures dimensions such as problem analysis, sensitivity, initiative, planning and organizing, written communication, judgment, and decisiveness.

Analysis exercises evaluate new graduates' ability to sift through data, come to a conclusion, and present a logical argument to support the conclusion. They are given data for a specific situation and asked to recommend appropriate courses of action. This type of exercise is particularly suited for measuring such dimensions as written communication, judgment, and analysis.

Interview simulations require meetings with employees, either one-on-one or as a group. New graduates are asked to conduct interviews that simulate meetings with employees, staff members, or other individuals with whom they will be in frequent contact. This type of simulation is particularly effective in evaluating candidates' proficiency in dealing with difficult situations, such as conflict resolution, disciplinary discussions, and problem solving, and enables evaluation of such dimensions as planning and organizing, leadership, sensitivity, oral communication, and tolerance for stress.

Scheduling exercises require graduates to schedule the work assignments of employees. This may include planning for work flow, arranging for resources, and arranging special work projects. Scheduling exercises simulate problems faced by professional employees and allow an evaluation of such dimensions as planning and organizing, analysis, judgment, and decisiveness.

Other types of job simulations or work samples can be a part of the selection process. They form an integral part of the assessment center process, described next.

Assessment Center Method. An assessment center is a formal system of simulations used to evaluate performance on job dimensions identified as important for success in a particular job. Although its primary application has been in the selection of supervisors, it has other applications for professional jobs for graduates, such as sales representative. It differs from other evaluation techniques in three major ways:

1. Multiple job simulations are used to elicit behavior.
2. Groups of individuals are evaluated at the same time.
3. Assessment is conducted, and evaluations are made, by trained observers (or assessors) who are familiar with the job for which candidates are being selected.

Several factors have stimulated interest in the assessment center method, including the accuracy of the technique, its nondiscriminatory features, and its positive impact on the morale of candidates. In addition, it has high acceptance by management, and it provides a learning experience for participants and assessors.

Defining the criteria to use in selecting candidates is a very important initial task in implementing a center. A successful candidate must possess a variety of characteristics, skills, and abilities, called "dimensions." These dimensions emerge from a logical, rational job analysis, which usually includes the following:

- a review of all job descriptions and other documents related to the job
- direct observation of job incumbents at various time periods
- interviews with job incumbents to determine how they spend their time and to identify the critical and challenging parts of their jobs
- a questionnaire, administered to all incumbents, describing the major job activities
- interviews with all management personnel to whom the job incumbents report to collect specific examples of the incumbents' effectiveness or ineffectiveness
- generation of a tentative list of dimensions
- a final questionnaire given to managers to determine which dimensions will be included in the selection system.

Although these steps may vary slightly, their purpose is to isolate the most important dimensions related to success. The dimensions for a professional job will vary considerably with the organization, its policies and procedures, the type of work, and the work environment. It is difficult, if not impossible, to suggest a group of dimensions apropriate for a job in an organization without applying the above steps. To illustrate the use of dimensions, here is a brief description of the key dimensions developed for a retail store salesperson (Byham, 1985).

- *oral communication*—effectiveness of verbal expression in individual or group situations
- *sensitivity*—understanding the needs and feelings of others
- *tolerance for stress*—stability of performance under pressure and/or opposition
- *planning and organizing*—establishing a course of action for self and for others to accomplish a specific goal
- *energy*—maintaining a high activity level.

A typical assessment center involves six participants and lasts approximately two days. The participants take part in exercises that display their skills in each of the job dimensions. Usually three assessors observe and record the participants' behavior. From this point on in the process, slight variations exist in the way a particular assessment center works.

The techniques used in an assessment center to measure potential can vary. As a general rule, no single technique provides information on all the dimensions indicated for the job. Considerable research has shown that certain techniques provide information that is highly relevant to specific dimensions (Moses and Byham, 1977). For example, the most effective way of evaluating interpersonal behavior is simply to have a candidate interact with others. Asking an individual to select a preferred leadership approach in a given setting is not as effective as simulating an actual situation that requires leadership capabilities. What is needed is a variety of exercises or job simulations that provide assessment center participants an opportunity to display their skills and abilities relative to each of the supervisory job dimensions. For a thorough analysis of the validity of the assessment center, see Thornton and Byham (1982).

Although the assessment center process has many positive features, several factors should be weighed before implementing it. First, there is the cost, which varies depending on the size of the organization and extent of outside assistance. For a company with 100 target employees, the cost for a consulting firm to implement an assessment center could be as high as $30,000. The cost thereafter might run to $500 per candidate (Phillips, 1985). Another factor is time. Assessment centers are time-consuming for the administrator as well as for the assessors. Assessor training usually takes three to five days, plus the time required to conduct an assessment center—nearly a week. When used to select college graduates, time and costs become more critical. It is difficult to pursuade graduating seniors to devote two to three days to the recruiting process, and when they do it adds significantly to recruiting costs. A third factor is the legal issue. The assessment center process is a fair, objective, and legally defensible system for selecting candidates, but only if the system is properly designed and is implemented under controlled conditions. This adds to costs and to the time required. However, the cost of defending the present selection system, should it be challenged, may overshadow the costs for implementing the assessment center. A fourth factor is the size of the operation. It is difficult to establish a cutoff point at which the process ceases to be feasible. It has been shown to work well in medium-sized organizations, with less than 2,000 total employees, so it should also work well for smaller companies. In fact, the system is currently used to select employees in organizations where the total number of people in the target jobs is less than fifty.

Decision Making. All the previous components of the selection system provide data for making the decision to accept or reject new graduates for job vacancies. This decision, which should be made by key management, is often a group decision. It is important for all the data from the selection system to be processed and summarized into a meaningful format for key decision makers. Most selection systems provide several decision points at which a candidate can be rejected (see Figure 2), allowing an organization to save the time and expense of moving all the candidates through all the steps.

Recruiting Communications

The college senior appeared to have everything going for him. An accounting major, with an "A" average from a leading state university, he was courted by five of the "Big Eight" accounting firms. He read their glossy recruiting literature, interviewed with their college recruiters, visited their offices, stayed at classy hotels, dined in elegant restaurants, and met senior partners. After receiving attractive offers from the five firms, which were accompanied by regular phone calls from firm partners, he finally made a decision and accepted one of the offers. His first assignment? To count toilet seat covers in a client's inventory. He soon discovered that newly hired accounting graduates usually spend their first two years living out of suitcases, doing very basic clerical work, and assisting in audits—one staff accountant among many and not the prestigious professional position he had expected (Dean, Ferris, and Konstans, 1985). This new graduate suffered from reality shock, inherent in the transition process. This shock could have been minimized, however, with more realistic recruiting communications.

Recruiting communications are a critical part of the college recruiting process. Through a variety of media an organization creates an image and provides information, and it is important that the image be accurate and the information be complete. Ideally, recruiting communications emphasize the strengths of the organization and career opportunities, while at the same time explaining the downside aspects of the organization and the difficult aspects of specific job requirements. This section outlines the importance of an effective communications program, which includes recruiting literature, audiovisual presentations, meetings, and job descriptions.

Students learn about organizations in a variety of ways. One major study, conducted with almost 1,000 students interviewed by a major corporation, discovered that students found out about the company through three primary sources: campus placement office (43 percent), friends and relatives (22 percent), and company literature (14 percent). In this study neither faculty members nor other sources, such as professional societies, brought the firm's name to the student's attention (Bergmann and Taylor, 1984). Therefore, it is important to ensure that the college placement office has ample information about the organization and that appropriate literature is developed to help the students learn about the organization.

What Attracts Graduates. The most important part of recruiting communication is to focus on what attracts graduates to organizations and then build on organizational strengths to attract new graduates. One important study of over 600 employees in thirty-three companies, mostly college graduates, focused on why they chose their first employer (Bewayo, 1986). Advancement opportunities was mentioned most often, followed closely by benefits and opportunity to use a wide range of skills. Pay was ranked fourth; challenging responsibilities, fifth; job security, sixth. Rounding out the bottom four were company prestige; informal, family-like working atmosphere; specialization opportunities; and other reasons. In the best-selling book, *The 100 Best Companies to Work for in America*, Levering, Moskowitz, and Katz (1984) used five categories to rate companies:

1. *Pay.* How well does a company pay, relative to other companies in its industry?
2. *Benefits.* How varied and strong are benefit programs? Does the company have profit sharing? Does it match employee savings? Can employees buy stock at a discount? Does it have some unusual benefits?
3. *Job Security.* Do employees have to live in fear of being placed on layoff?
4. *A chance to move up.* Is it possible for an employee to rise from a low level to a high one? Does the company have a good training program?
5. *Ambience.* What unique qualities does a company have? What styles of working or playing set it aside from all others?

In general, graduates seek these qualities in their employers:

1. *Advancement opportunities.* Graduates are ambitious and want most to move up in an organization. They want to see tangible evidence of growth potential, usually in terms of distinct career paths.
2. *Salaries.* Graduates usually want maximum salary and to some salary is the most important consideration. However, most of all they want a salary competitive in the community and industry.
3. *Reputation.* Graduates want to work for a company with a positive, favorable image in the community or business world. They are also attracted to organizations with an outstanding reputation in their major field of study.
4. *Employee benefits.* Graduates want a competitive benefits package to meet their basic needs and give them ample opportunities for rest and relaxation. Having the best package

is usually not as important as having one that is competitive with other organizations.

5. *Quality of work life.* Students are interested in an organization that has an enjoyable and pleasant work life. They want to feel a part of the organization and be treated with dignity. They want to make a contribution and feel pride in their work and the products and services they produce. They prefer open communications and want to be kept informed about important activities and events in the organization.

These qualities that attract students to an organization are consistent with findings in the study by Bergmann and Taylor (1984). Also, this data supports recent theories concerning human needs. The Existence, Relatedness, and Growth (ERG) Theory (Alderfer, 1972), for example, outlines human needs similar to the qualities above. Existence needs include (1) salary level, (2) fringe benefits, (3) fairness in pay, (4) physical safety at work and in daily life, (5) physical aspects of working, and (6) living conditions. Relatedness needs include the need for (1) working or living with friendly people, (2) respect from others, (3) support from others, (4) open communication with others, and (5) a feeling of prestige among others. Growth needs indicate (1) a degree of challenge at work or leisure, (2) the desire for activities in which the individual is independent, (3) the degree that abilities are fully used, (4) personal involvement at work, and (5) the feeling of self-esteem. This three-category system seems to be in accord with data accumulated over the last decade (Wahba and Bridwell, 1976; Wanous and Zwany, 1977). Throughout the recruitment process the organization should focus on matching the needs of students with the needs of the organization. With regard to recruiting literature and other communication, it is important to focus on the areas that attract students and clearly and accurately state the organization's philosophy on each category. Complete descriptions may not be appropriate, but the more information provided the less chance there will be misunderstandings.

Recruiting Literature. For some students, recruiting literature may be the primary source of information whether it is obtained through placement offices, career centers, job fairs, or directly from the organization. Not only is recruitment literature useful as an initial contact, it often serves to provide answers to questions students fail to ask during interviews.

Literature should be developed to meet the needs of students who are the target for the literature. In a study of recruiting literature, conducted by the Eastern College Personnel Officers, Research and Projects Committee (Stantial and others, 1979), students were asked to evaluate the importance of seventeen components as they currently appear in recruiting literature. They were then asked to evaluate how important the components should be in the "ideal" recruiting literature. Table 6A shows that these two student evaluations differ significantly. At the top of the ideal list are details about entry-level positions, and in second place is the training program outline. Five of the top seven items are directly related to the job. The current evaluations of these items did not fare as well.

These results clearly show that students want information about specific job duties, which can improve the selection process and avoid transition problems. However, most organizations are still reluctant to provide details about job opportunities, perhaps because recruiters do not always know which jobs students will understand or fill. In many instances, graduates enter formal education/training programs to prepare them for their assignments, in which case specific job assignments are usually unknown.

Although recruiting brochures come in a variety of formats, they should be professionally prepared, accurate, and describe the work environment. Brochures should contain the following information:

1. *Typical job opportunities,* an extremely important part of the process. More on this later.
2. *Descriptions of the organization,* including products and services, organizational performance, the position in industry, business policies, and future outlook.
3. *The education/training program,* outlining what to expect during the initial weeks and months of employment.

Table 6A. Student Evaluations: Ideal Compared with Current Recruiting Literature.

Ideal Rank (Importance)	Average Rate	Component	Current Rank (Quality)	Average Rating
1	6.07	Details of Entry-Level Positions	7	3.71
2	5.81	Training Program Outline	5	4.14
3	5.71	Hiring Process (timing, evaluation criteria)	15	3.18
4	5.61	Basic Company Information (size, history, philosophy, location)	1	4.64
5	5.58	Benefits (including education)	3	4.22
6	5.57	Requisite Qualifications for Entry-Level Positions	11	3.51
7	5.33	Typical Career Paths	6	3.81
8	5.32	Introduction to Company Products/Services	2	4.43
9	5.29	Starting Salaries/Compensation Forms	16	2.89
10.5	5.17	Employee Review/Evaluation Process	12	3.30
10.5	5.17	Travel Relocation Expectations	10	3.52
12	5.06	General Hiring Patterns	14	3.21
13	4.96	Regional Life-Style/Cost of Living	17	2.64
14	4.84	Exercises Promoting Self-Analysis and Career Goal Definition	13	3.27
15	4.36	Organizational Chart/Structure	9	3.63
16	4.29	Profiles of Typical Employees	8	3.64
17	4.25	Simplified Annual Report	4	4.19

Source: Stantial and others, 1979.

4. *Preferred degrees or majors,* pinpointing the educational background appropriate for the specific job opportunities.
5. *Compensation and benefits,* presented in general language, possibly in terms of competitiveness. Some organizations want their starting salaries to be at the average of survey data

compiled by the placement office; others want to be greater or less than average. Employee benefits packages should be presented in detail and possibly compared with others in the industry.

6.   *Work locations*, including specific facilities, if known. If not, the most likely regions or areas should be outlined.

7.   *The application process*, including steps new graduates take to secure employment with the organization.

Sometimes brochures are targeted for specific purposes. For example, brochures can be designed for different career areas, such as engineering, management, finance. Other variations include brochures focusing on the education or training program, an important aspect of the transition program, or on compensation, benefits, or work life issues.

Descriptions of the Job. Students desire as much information as possible about job opportunities. The more information communicated, the more likely it is that there will be a better match between the graduate and the organization, lessening potential transition problems in the future. Specifically, organizations should communicate the following:

1.   *Job duties and responsibilities.* The jobs for which graduates are recruited should be described in as much detail as possible. Samples of work can show new graduates the actual tasks to be done. If possible, invite graduates to observe incumbent job holders and allow them to discuss job duties. If this is planned, new graduates should visit during typical workloads, not in peak or slow periods. The important point is to be realistic and not overwhelm graduates.

2.   *The education/training program.* The different phases of the formal education/training program, including specific assignments, should be presented as accurately as possible. Graduates should understand the objectives of the program and their role in the process, that is, as observer or contributor.

3. *The basis for performance evaluation.* Graduates need to know how they will be evaluated in initial assignments, who will be evaluating them, and what it will mean in terms of promotion or pay increases.
4. *Typical employees in the target job (or program).* Graduates should know the types of employees who usually succeed in target jobs. A few case histories of current employees in those jobs would be helpful.
5. *Promotions and advancement opportunities.* Career-path information showing typical progressions, if there are any, should be included. This information is typically presented in general terms, as progress will depend on performance. However, graduates expect and need to know about typical progressions.
6. *Expectations.* The expectations of graduates in terms of performance, work habits, and attitudes should be clearly communicated. This avoids misunderstandings that can lead to potential transition problems.
7. *Determinants of success.* Related closely to performance evaluation and "typical employee" information, this material outlines the factors necessary for a successful track record in the job.

Job information is intended to provide prospective employees with a realistic preview of the job or of the education/ training program. This realistic job preview process has been used successfully to reduce the turnover of new graduates and is discussed later in this section (Wanous, 1980).

Audiovisual Material. More organizations are turning to audiovisual aids and video media to supplement recruiting literature and enhance the communication process. Audiovisual material ranges from a brief slide show to sophisticated videotape presentations that students can view at their convenience. Videotapes have important benefits. They enable prospective employees to view the jobs in action and listen to people in those jobs discuss their experiences, responsibilities, and reactions to the organization. Ideally, video material should supplement and reinforce the information in the recruiting literature and the campus interview rather than replace it.

Several companies, including AT&T, Bell Communications, and AeroJet-General, have attempted to make college recruiting efforts more cost-effective through teleconferencing. For example, on October 8, 1985, a teleconference was transmitted from Washington, D.C. to graduating students, mainly in high-tech disciplines, on twenty-one campuses across the country. After the participating companies concluded their remarks, the students and company representatives participated in a question-and-answer session ("Give the Full Recruiting Picture," 1985). Teleconferencing may be an important means of communication between employers and potential employees in the future.

Meetings with Students. Direct communication with students in discussion groups is another important medium. These meetings, arranged by the placement office, a key faculty member, or a professional society, allow the organization to present important information about career opportunities and typical jobs for new graduates. Question-and-answer sessions usually follow. Prior to committing to a campus interview, graduates collect additional information in this type of meeting, ensuring that time is not wasted—by the recruiter or the student—when there is an obvious mismatch in interest or needs. On the other hand, these meetings may attract students who otherwise may not have been interested in the organization. Thus, it serves as a cost-effective screening device. The timing of meetings is important. Some organizations hold them on the night before the interviews. Others conduct them well in advance of recruiting trips in conjunction with a professional society meeting or other student event. These career discussion meetings can spark student interest and provide an excellent opportunity for employers to communicate their message.

Realistic Recruitment. At several points in this chapter the need for realistic recruitment has been emphasized. This approach contrasts with traditional recruitment methods and has shown surprising and impressive results. The traditional approach to recruiting involves presenting positive characteristics of the organization to potential job candidates, rather than the information that insiders find unsatisfactory about the organization. Traditional recruitment is aimed at bringing in as many candidates as possible with the results typically measured by the selection ratio.

Realistic recruitment, rather than selling the organization and the job, focuses on presenting candidates with all pertinent information without distortion. Traditional measures of recruiting success, such as selection ratio, ignore what happens to new graduates after they are employed by the organization. A broader perspective includes not only attracting and selecting competent new graduates but also managing to retain them through a formal transition program. Thus, a realistic approach to recruitment can help ensure that the effects of culture shock are minimized.

Several studies have analyzed the impact of realistic recruitment, or realistic job previews as they are called in the literature. The proponents of this process claim that by providing job applicants with an accurate description of the job, those who accept the job will be more satisfied with it and thus less likely to leave voluntarily. Dugoni and Ilgen (1981) and Wanous (1980) conclude that there is considerable empirical support of the hypothesized effects of the realistic job previews on satisfaction and voluntary turnover. Wanous presents a summary of thirteen studies of experimental results on the realistic job preview process. The view that realistic job previews reduce dissatisfaction and voluntary turnover have been accepted by other researchers (Reilly and others, 1981; Rynes, Heneman and Schwab, 1980). Although this process is very attractive, it is not without its weaknesses. Breaugh (1983) points out flaws in some of the research conducted on realistic job previews and indicates that additional research data is needed before drawing specific conclusions about this process.

The methods for developing realistic previews can vary considerably. The process usually starts with the recruiting literature and continues through the interview stage, where the interviewer accurately describes working conditions and job duties. It continues through the selection process, where, in some cases, work samples are included as a selection component. These job simulations, described earlier in this chapter, are aimed at presenting realistic situations related to part or all of the job, and the applicants are rated on how well they perform on the simulation. In some cases, job-related tests can measure the candidates' ability to handle certain job situations while providing them with a more realistic preview of the job. As mentioned earlier, recruiting brochures are beginning to show a realistic picture of job settings. One example is a booklet used by Prudential to recruit life insurance agents. A portion of the booklet, shown in Exhibit 2, provides a realistic description of the problems experienced by agents and the difficult parts of the job.

In summary, realistic recruitment is a relatively new process that offers significant organizational advantages, particularly when emphasis is placed on minimizing adjustment problems for new graduates. It can help ensure a better match between the graduate and the organization, thus minimizing the transition problems. For additional information on realistic recruitment, see Wanous (1980).

Candidate Requirements

Although it is difficult to address specific requirements that determine the basis for selecting new graduates, it is important to discuss three important areas: experience requirements, skills and abilities, and career needs.

Experience Requirements. Ideally, graduates with work experience should take preference over those without experience, assuming all other factors are equal. Some work experience is better than none and related work experience is preferred. Although most college students have had some type of summer work experience, this alone is not enough to develop work expectations in their chosen profession. Most students perceive summer work as a necessary evil, something to be tolerated for a three-month period until they can return to campus. Few see it as an opportunity to gain insight into the organization and learn

Exhibit 2. The Door to Success Does Not Open Easily (from a Prudential Insurance Recruiting Booklet).

The situations presented on these pages represent some of the problems which face every Agent. Thinking about what your reaction to them would be should help indicate whether or not you should pursue a life insurance sales career.

1. An Agent spends several hours preparing a sound insurance program for a family . . . only to be turned down during the second interview.
2. An Agent completes the sale of a policy only to have the policyholder allow it to "lapse" by not paying a subsequent premium.
3. An Agent is sincerely interested in helping people plan their futures wisely, but, time after time, people say "No" to his recommendations.
4. An Agent makes the personal sacrifice of making a sales call on a stormy night only to find that the prospect has forgotten the appointment and is not at home.
5. An Agent plans to attend an eagerly anticipated social event . . . but he has to postpone it because it is the only night a prospect can see him.
6. An Agent pays a call on a prospect to discuss insurance, only to be subjected to uncomplimentary . . . even though unwarranted . . . remarks about salesmen.
7. A conscientious Agent wants to qualify his prospects carefully and take time to visit policyholders whose insurance is about to lapse . . . but he knows that new prospects and new sales are also essential.
8. An Agent realizes that the Home Office tries to provide him with the best possible service, but he cannot help recalling the time an important case was lost because "the prospect cooled off" or "the competition moved in" while an application was being processed.

Source: Wanous, 1980.

what is expected of them when they graduate. The problems encountered in full-time professional employment are vastly different from those encountered in summer employment. The expectations of the employer are not nearly as high for summer employees, and students are not overly concerned about performance. Therefore, summer employment, although better than no work experience, may not provide help with transition problems.

Students participating in structured pre-employment programs such as cooperative education and internships will usually have work experience closely related to their actual field or major course of study. A recent survey of more than 100 organizations provides insight into the importance of experience in hiring entry-level college graduates (Kaplan, 1985). In this study, personnel professionals reported that work experience related to the concentration or major is the most important type of experience. Among the personnel professionals, outside work experience, such as part-time jobs, ranked higher than field experiences, such as internships. In the same study, college seniors completed the same questionnaires as the personnel professionals; the students generally agreed with employers on the importance of outside work experience but ranked field experience higher.

Skills/Abilities Requirements. The skills and abilities of graduates, important aspects of the selection process, usually cause organizations more problems than any other. The precise skills and abilities essential to success can be determined from detailed job analyses. This subject was briefly discussed earlier in this chapter, where it was noted that dimensions (another term for skills and abilities) should be developed for use in the selection process. The use of job dimensions appears to be a very effective, acceptable, and legally defensible approach to selection (Byham, 1985). Table 6B shows a list of common dimensions used in the selection process. Some jobs require only a few dimensions, while others require as many as fifteen. Only a thorough job analysis can determine which dimensions are important to success in a particular job. One dimension deserves a few additional remarks. Written communication skills are becoming increasingly important for most entry-level professional, technical, and supervisory positions. More organizations are requiring new graduates to be able to express themselves in writing, clearly and succinctly. Because of this requirement writing ability tests are increasingly used as part of the selection process.

Notice that intelligence is not listed as a dimension. Intelligence is not considered a skill or ability, although it appears in selection criteria for many college students. In the study of personnel professionals and students discussed above (Kaplan, 1985), both groups ranked intelligence at the top of the list as the most important selection criterion. The difficulty in using intelligence as a dimension, however, is the problem of how to measure it and its relationship to job success. Some organizations have

Table 6B. Typical Job Dimensions.

1. Impact
2. Oral communication skill
3. Oral presentation skill
4. Written communication skill
5. Creativity
6. Tolerance for stress
7. Work standards
8. Leadership
9. Persuasiveness/sales ability
10. Sensitivity
11. Behavioral flexibility
12. Tenacity
13. Risk taking
14. Initiative
15. Independence
16. Planning and organizing
17. Delegation
18. Management control
19. Analysis
20. Judgment
21. Decisiveness
22. Development of subordinates
23. Adaptability
24. Technical translation
25. Organizational sensitivity

Source: Development Dimensions International, P.O. Box 13379, Pittsburgh, PA 15243.

developed standard tests that measure intelligence to a certain degree, while others rely on a combination of other factors or dimensions to approximate the intelligence level. Still, some rely on grade point averages, assuming a relationship between intelligence and grades, although grades may not be a reliable indicator.

In this same study (Kaplan, 1985), work motivation (that is, personal work standards) was ranked second among employers, although it was ranked fifth by students. Oral communication skills were ranked second by students and fourth by employers. Initiative was third on the personnel professionals' list, but it was ranked in the lower part of the top ten by the students. These results clearly indicate students have limited understanding of the skills and abilities that personnel professionals consider important in college graduates for entry-level professional positions.

Career Needs. Candidate requirements should also consider long-range career development needs of potential employees. According to Derr (1986), employees can be grouped into one of five categories depending on their career aspirations:

- *getting ahead*—pursuing traditional career success in terms of rapid advancement in the organization
- *getting secure*—seeking job security and organizational identity more than advancement or challenge
- *getting free*—wanting autonomy and independence and the option to solve problems in one's own way
- *getting high*—valuing excitement, challenge, and the content of the work
- *getting balanced*—giving equal priority to careers, family, friends, leisure, and self-development activities.

No organization can afford to have all "getting ahead" graduates. Their combined ambition would create an overly competitive atmosphere. Likewise, few organizations would want all of their graduates to be primarily interested in getting secure. The result may be a lack of innovative and creative spirit necessary for most companies to grow and prosper. What is optimum is a balance of graduates with career aspirations consistent with the needs of the organization. For example, fast-growing, high-tech firms developing many new products and services need graduates who desire to get ahead, get free, or get high. Stable organizations with little or no growth and delivering products and services that rarely change (such as a government agency) might focus on graduates who desire to get secure or get balanced. A variety of instruments are available through which an organization can pinpoint the career aspirations of potential professional, technical, and supervisory employees. One such instrument is the Career Anchoring Pattern developed by Pavloff (1986).

Follow-Through

After the initial campus interviews have been conducted and candidates have been invited to the organization for a site visit, the recruiting process is far from over. The follow-through from this point is essential to ensure that all other components of the selection process work effectively.

Organizational Visits. An important part of the recruiting process is the graduate's visit to the organization's facility. Thorough preparation with attention to every detail is necessary so the graduate's time is organized efficiently and personal visits are arranged properly. Even the written invitation is important. It must clearly define the purposes of the visit and provide adequate details on the arrangements.

New graduates can become very disillusioned on visiting an organization and realizing that the visit has not been adequately planned, catching key managers by surprise. Even worse is the manager or staff support person who shows little support for the recruiting activity and indifference about the new graduates' career interests. Even with today's sophisticated recruiting, these situations still occur.

The selection of interviewers for the site visit is another important element. Interviewers should know the organization and have a positive attitude toward the recruiting process. They must be able to portray the organization's image in a positive manner and, as mentioned earlier, provide a realistic view of the challenges and problems graduates may encounter. Interviewers should be briefed, not only on which individuals will be visiting, but also on what is expected of them as they conduct interviews and meet new graduates.

Part of this visit often includes the plant tour, particularly if the graduate will be working directly in a plant. Plant tours should be conducted by individuals who know the plant's operations and can communicate them well. Some organizations assign staff to give plant tours as their regular duty; even these individuals need to be briefed on the importance of making the proper impression on the new graduates. Some parts of the visit may include a tour of the community, city, or area surrounding the location, particularly for graduates who are unfamiliar with the setting. This may include a visit to local attractions to examine available entertainment and leisure activities.

Overall, the visit should be pleasurable and meaningful to graduates. It should not be too hectic nor too slow. The expenses incurred by the graduate should be reimbursed promptly. In essence, the organization should portray a very positive image, while at the same time providing a realistic view of the work setting. New graduates should leave with a clear understanding of the next step in the recruiting process whether the company will follow up or the graduates must initiate the contact. It is best not to leave the follow-up to the graduates, who may have many other offers and opportunities.

Rejections. Although frequently disappointing, rejections are important information to monitor, whether they come from graduates or employers. From the organization's point of view, after making an investment in the new graduates it is essential to find out why some declined to be considered further or turned down job offers. This kind of investigation helps correct recruiting mistakes or problems. If the organization approaches the subject in a diplomatic manner, it can learn reasons for the rejection. Sometimes organizations send a survey to graduates asking for the reasons for rejections. A simple, easy-to-complete form and a self-addressed, stamped envelope can help ensure its return.

When the organization rejects an individual, the individual should understand, at least in general terms, the reason. Rejection discussions should be conducted in a positive manner. An adverse reaction, due to the poor handling of a rejection, can hamper future recruiting efforts with other graduates when they learn how the rejection was handled. Although no graduate likes to be rejected, rejections are sometimes expected and when handled in a sensitive and diplomatic manner, both parties should benefit from the learning experience. Communicating the reason for rejection may help the organization to maintain its objectivity in the employment process since graduates would be rejected only for tangible, objective reasons.

Job Offers. Job offers should be extended to new graduates as soon as possible, particularly in competitive professions or in locations where college graduates have numerous opportunities. The decision-making process for college graduates must be streamlined so offers can be expedited. When faced with multiple opportunities, some graduates will take the first job offer that meets their basic employment needs. Any delays in this process may result in the organization losing many good prospects.

Job offers should be documented with a friendly, personal letter that includes all the pertinent information: the position, location, starting salary, benefits, relocation expenses information, and approximate starting date. Planned education or training programs should be described. If the time between the job offer and the applicant's decision is more than a few weeks, the organization should contact the candidate again to reaffirm the organization's strong interest and answer any remaining questions. This contact is essential to keep the organization's job offer in the mind of the individual, particularly if other offers have been extended.

Acceptance of the job offer completes the recruiting process, but it is only the beginning of efforts aimed at ensuring the new graduate is successful on the job. This marks the beginning of pre-employment education, which is covered in Chapter Four.

4

Introducing and Orienting
New Employees
to the Organization

This chapter focuses on the second and third stages of transition: pre-employment education and orientation. After students are recruited, the organization must begin to prepare them for a permanent professional job. A few organizations take advantage of the time between the selection decision and when the new graduate arrives. Through pre-employment education programs, these organizations provide information, typically presented in orientation sessions. It helps the new employees begin to adjust to the organization and understand their jobs prior to arrival.

Upon arrival, new graduates begin their orientation process, which is designed to help them understand the organization and become a productive member of the team as soon as possible. Whether developing a new orientation or revitalizing an existing one, the designers of the system should address several issues, including strategy, orientation components, and the content of the orientation.

Pre-Employment Education

An often overlooked opportunity to prevent transition problems is available during the time period from recruitment to the first day on the job. This time frame, which can extend to almost nine months for graduates recruited in the fall to report to work the following June, represents fertile ground for pre-employment education; in essence, this period is the beginning of orientation. Because the employer has the student's loyalty and attention, the climate is right for a variety of organizationally focused educational activities. Often, much of what new recruits need to know about an organization can be transmitted before they are actually employed. Preliminary information about the organization, its structure, and its purpose often can be conveyed in such a fashion that new graduates can share this information with family and friends, thereby reinforcing the decision to join the organization.

Typical Activities. The range of pre-employment educational activities varies considerably. Here are a few possibilities:

• *Organizational publications.* Internal publications and communications provide new recruits with information about the activities, people, products, and services of the organization. Official organizational publications, special newsletters, product information sheets, annual reports, company directories, employee handbooks, and other useful documents can increase their understanding of the organization. As a minimum, new graduates should be placed on the organization's mailing list for its official newspaper as soon as the job offer has been accepted. This not only begins the education stage but reassures recruits that they have the job.

• *Direct communication from key executives.* Telephone calls, letters, and notes of encouragement from senior executives, human resources managers, and line executives can help motivate newly recruited students. Personal letters can mean much to new graduates who are eager to become a part of the organization. The tone of these letters should be warm and congratulatory, but they can also provide additional information, introduce other required reading material, or outline expectations.

• *Schedules.* Detailed schedules of planned orientation sessions, training programs, or education sessions could be sent to graduates prior to employment. This lets new graduates know what to expect and when it will occur.

• *Job-related documents.* Job-specific information is helpful for future graduates to begin preparing for full-time employment. Policy manuals, procedures manuals, design specifications, process standards, job information sheets, standard practice instructions, and other work-related documents are appropriate for new recruits. These documents may be mailed directly to students or presented to them in meetings.

• *Self-study materials.* Some organizations, particularly ones that have an extensive education or training program for new graduates, may begin the learning process by assigning books, manuals, programmed instruction booklets, or other materials of a self-study nature. This is a cost-effective way for future employees to learn important job-related information.

• *Meetings/Workshops.* Short meetings or workshops with new recruits prior to employment present another opportunity to conduct orientation, education, or training sessions as part of the transition program. For added impact, these meetings could be held in conjunction with additional plant visits and tours.

The above actions are simple and straightforward, yet they are not practiced very widely in the United States. However, pre-employment education programs are common practice in Japan (Tanaka, 1980). Pre-employment education starts immediately after selections are made, usually in late fall, six months before the graduates arrive in mid-April. These programs familiarize the students with the company; monitor the student's activities at the university; make students comfortable with the company; answer questions they may have; and improve basic skills, such as writing. During the pre-employment education period, several items of the type mentioned above are sent to the new recruits. Sixty percent of the companies interviewed in the Tanaka study hold one- or two-day meetings with students. One-third of these companies hold more than two meetings. These meetings provide future employees with an opportunity to get to know one another through dining and participating in sports activities together. Recruits are sometimes sent to formal training centers where they work and live together. At a formal entrance ceremony after the pre-employment education period the graduates are formally welcomed into the organization. One reason for the popularity of this approach in Japan is that lifelong employment with one company is the norm, particularly for male, professional employees.

A study of socialization practices in western Canada revealed the extent of commitment to pre-employment education in that region. Sixty of the eighty-five respondents indicated that they usually contact new recruits before their first day of employment. This figure is somewhat misleading, however, as in many organizations the time between acceptance of the job offer and the start date is less than one week, so little time is available for pre-employment education. Moreover, many of those who do contact future employees do so for documentation rather than education purposes. In other words, much of the pre-employment contact occurs so that the company can gather more information about the individual rather than vice versa (McShane and Baal, 1984.)

Advantages. Pre-employment education has several advantages. First, it is inexpensive compared to other stages of the transition process. Prospective employees are usually involved in this activity on their own time. A possible exception might be required meetings where the recruits are assembled at a convenient place, usually at the organization's facilities. They may be paid for this time, but certainly a viable option is to not pay them. Also, these meetings cover information that would normally be presented on company time and possibly take longer than the time required for the activity in the pre-employment period.

Second, this process gets the new graduates thinking about the culture of the organization, adapting to the organization, and aligning their values to those sought by the organization. Bits and pieces of information scattered over a longer period appear to have a more lasting impact on the new graduate and eases the adjustment process for the remaining transition stages.

Third, this approach gets more individuals in the organization involved in the recruiting and transition process. During meetings, special communications, or in visits, key employees have an opportunity to meet new recruits and learn more about them. It facilitates interaction between the groups.

Fourth, this careful attention helps ensure that new graduates will not accept other job offers, a problem that has sometimes plagued campus recruiters. Graduates will sometimes accept an offer and continue to interview, looking for a better one. In good economic times this problem is magnified because of the high demand for graduates. Pre-employment education requires immediate interaction and commitment and helps to "lock" the student into the organization.

Fifth, the new recruits appreciate the special attention they receive and the information they secure. New employees are eager to find out more about their future jobs. They are highly motivated, enthused about the organization, and will absorb almost everything they are presented. Pre-employment activities increase their motivation, dedication, and loyalty—with little effort and expense. With these advantages, more organizations should consider educational activities during the pre-employment period; they could reap an impressive return for a small investment.

Orientation Strategy

Orientation systems for new graduates vary considerably. Sometimes the content of orientation sessions and the content of formal education or training programs overlap, and in some organizations the two stages of transition are integrated into one continuous process. McShane and Baal (1984) define orientation as the process of familiarizing new employees to the work setting, which includes the supervisor, co-workers, organizational values and expectations, the physical setting, the corporate structure, and usually the formal employee-employer exchange relationship. Orientation is only one of many components of a well-managed transition process, but it makes a significant contribution to the new graduates' adjustment to the organization and job for it is the first formal activity upon employment. Although orientation may be difficult to distinguish from employee training, orientation generally concerns the transfer of knowledge about the job rather than the actual development of job skills. Orientation also attempts to develop expectations and beliefs in new graduates that will help them to contribute to organizational effectiveness and their own career success.

An effective orientation system evolves from a careful planning process that is part of the organization's overall strategy. This process focuses on the importance of orientation and its impact on organizational output. Developing or revitalizing an orientation system requires addressing such issues as objectives, timing, length, and responsibilities, as well as the preparation of the orientation staff.

Importance of Orientation. Few will dispute the importance of the orientation process and its impact on new college graduates. Yet too many organizations still take this process lightly and do not have adequate programs to address the concerns of new graduates on their first few days of employment. The importance of orientation for new graduates is underscored by four basic assumptions:

1. The new graduates' enthusiasm and motivation may be at its peak at the beginning of employment in the professional work force. New employees are highly motivated and eager to make a contribution.
2. The initial perceptions of co-workers, work environment, and culture will have a long-term impact on the graduates. The first days of employment are critical and will not likely be forgotten; negative impressions during this time are difficult to erase.
3. The first few days of employment represent an excellent opportunity—perhaps the best opportunity—to shape attitudes and influence new graduates.
4. The new graduates' perceptions and impressions will be transmitted to other prospective employees through campus connections, friends, and relatives who are anxious to find out about the new graduates' reactions to their employer.

Given these basic assumptions, the orientation process becomes a very critical part of a new graduate's career. The orientation should be carefully planned and executed. For example, the initial introductions to key individuals and lunch companions on the first day are two important details that can leave lasting impressions. Because it is an excellent time for communication, the orientation should contain positive experiences; the graduate will discover the negative aspects soon enough, without assistance.

A properly designed orientation program can have a tremendous bottom line impact on the organization. As discussed in Chapter One, a redesigned orientation system for professional personnel at Corning Glass Works resulted in a 17 percent decrease in the number of voluntary separations among those with three years or less service. In addition, the time to reach a desirable level of performance decreased from six months to five months. On these two items alone, Corning calculated an eight-to-one benefit/cost ratio for the first year and a fourteen-to-one benefit/cost ratio annually thereafter (McGarrell, 1984).

Given the importance of orientation, why are some organizations reluctant to develop a formal process? In order to understand more fully the barriers to implementing formal programs, one study asked thirty organizations without an orientation program why they had not implemented one. The study found that the single outstanding reason why these organizations had no formal program was that the company had higher priorities. In some cases, these higher priorities were within the human resources department. However, several respondents frankly indicated that their organization did not consider *any* human resource management activity to be a high priority. This response corresponds to the second most important reason given for the lack of a formal orientation: the human resources department did not have enough human or financial resources to develop such a program. However, contradicting these statements is the relatively low importance of "lack of management support" as a reason why no formal orientation program exists. Lack of knowledge to develop an orientation program was indicated as the least important reason for not having one. Most respondents felt that someone in human resource management within the company was familiar enough with the theory and applications of organizational transition to mount a new program. Similarly, only five of the thirty companies interviewed felt that orientation is not cost-effective, and only a few believed that orientation is unnecessary because employees already know their jobs (McShane and Baal, 1984).

Developing the Orientation System. The factors that make an effective orientation system can be difficult to pinpoint. What works for one organization may not work for another, and some organizations seem to take the simplest approaches and produce the best results. A few factors important to the success of an orientation program were identified by Tracey (1983):

- personal involvement of managers, supervisors, and HR staff in the program
- careful and thorough preparation and planning
- clear and specific objectives
- clear definition of the roles of the HR staff and line supervisors
- identification of the information needs of new employees
- adequate facilities, materials, and funding
- capable and dedicated instructors and discussion leaders
- ample time.

Some researchers contend that training of supervisors to conduct their portion of the orientation program is a critical element (Shea, 1985). Others argue that the evaluation of the overall process is extremely important and that it should be incorporated as a major part of the program in the design stage (Phillips, 1981).

It is unusual to find an organization without an orientation program of some kind. The problem often lies in the monitoring of the program. Even a program that is effective when it is implemented can become ineffective as the needs of the organization change or when the individuals responsible for it change. Therefore, it is important to periodically review the orientation process to see if it meets the needs of the organization, particularly as it affects newly recruited college graduates. The steps involved in developing or revising an orientation system are relatively simple.

1. The objectives should be reviewed, or established if there are none. Objectives should focus on what new graduates need to know to be productive as soon as possible, to learn the organization, and to develop a proper attitude.

2. Input should be secured from the management group and staff support personnel involved in orientation to ensure that objectives are adequate and the approach and content of the orientation process are timely and appropriate.

3. Candid input should be obtained from recently employed graduates who have participated in the orientation program. This provides valuable insight into the areas where the orientation system is weak or needs changing. Also, it may be appropriate to solicit input from other employees not involved in the formal orientation program. This input can easily be secured through interviews or questionnaires.

4. Successful approaches used by other organizations should be examined for their applicability. Many organizations have implemented successful orientation programs, and a review of their design and content can be an excellent source of ideas for improving an existing program. When Corning Glass revised its orientation program, it examined an effective program developed by Texas Instruments.

5. The orientation process should recognize that graduates are different and have different needs. It is likely that each graduate is going to a different work area or job, which will demand different types of information. Therefore, to the extent possible, the orientation system should be designed to be flexible to individual needs and requirements.

6. If the orientation involves enough individuals and its impact is significant, it might be appropriate to pilot test the system before finalizing all the materials to be used in the program. However, if the input for revision is reliable, pilot testing may be unnecessary for most organizations.

7. The new or revised program should be produced, packaged, and prepared for presentation using formats and media compatible with existing materials and methods of presentation.
8. The employees responsible for the orientation process, including supervisors, must be trained to use the new system effectively. Thorough preparation is an important element for success.

These basic steps for developing or revising an orientation program will enhance effectiveness of the orientation process and ensure that it meets the needs of new graduates.

Objectives. Most organizations develop specific objectives for their orientation process and monitor progress accordingly. Although they vary considerably with the organization, common objectives are:

- to ensure that the appropriate forms and documents are completed so that the employment process can be finalized
- to welcome new graduates and assure them that they are an important part of the organization
- to provide comprehensive information about the organization
- to help new graduates understand the organization's structure, history, mission, philosophy, and the like so that they can function effectively as soon as possible
- to introduce new graduates to their jobs and work environment
- to develop a thorough understanding of pay practices and benefits
- to communicate the policies, procedures, rules, and standards within which the graduates must work
- to outline the general expectations for new graduates
- to build within graduates a positive attitude about the organization and the community.

Other objectives may address such issues as problem solving, necessity to make a profit, nonunion philosophy, or gaining a commitment from new graduates. Orientation objectives are plentiful and must be developed to reflect the needs of the organization *and* the new graduates.

Timing and Duration. The timing of the orientation process is another important issue. Ideally, new graduates should begin the orientation process on the first day of full-time professional employment. This is the typical goal for many organizations. However, because of the numbers involved, it may be difficult to start an orientation system whenever a new graduate or group of graduates joins the organization. Because of this, some organizations wait until they have several graduates recruited and then schedule a group to begin employment at the same time. Others involve new graduates in other activities until the formal orientation program is scheduled. Still others individualize the process so that it can begin immediately upon the graduate's arrival, utilizing on-the-job coaching, self-study materials, and audiovisual presentations.

The urgency for the graduate to learn job-related information and understand the organization is the determining factor for the timing of orientation. In some cases it is important to schedule it early in the transition process; in other cases it may be advantageous for the new graduate to be on-the-job for a short period of time before participating in the orientation process. The decision hinges on what is to be accomplished and the content of the orientation. Among the fifty-three organizations with a formal orientation program studied by McShane and Baal (1984), over two-thirds begin it immediately. Another 15.1 percent orient newcomers within the first two weeks. For the remaining firms, orientation begins between two weeks and six months after the employee starts work.

The duration of orientation may vary from one hour to two weeks. A short one-hour presentation provides only enough time for a very brief introduction to the organization, the job, and the people. Then the new graduate is available to participate in the formal education or training program or possibly on-the-job training. A longer presentation includes a broad range of detailed activities. Some organizations divide the orientation into segments conducted at different time intervals. Exhibit 3 shows the timetable

Exhibit 3. Timetable of Events in Corning's Orientation System.

Material distribution. As soon as possible after a hiring decision is made, orientation material is distributed: The new employee's supervisor receives a pamphlet titled *A Guide for Supervisors*; the new employee receives an orientation plan.

The pre-arrival period. During this period the supervisor (1) maintains contact with the new recruit, (2) helps with housing problems, (3) designs the job and makes a preliminary MBO (management by objectives) list after discussing it with the new employee, (4) prepares the new employee's office, (5) notifies the organization that all these tasks have been done, and (6) sets the interview schedule.

The first day. On this important day, new employees have breakfast with their supervisors, go through processing in the personnel department, attend a *Corning and You* seminar, have lunch with the seminar leader, read the workbook for new employees, go on a tour of the building, and are introduced to co-workers.

The first week. During this week, the new employee (1) has one-to-one interviews with the supervisor, co-workers, and specialists, (2) learns the how-tos, wheres, and whys connected with the job, (3) answers questions in the workbook, (4) gets settled in the community, and (5) firms up the MBO plan with the supervisor.

The second week. The new employee begins regular assignments.

The third and fourth weeks. The new employee attends a community seminar and an employee benefits seminar (a spouse or guest may be invited).

The second through the fifth month. During this period, assignments are intensified and new employees have biweekly progress reviews with their supervisors, attend six two-hour seminars at intervals (on quality and productivity, technology, performance management and salaried compensation plans, financial and strategic management, employee relations and EEO and social change), answer workbook questions about each seminar, and review answers with their supervisors.

The sixth month. The new employee completes the workbook questions, reviews the MBO list with the supervisor, participates in a performance review with the supervisor, receives a certification of completion for Phase I orientation, and makes plans for Phase II orientation.

The seventh through the fifteenth months. This period features Phase II orientation: division orientation, function orientation, education programs, MBO reviews, performance reviews, and salary reviews.

Source: Adapted from McGarrell, 1984.

of events in Corning's orientation program for professional employees.

The total length of the orientation process depends on these factors:

- size and complexity of the organization
- complexity of the jobs new graduates will assume, particularly in terms of standard practices and organizational policies and procedures
- importance the organization places on having a thorough orientation program; the organization's commitment to the orientation process
- resources available to schedule, coordinate, and conduct the orientation process, including the availability of audiovisual equipment or self-study material
- specific objectives of the orientation process—the greater the number of objectives, the more orientation time required.

In the McShane and Baal (1984) study, approximately 50 percent of the formal orientation programs are conducted in less than a half day. Only about one in every five organizations spread orientation over more than one week (not including follow-up). The survey also revealed that 60 percent of the respondents conduct their orientation all at once rather than intermittently over a period of time. Yet this procedure is at odds with the training literature, which prescribes distributed rather than continuous information dissemination when material can be divided into logical units (Wexley and Latham, 1981). Spreading out the learning process helps prevent new graduates from becoming fatigued, bored, or overstressed due to information overload, and ultimately they will be able to retain more information. Avoiding information overload is also emphasized in much of the employee orientation literature (Hollman, 1976; McGarrell, 1984; St. John, 1980). For example, St. John (p. 374) makes this recommendation:

> It is important to avoid jamming all orientation, especially detailed information, into one long session

at the beginning of the job, since there are limits to what any new employee can be expected to absorb, digest, and retain during the initial induction session. Brief sessions, not to exceed two hours at a time, are recommended, especially for nonmanagerial-level positions.

Preparing Supervisors to Handle Orientation. Supervisors who have a formal part in the orientation process should receive training on how to properly and effectively handle their responsibilities. They must understand the orientation process, the rationale behind it, their role in it, and how to use the material developed for them. Without training, supervisors in different sections or departments may handle the orientation inconsistently and in some cases inadequately or incompletely.

One of the most effective techniques used to prepare supervisors for this responsibility is behavior modeling. One such program has been developed by Development Dimensions International in Pittsburgh as part of their Interaction Management program. Supervisors are instructed in general orientation principles and are provided critical steps necessary to conduct the orientation effectively. A model depicts an effective, positive orientation session, using the critical steps. Next, supervisors practice their skills by conducting orientation sessions. They also have the opportunity to participate in the orientation discussion from the new graduates' viewpoint. Last, but not least, the supervisors are taught techniques to ensure transfer of this general orientation skill to the job. With this or a similar approach, supervisors acquire the proper information to conduct an orientation and develop the necessary skills to handle it effectively. They must make new graduates feel welcome, address the critical issues, and answer the questions raised during discussions. Some of the problems encountered may involve "older" employees who did not receive such a formal introduction. In these cases, supervisors must counter antagonistic feelings toward new graduates and ensure that the work unit functions as a team.

Responsibilities. As with most human resources programs, the orientation process entails multiple responsibilities. There are usually five key groups who have important formal responsibilities.

Policy-making executives must develop the overall policies of orientation and commit resources, both in staff time and money, to provide an effective orientation process. In addition, they must provide support and, to a certain extent, be involved in the process either by making introductions in person or on film, or by meeting new graduates when they arrive. These policy makers are usually the senior executives or even the chief executive officer.

The *human resources department* plays a key role because it must determine needs, develop the system, and control it. The department's responsibility usually includes planning, program development, coordination, and conducting parts of the orientation. Although the employment section or the human resources development section may have the primary responsibility for orientation, others, such as recreational directors, safety managers, or communication specialists, may be involved as needed to develop and present the orientation. When there is a formal transition program, the *program coordinator* usually has an important role in orientation, such as conducting portions of the program, providing input into its development, and monitoring the process with other staff members. As discussed earlier, *supervisors* of new graduates play a critical part in the orientation process. (Of course, this assumes the new graduates have a defined work assignment under the direction of a supervisor.) Supervisors introduce new graduates to the work area, facilities, and job. They must provide support, encouragement, and assistance to make the process work. In some cases they must prepare for the orientation so they can conduct it in an effective manner. Last, but not least, other *executives and middle managers* are responsible for supporting the orientation process and providing time to work on orientation. In some cases these managers are actively involved in the process.

Overall these different groups, through their *formal* responsibilities, help ensure that the organization has an effective orientation process. Other groups and individuals have *informal* responsibilities to help ensure new graduates are properly welcomed and are provided with the necessary information. Thus, working together, the entire organization is charged with the responsibility to make orientation work.

Orientation System Components

An effective orientation system consists of a variety of components that must work together. The most important component is probably the actual presentation, including the format, media, and packaging. Other important components include written material distributed to new employees, tours of facilities, the involvement of other individuals in addition to the human resources staff, orientation follow-up, the informal orientation, and finally a continuous evaluation process that examines the different components and makes adjustments as they are needed.

Presentation. The format and method of presentation include such issues as location, the mechanics of presentation, the sequence of information, and how audiovisual equipment and self-study material are to be used. Although orientations may be conducted at various locations, they are normally conducted at the location where new graduates are based for initial assignments or education/training programs.

The mechanics of presentation can be critical to a program's success. The presentation must be dynamic and enthusiastic to hold attention. Although the sequence of information may vary, it usually begins with overviews and general information and culminates with specific, job-related details. Some organizations use a checklist to ensure that every detail is presented.

Some orientations include videotaped presentations, audiovisual slide shows, or audiotapes; others rely on face-to-face, live presentations. Audiovisual presentations may be necessary to include messages from top executives or to economize when sessions are repeated frequently. Programmed instruction booklets or other self-study materials may be helpful to secure the active involvement of participants and enhance the learning process.

Factors that influence the choice of format and media are cost-effectiveness, available resources, and specific objectives.

Wall posters, illustrations, or photographs for live presentations or slides can be an effective way to present the organization's message. Slides can be enhanced with an audiotape or combined with films or live presenters to form a powerful sound-and-sight show. Inexpensive slides documenting internal operations or listing key points that new recruits must know are very effective, particularly when supplemented with music or narration from the presenter. Effective and even dramatic multimedia shows can be prepared inexpensively using present staff and existing pictures. More expensive productions may be artistic successes but do not necessarily get the message across more successfully. The key point about media selection is that different people learn and retain information best through different media. A multimedia approach should be able to attract and hold new employees' attention, offer a variety of interests, and at the same time foster learning and retention (Shea, 1985).

Written Material. Another essential component in the orientation system is the written material prepared as handouts during orientation. The scope of the written material varies considerably with the organization and with the specific jobs of the new graduates. This stage in the transition process is an ideal time for new graduates to learn more about the organization through brochures, booklets, and handbooks that go beyond the essential job-related information.

Probably the most important printed material to distribute during orientation is the employee handbook, assuming that it has not been distributed in the pre-employment education activity. The typical employee handbook outlines the philosophy and mission of the organization, company history, and information about products, markets, and services. Basic policies are usually included, along with general explanations of employee benefits, services, and employee activities. New graduates are usually more motivated to read an employee handbook during orientation than at a later stage of transition, so it may be the best time to communicate this important information.

Detailed information on employee benefits—including services or activities related to improving the employee's perception of the organization—is usually distributed to new graduates at orientation time. Some information is necessary because of the Employee Retirement Income Security Act (ERISA), which requires employers to provide employees with a summary plan description of each of their welfare benefit plans. However, the documents required by federal law usually are difficult to read and often leave employees confused about benefits. Therefore, most organizations develop small brochures or booklets describing benefit plans in simple, easy-to-understand terminology. A word of caution is needed here: A deluge of information on benefits may further confuse new graduates to the point where they will not read or understand it. The material may need to be coordinated with a discussion of important points for each benefit. Other handout material on benefits may include such items as a schedule of employer-provided training courses, tuition refund plan, and information on management club membership, if applicable.

Other types of printed material typically presented to new graduates at orientation are basic company policies, procedures, and work rules related to the job. This may include a condensed version of major policies that outline important rules and regulations to keep graduates informed. Other informtion may be included as orientation handouts depending on the organization and the job. For example, in one organization all accounting graduates are provided information on how to join the local chapter of the National Association of Accountants. In another organization, new graduates are provided a booklet that describes the cultural activities available in the city. This booklet is provided to all new graduates—out-of-town recruits as well as local residents.

Tours. Almost every organization includes a tour as part of the orientation process. New graduates should see as much of the organization as is feasible during the orientation period. They need to meet employees, learn about the facilities, and see the organization producing its product or providing its service. Tours can be more effective if the following guidelines are considered in their execution:

1. Design the tour around each individual to the greatest extent possible: Some graduates need more exposure to specific facilities and individuals, and others may need to tour only isolated parts of the organization.
2. Integrate the tour with formal classroom sessions to break the monotony of a full day or several days of sitting and listening. Brief tours interspersed with the formal group discussions can make the process more interesting and enjoyable while enhancing learning.
3. Assign someone from the local area to conduct the tour. For example, if outlying plants or other facilities are a part of the tour, have someone most familiar with that plant or facility conduct the tour. This may appear to be a burdensome duty for these individuals, but their additional credibility makes an important difference.
4. Plan the tour carefully with a predetermined itinerary and sequence of events, including a list of staff new graduates should meet during the tour. Proper planning will help ensure that the tour is complete and is scheduled in the most logical manner.
5. Ensure that the tour guide is well prepared for the assignment and is an effective communicator who can be understood by all tour members.
6. Combine lunch with the tour and invite key employees or executives from that particular area. This kind of luncheon impresses new graduates and provides them an opportunity to meet additional key people. It also give key employees an opportunity to interact with the new graduates.

Involvement of Others. Although the human resources department is typically charged with the summary responsibility for orientation, various staff and management groups should also participate. It is important to have upper management involved in the process, even if it is only via film or videotape. New graduates want to know and meet top executives and their input into the orientation process will be a pleasant surprise. Their input is typically limited to welcoming addresses and introductions to the organization. One large service organization schedules a member of senior management to meet with new graduates over dinner to speak on company philosophy and mission. Anything more is helpful but may be unrealistic because of the timing of the orientation and the demands on executive time.

Another possibility is to involve middle managers from the area, plant, or department where new graduates will work or receive initial education and training. This brings face-to-face interaction between new graduates and key managers who will help shape their future. In some cases, where job assignments are known, immediate or prospective supervisors of new graduates are assigned the responsibility of providing part of the orientation. This helps to individualize the process and brings a personal touch to orientation. In these cases, an orientation guide is helpful so that supervisors thoroughly cover the material planned for the orientation. A checklist is a plus. Also, as discussed earlier, supervisors may need to be trained to conduct this orientation in the most effective manner.

Follow-Up Orientation. An orientation follow-up with new graduates is an often overlooked opportunity. A follow-up can be conducted thirty, sixty, or ninety days from the date of employment and serves several purposes. First, it gives the organization an opportunity to fill in gaps of information missed in the orientation process. Second, it gives participants the opportunity to ask questions and clarify their interpretation of policies, procedures, benefits, and other items covered during the orientation. Third, it provides the organization an opportunity to gauge the attitude and reaction of the new graduates after they have had a brief tenure with the organization. Fourth, it gives the new graduates an opportunity to air their concerns about the organization or discuss problems they have encountered.

The follow-up orientation is particularly important when there is no formal education or training program for new graduates after the orientation process. This component of orientation must be carefully planned and should coordinate smoothly with the earlier components of orientation. The McShane and Baal (1984) study revealed that more than two-thirds of the firms with formal orientation programs include a follow-up session. About one-third conduct this session within one month, and another one-third of the respondents schedule their follow-up one to three months after employment begins. The optimal length of time between orientation and follow-up depends upon the nature of the job (for example, the complexity and time span of the tasks). Typically, three months should be the upper limit on the time of the follow-up session, although Hollman (1976) and St. John (1980) recommend that this session be conducted within one month. It may also be advisable to use an orientation checklist (similar to the one used at the end of orientation) to cover any missing information. Of course, *informal* consultation and follow-up should be ongoing during the fist months of the new graduate's tenure with the organization.

Informal Orientation. Informal orientation, just as important as formal orientation, includes information conveyed by, and interactions with, the individuals who will be in frequent contact with new graduates. These include co-workers, support personnel, receptionists, secretaries, and other individuals with whom there is frequent contact. Without proper attention to the informal process, these individuals and others assume that orientation is a formal process conducted by selected specialists and that they have no responsibility. However, all individuals ultimately have a part in welcoming new graduates to the team. Everyone must be aware of the importance of orientation as these new recruits try to adjust to unfamiliar surroundings and their new career path.

Organizations can enhance the informal orientation component in two important ways. The first is through the expectations conveyed to all employees by the culture of the organization, by role models, and by reinforcement from various levels of management. The overall attitude toward orientation is established at the top and filters throughout the organization. When top executives stress the importance of bringing a new person into a friendly and encouraging atmosphere, others will do the same. All levels of management should communicate what is expected in interactions with new recruits.

The second way to enhance the informal orientation process is to communicate the arrival of new graduates through memos, bulletin boards, or personal introductions. All employees in the immediate work area, as well as those who will have frequent contact with the new graduates, should know they have arrived and what their positions and duties in the organization will be. Informal orientation is an intangible component that can have a significant impact on the effectiveness of the orientation process.

Evaluation. The final component of an effective orientation system is evaluation. Because of the importance of orientation and the extent of resources dedicated to it, it is imperative for the organization to ensure that the effort is worthwhile. For this reason, the program design should provide for evaluation of the process and for making adjustments as needed. Several methods can be used to collect data for evaluation purposes. First, anonymous reaction questionnaires, filled out by graduates at the end of the formal orientation program, can provide useful information about the effectiveness of the orientation. This provides a means to check for understanding of information, the quality of the delivery, and the perceived usefulness of the information.

Second, random in-depth interviews with participants who complete the program can provide additional insight into the effectiveness of orientation. Frank comments can be solicited regarding all phases of the orientation, along with suggestions for improvement.

Third, a follow-up questionnaire completed at some fixed time after the program can provide input on the lasting impact of the orientation process. Much of the information presented in orientation, such as policies, benefits, rules and regulations, and other general company information, should be retained by the new graduates. It is one thing to understand the material initially, but quite another to know the material at some later date. A follow-up evaluation will check for retention. Problem areas might suggest that repetition of key information is essential. These questionnaires can easily be administered during the orientation follow-up.

Fourth, turnover rates of new professional employees should be examined to check for a possible correlation with the orientation. In the Corning Glass Works example, discussed in Chapter One, the turnover rate for new professional employees was reduced by 17 percent after the implementation of a new orientation program, which indicates there was a relationship between orientation and turnover. Many studies have shown that turnover is linked to the orientation process (Wanous, 1980). Admittedly, a number of other factors can cause turnover and a sudden shift in turnover would not necessarily mean the orientation program is ineffective. However, if during exit interviews professional employees indicate that they are leaving because of reasons traceable to the orientation, it might indicate some type of causal relationship.

Fifth, initial employee performance may be another measure of effectiveness in the orientation process. This may be a very weak correlation, but nevertheless the speed at which an employee reaches a certain level of performance is directly related to the quality of the information received in the early stages of employment. In the Corning Glass Works study (McGarrell, 1984), the time required to reach a certain level of performance was reduced from six months to five months through an improved orientation process. Shifts in initial performance may indicate a problem with the orientation process.

Orientation Content

Just as the strategy and components of the orientation system vary with the organization, so does the content. The organizational setting, target jobs, the importance placed on running an effective orientation process, and the desired speed at which new graduates need to learn about the organization all affect the specific content. Also, orientation content should address the culture items discussed in Chapter One. Each of the major content areas is discussed below.

Organizational History, Goals, and Mission. Virtually all organizations discuss this area, which includes early history, significant milestones, organizational structure, goals, objectives, mission, and philosophy. All of these aspects define, to one extent or another, the culture of the organization, and new graduates must understand them as soon as possible. This content area usually is supplemented by brochures, annual reports, booklets, and organizational charts. These materials may also include short- and long-range plans, information about employee and labor relations, and other factors affecting the climate in which the new graduate will work. New graduates need to see how they fit into the organization and how they will interact with others.

Products, Services, and Facilities. Information on the organization's products and services is an essential part of orientation. An end-use slant is particularly helpful, stated in a way in which new graduates can easily comprehend. For example, a manufacturer of pollution control equipment might outline how the equipment is used in a chemical company to control toxic waste, with typical examples of installation. This content area is usually supplemented with pictures, catalogs, brochures, and tours of the facilities. For larger organizations, an audiovisual overview of the facilities identifying locations and describing the functions performed at each location might suffice. Information on how the products actually work or how services are provided and how these differ from competitive products and services is helpful.

Policies and Procedures. This content area typically includes all the procedures that immediately affect the new graduate's work or education/training program. For large, complex organizations, this can be quite involved. It might include work flows, production processes, personnel policies, accounting practices, work rules, and official policies that may have an important impact on new graduates. The problem with presenting policies and procedures is the likelihood of overloading new graduates with too much detail too soon. A proper balance of information should be presented along with explanations of "why" for the curious minds.

Compensation. Few items are as important to new employees as their pay and benefits. The competitiveness of the pay system, how pay raises are administered, and the extent of the information available on compensation are important items to discuss in orientation sessions. Benefits are covered in more detail. Explanations of the benefits package, how benefits are administered, and how new graduates can make the best use of their benefits plans are discussed. Information on the competitiveness of the benefits package relative to other organizations can be a plus.

New graduates have their own frame of reference concerning pay and benefits. These different perspectives are not easy to address, unless new recruits are provided ample information to clear up questions, concerns, and potential misunderstandings. Appropriate policies or guidelines affecting compensation and benefits should be distributed along with clear verbal explanations. New graduates should have ample opportunities to ask questions and receive adequate responses. Misunderstandings about compensation are a source of employee dissatisfaction and can damage an otherwise excellent employee-employer match.

A major problem with discussing benefits packages is that they are usually very diverse and complex. Graduates, struggling to learn a host of new facts and ideas, may leave an orientation confused and ill-informed. For this reason, it may be important to include benefits information in various stages or in follow-up presentations to ensure the information is not confusing. One important reason for discussing compensation and benefits is to avoid future surprises that may distract from the remainder of the orientation and the education/training process.

Job Content. Descriptions of the jobs new graduates will assume are included in some orientations. Because this factor varies considerably, some organizations discuss it individually or defer it to the education or training program. As was discussed in Chapter Three, all job-related information should provide a realistic preview of the future job. It should present both positive and negative features and should include work schedules, work rules, overtime requirements, reporting relationships, and other items concerning job content or work environment. New graduates have a right to know what is expected of them and should have a clear explanation of their job as soon as possible. For most organizations, this matter is handled by the new graduate supervisor, so discussions about specific duties are sometimes deferred until the new graduate assumes the job. However, adequate explanations of work rules at the orientation stage can avoid subsequent problems, such as violations of a rule or procedure that was never explained or had been misinterpreted.

Expectations. Orientations often include what the organization expects of the new graduate, in terms of work habits, performance, ethics, and other sensitive issues affecting the new graduate's success in the work setting. In addition, expectations should include what new graduates can expect from the organization in terms of career potential, promotions, equitable treatment, and pay increases.

Safety and Health Requirements. In most organizations, and primarily in manufacturing firms, part of the orientation process is devoted to safety and health requirements. Nothing affects the well being of new employees as much as a thorough understanding of safety and health procedures. Yet, because safety hazards are often undetected and emergencies are rare, they tend to be overlooked by new employees and their supervisors—which is why so many organizations have ongoing safety awareness and training programs. Even then, safety and emergency training tend to be greatest where the dangers are greatest. This is a rational approach, except that people in work areas considered entirely safe, such as in offices, tend to get little training or reinforcement.

It is important that new graduates understand safety rules and regulations, safety hazards, and personal safety equipment and protection so they can be aware of their own personal safety needs as well as provide a role model for others in the use of protective apparel and safety equipment. In some settings, organizations have a legal or contractual obligation to provide safety information to all new employees, including new college graduates. In some orientation sessions, new graduates are provided safety and emergency checklists that outline what they must do in case of fires, accidents, or other emergency situations.

Summary

This chapter focused on two important stages of the transition process. The first, pre-employment education, includes a variety of activities aimed at educating the new graduate about the organization and the job prior to the actual employment date. Though many organizations do not take advantage of this stage, it can be an inexpensive way to begin the graduate's adjustment to the organization. The next stage, the orientation process, begins on the first day of employment and usually lasts for one to two days, but in some cases up to two weeks. This formal indoctrination provides information about the organization and its history, policies, procedures, and goals, as well as job-related information. An effective orientation system places new graduates on the right path, easing the adjustment process and minimizing culture shock as they move on to their work assignments or education/training program. Orientation is a standard approach used by most organizations, but most orientation programs could be substantially improved to make this stage an integral part of the transition process.

5

Educating and Training
New Employees

Probably the most important part of the formal transition process is the fourth stage of transition—the education and training programs developed to help new graduates adjust to the organization, environment, and job. Although the design of programs for new graduates may be the same as education and training programs for other groups, they do have some unique features. This chapter focuses on the information needed to develop effective programs, particularly approaches aimed at minimizing transition problems.

Developing Education and Training Programs

Before examining specific strategies to deal with the transition issue, it is best to distinguish between the terms *training, education, development,* and *human resource development (HRD),* which encompasses all three activities. It is important to understand the conceptual differences among these three terms, particularly as they relate to new graduates. One description of the differences is presented by Nadler (1980), who suggests that training, education, and development be differentiated according to the three categories shown in Table 7.

Training prepares employees to improve performance on present jobs and is usually regarded as an expense item necessary to make the organization more effective or increase productivity.

Table 7. Differentiation of Learning Experiences.

Label	Focus	Economic Classification	Risk Level
Training	Present job	Expense item	Low
Education	Future job	Short-term investment	Medium
Development	Organization	Long-term investment	High

This effort represents a low-risk activity because it leads to an immediate payoff; it is the principal focus of most HRD departments. New graduates placed directly into regular jobs usually receive training to enhance their skills.

Education represents learning experiences that prepare employees for future jobs. Education represents a short-term investment and carries only medium risk. Although there may not be an immediate return, educational programs are important to the organization in periods of both growth and downturn. In growth periods organizations need to prepare employees for promotional opportunities brought on by expansion. During periods of economic downturn educational programs may be needed to prepare employees to take on other jobs. Some of the approaches to learning described in this chapter prepare new graduates for their initial job assignments. Thus, the formal, full-time learning programs are actually education programs, although they are often mislabeled as training programs.

Development focuses on the organization and future organizational activities. It is based on the assumption that organizations must grow and change in order to remain viable. Development programs prepare individuals to move in the new directions that organizational changes may require. They are investments for which it is almost impossible to calculate a return; and because of this, they are high-risk ventures. Developmental activities are long-range in scope and are provided without reference to a particular job. True developmental experiences are not common in most organizations, at least on any formal basis. Few, if any, learning activities for new graduates represent development.

Although the learning experiences for new graduates may not always carry the labels *training, education,* and *development,* such programs should be analyzed and placed in these categories. This can help management decide which programs are needed at what time and for what purpose. In practice, most programs fall in the category of either immediate job training or educational programs. Thus, the label *education/training program* is often used to describe the learning experiences for new college graduates.

Organizational Needs Analysis. An important step in determining the structure of education/training programs is to determine the content through an organizational needs analysis. Although most needs analyses for training purposes focus on performance deficiencies, the needs analysis for an education program focuses on the jobs that new graduates will assume. A job analysis thus provides the basic needs analysis for the transition program (education/training) and is an essential element in the design of the overall program.

The underlying assumption of a formal transition program is that newly recruited graduates are not sufficiently prepared to assume a professional job without additional training or education. As Figure 3 indicates, a job analysis typically leads to a job description, and together they provide information on recruiting requirements as well as education/training needs. A job analysis identifies what new graduates must know to perform the job in a satisfactory manner. It outlines the skills, abilities, and knowledge required for success on the job. The job description outlines the duties of the job, usually in terms of expected outcomes.

Jobs can be analyzed using a variety of approaches (see Gael, 1983; McCormick, 1979; and Rock, 1984). *Questionnaires and surveys* are probably the most common vehicle for determining the key elements of the job and the importance of different tasks. Job incumbents, as well as their supervisors, complete a variety of questionnaires and surveys about the details of their jobs. Typical questions include the amount of time required for certain parts of the job, the decisions required, and the knowledge necessary to make those decisions.

Figure 3. Relationship Between Job Analysis, Job Description,
Recruiting Requirements, and Education and Training Needs.

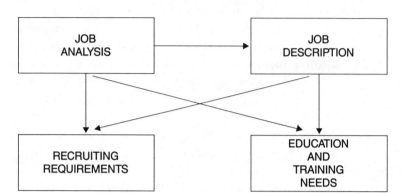

Another technique for job analysis is a *work sample* that consists of pieces or a sample of a job, typically captured in time increments of a day or less. Work samples can be conducted systematically or randomly and provide additional information on the activities of the job as well as on the knowledge, skills, and abilities necessary to perform it satisfactorily.

Interviews, either individually or in group settings, provide additional information on job requirements. The face-to-face interaction inherent in the interview process allows job incumbents to explain exceptions and deviations and to amplify the information provided on questionnaires.

Observation is another useful technique when a job requires substantial physical activity or when there are many interactions with other individuals. Job incumbents are observed in a variety of settings and activities, and the interactions or movements are recorded. The observer tabulates the frequency and nature of the activities. This approach is particularly helpful in analyzing supervisory jobs that have a high level of interaction with others.

Force-field analysis is a technique for gathering information from groups or individuals about jobs. This process examines the environmental forces, either causing or restraining, which affect the performance of employees or groups of employees. Causing forces are the environmental pressures that cause employees to perform in a particular manner or react in a certain way. Restraining forces inhibit or restrict employee performance. A force-field analysis provides important information about jobs by revealing the environmental pressures and external forces on the job holder.

Finally, the *critical incident technique* focuses on behavior and is typically used in analyzing supervisory jobs. Supervisors of job incumbents provide examples of incidents that represent both effective and ineffective job-related behavior. These incidents provide insight into the different skills and abilities needed for success on the job.

When combined, these various approaches provide a systematic, professional way to obtain a detailed analysis of the skills, abilities, and knowledge necessary to perform in a job.

Specific Objectives. According to Kirkpatrick (1983), education and training programs have four kinds of objectives: (1) *attitude objectives* focus on new graduates' attitudes toward some aspect of the job, employees, management, or the organization; (2) *knowledge objectives* focus on specific parts of the job and include policies, procedures, processes, and technical aspects of jobs; (3) *skill objectives* focus on the identifiable changes in how new graduates perform tasks or assignments; and (4) *job behavior objectives* focus on measurable results obtained on-the-job after completing the program.

In a recent unpublished study which I conducted with more than 100 organizations recruiting MBA graduates, objectives were presented in the order presented below. The first two were identified as objectives by all of the responding organizations with formal training or education programs for MBA graduates.

- to familiarize new graduates with products, services, and facilities
- to familiarize new graduates with the people and structure of the organization
- to develop an understanding of the organization's policies and procedures

- to enable new graduates to make a contribution to the organization as soon as possible
- to shape the desired attitudes and work habits within new graduates
- to teach new graduates the content of the planned permanent job
- to explore a variety of career opportunities in the organization before permanent job assignment for new graduates
- to allow new graduates to work in several different assignments.

Specific objectives in organizations in other countries are similar to those in the United States. In a study conducted with Japanese companies (Tanaka, 1980), the following overall objectives of these programs were:

- to educate as members of the company, emphasizing self-discipline and the transition from student life to company life
- to teach professionalism and the significance and meaning of work
- to provide background information about the company and to familiarize employees with distinctive management trends
- to familiarize employees with basic company procedures and fundamental business rules and etiquette
- to cultivate a spirit of harmony and teamwork among employees.

Specific objectives serve as guiding principles in the structure and administration of the program. They inform program participants, the HRD staff, and management about the desired outcomes of the program. Also, objectives form the basis for evaluating the effectiveness of the transition program. It is essential that they be developed, communicated, and understood.

Formality. The degree of formality frames an important issue in the transition process. A highly formal program is characterized by written objectives, detailed plans, structured training, guidelines, and specific schedules. It represents a precisely scheduled approach in which every detail, event, or activity is planned and documented. A very informal program has none of the above features but rather functions on verbal understandings and agreements between management and among the individuals in transition. In essence, a very informal program is equivalent to no program, because there will be little documentation to indicate how the program should function. Obviously, an organization's approach will usually fall somewhere between these two extremes. The degree of formality will depend on the organization and what it plans to accomplish in the transition process.

Formal approaches have several advantages. First, specific objectives usually require a formalized approach. Formal mechanisms are necessary to ensure that plans will be executed in a timely manner. It is difficult, if not impossible, to meet objectives through an informal process.

Second, a formal approach ensures consistency in how transition problems are addressed in the organization. New college graduates share similar problems, and they will need similar education and training activities. A formal approach, through structured sessions and experiences, can ensure some common solutions to transition problems.

Third, a formal approach helps to ensure that transition is addressed in an efficient manner. Plans and objectives with a structured program, coupled with evaluation and feedback, ensure that education and training are accomplished on time, utilizing the resources of the organization in an efficient manner. An informal approach can breed inefficiency and disorganization, resulting in misuse of new graduates' time as well as the resources of the organization.

The most important disadvantage of a formal approach is that it can be too rigid for an organization whose values and culture are based on many informal practices. Somewhere between the two extremes is a level of formality appropriate for an organization. This issue needs to be addressed early because it determines the extent that plans, policies, and procedures will be developed for the program.

Structure. The structure of transition programs includes design issues, such as the extent to which all graduates are involved in the same training activities, the timing and scope of various experiences and training assignments, and the schedules for progress reports, performance reviews, and other pertinent activities in the program.

A structured program defines what will be done, at what time, and by whom. It may leave little room for judgment as to whether participants are involved in certain experiences or activities or as to the timing of events in the program. Structure minimizes misunderstandings and miscommunications with graduates and with the management group. Some new graduates need structure; without it they appear lost, unmotivated, or misdirected. They equate an unstructured program to an ineffective one. They believe a thoroughly documented program will be executed the way it is planned, although this is not always the case.

A structured program is more likely to be followed than an unstructured one. Specific events can easily be tracked and monitored, which enhances the evaluation process for both the program and participants. A structured program helps ensure that all participants are treated fairly and equitably and that they are involved in the same scheduled activities. In this environment, charges of unfairness against the organization are usually unfounded.

Flexibility, the opposite of structure, becomes an important issue in scheduling education and training assignments, coordinating on-the-job experiences, and timing special events such as performance appraisals, progress reports, and meetings. Flexibility has several advantages. A flexible program adjusts to the needs of individual graduates. If a graduate needs additional training or preparation in an area, it is provided. Because of previous work experiences, a new graduate may not need a planned work experience. Flexibility is an efficient way to provide education and training because it avoids spending resources on unnecessary activities. Flexibility is an important asset for the management group when scheduling their involvement in the transition program. With a flexible program, management can plan assignments when appropriate, attend training programs when it is convenient, and schedule performance review meetings around the needs of the organization. This flexibility helps management plan and coordinate activities, which, in turn, build additional support for the program and its objectives.

Fortunately, a transition program does not have to be highly structured or extremely flexible. It can structure essential activities and events that must occur as planned and be flexible enough to react to individual differences and adjust the program accordingly. Ideally, the program should have a good mixture of both structure and flexibility centered around the needs of the organization and the individuals.

Individual Interests and Needs

Another important issue concerns the interests of the participants when compared to the needs of the organization. Graduates want to be involved in the type of work or functional area in which they have the most interest. From the organization's viewpoint, graduates should be available to take on any assignment regardless of their level of interest. After all, they have been recruited to satisfy the needs of the organization. A blending of the needs of the two is ideal and can usually be achieved in most organizations.

Determining Interests. In the early stages of the recruiting process, the organization usually determines the job interests of the applicants. Job interest is sometimes a factor in the decision to hire the graduate. For example, an engineer with an interest in sales would not be hired for an engineering assignment. Instead, he or she might be recruited for a technical sales position. The matching of interest with organizational needs is an important element of recruiting that cannot be overemphasized. Serious problems can surface when the graduate's interests are not fully detailed in the recruiting process or if they change during the transition process.

Some organizations prefer not to address the issue of individual interests, believing that graduates should be flexible enough to take on any assignment within their chosen profession or within the scope of the education or training program. Although this strategy may be optimum in terms of organizational needs, it may produce high turnover of entry-level, professional employees. Too many graduates leave organizations because they cannot work where they want to or think they should.

Job interest should be determined early in the education or training program through discussions, interviews, and possibly even questionnaires. Also, progress reports or follow-up evaluations of graduates should focus on career interests. An example illustrates the importance of listening to graduates about career interests. A manufacturing firm recruits marketing graduates to enter a sales representative education program. After new graduates finish the formal program, ranging from one to two years, participants are assigned to various geographical locations. Although all graduates are recruited with the understanding that they can be assigned to any domestic location, their preferences for geographical assignments begin to surface during the program. Some may have a particular preference for the sunbelt region, while others may prefer a west coast assignment. And almost all participants have a few undesirable locations, although they might have the flexibility to move to those areas, if necessary. For years the firm ignored the participants' preferences, assigning geographical locations strictly on the basis of present needs. As a result, turnover was high among sales representatives. Some graduates even refused to relocate, resulting in a tremendous cost of almost two years of education. Finally, the organization began to consider location preferences. It would make assignments, wherever possible, within the scope of interest of the individual. The organization was very discrete in how they obtained information about interests and did not make a big issue out of the probable assignment, except to let the participants know they would take their interests into consideration. This change in philosophy significantly improved morale *and* the turnover of outside sales representatives.

An organization must exercise caution not to allow participants to develop false hopes in meeting their individual interests. New graduates pay attention to organizational communications on this topic. If they are told their interests will be met and they see the organization acting otherwise, a serious morale problem may develop. If interests cannot be considered, then the participants must know so.

Defining Individual Needs. Because individual graduates have different education and training needs, an early step in the transition program should determine specific training needs, assuming the program has some flexibility. Individual needs can be identified through self-evaluation, interviews, questionnaires, surveys, examinations, observations, and simulations. The extent to which individual needs are assessed usually depends on the organization's resources and the planned investment in the graduates. A simple self-evaluation suffices for many organizations, where participants are provided a description of the skills necessary for the future job and asked to identify experiences or subjects in which they may have deficiencies. If this approach is used, it must be tackled in a positive manner to avoid embarrassing graduates or giving them feelings of inferiority because of a lack of knowledge, skill, or ability. Typical questionnaires are headed with such phrases as "additional training is needed in these areas." Some organizations provide a list of education/training activities and work experiences and give new graduates the opportunity to develop an individual program. This approach works only if the program has some flexibility to adjust work experiences, training assignments, or educational activities to meet individual needs. Additional information on how to determine individual training needs can be found in Nadler (1982).

Matching Needs and Interests. Based on the information above, an ideal situation exists when individual needs are met in the education and training program and at the same time individual career, occupational, or task interests are matched with organizational needs. The extent to which this goal can be achieved depends on the organization, the resources available, and the number of participants involved in the transition process. Although practical limitations usually prohibit this ideal matchup, it should be an organizational goal. The result will be increased satisfaction, higher morale, and greater productivity of the new graduates.

Attempts to match organizational needs with career interests and needs naturally breed conflicts, which should be handled diplomatically so they do not damage the integrity of the program. Disenchantment with mismatches quickly spreads to other participants and can destroy an otherwise effective program. One way to minimize conflicts is to take steps to prevent them. This requires the organization to address the issue early and explain the policy and practice at the time of recruitment so there is no misunderstanding. Also, early in the transition process, explanations of how training needs will be determined and met and how well career and vocational interests will be satisfied are essential. As problems develop, they can be resolved best by explaining the positions and the rationale for those positions while trying to provide alternatives at this point in the program. This may result in a transfer to another job, removal from the program, or encouragement to leave the organization altogether should the conflict be significant.

Developing Career Paths. One important way to help match interest with organizational need is to develop career paths for new college graduates and outline the requirements necessary to move along the path. Time, experience, and ability requirements necessary to move to the next job level are sometimes communicated. Career paths provide new graduates with likely prospects and can remove much of the mystery about their career in the five-to-ten-year time frame. Figure 4 shows a career path for management trainees in a retailing chain. In this firm, graduates have several paths from the management trainee program, all leading to a vice-president's job.

The career path approach has some disadvantages. First, paths are not always available for many of the jobs of new college graduates. In highly specialized fields it may be difficult to outline career paths because of the limited advancement opportunities. For example, it may be difficult to outline a career path for someone recruited to become an editor of a company's newspaper or for a

Figure 4. Career Path in Retailing for New College Graduates.

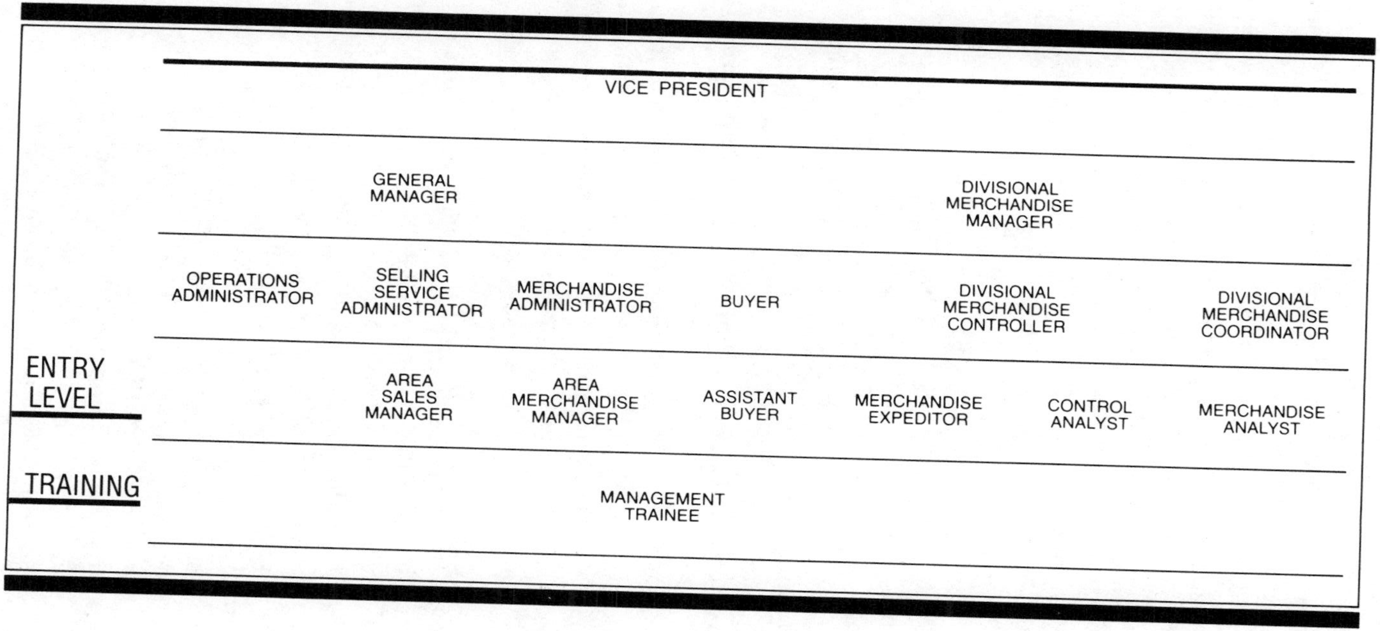

Source: "Management Careers: Capitalize on our Retailing Excellence." Woodward and Lothrop, Washington, D.C., n.d.

new graduate who joins an organization as its only public relations specialist.

Second, career paths show the likely sequence of moves, whereas actual moves may depend on the individual interest and needs of the organization. Therefore, significant deviations from career paths may cause morale problems among graduates who aspire to move along the path.

Third, much of the progression depends on individual performance. Consequently, graduates could become disgruntled if they are not moving along the path as planned, causing morale problems that are difficult to rectify.

Even with these drawbacks, career paths may be one answer to providing graduates with long-range outlooks for their occupations. Ideally, career path information is presented in the recruiting process to help the new graduate make a decision to join the organization.

Developing and Communicating Program Information

A formal approach to education and training requires the development of policies, guidelines, and other documents to ensure that consistent information is presented and understood by all parties. This includes the communication of policies as well as their development.

Scope of Policies and Guidelines. Education and training program policies describe how the program is intended to operate, detailing particular requirements and essential conditions that must be met by those involved. It outlines responsibilities of participants, managers, mentors, staff support groups, and others who have a part in making the program successful. Policies may appear in official organizational policy manuals, in operating guidelines from the human resources department, or in separate documents developed specifically for the program. Policies and guidelines should address all significant elements of the program and include basic expectations and the organization's position on various issues that may arise in the program. Policies and guidelines should be developed with input from the participants, or at least part of the policies should reflect comments or concerns of the participants. Management input is also important to help secure additional support and commitment for the process.

Communication of Policies. Policies are useless unless they are communicated to those who need to know them. Transition program policies should be communicated to several important target groups. The students contacted during the recruiting process should be the first group. This is the time to let potential program participants know and understand the "rules of the game" and the basic policies that guide the organization and administration of its education and training program. This communication, even if it is presented in a brief format, can help alleviate problems and clear up issues prior to actual selection. During the orientation process, newly recruited graduates (the second group) should receive a thorough presentation of the policies. This information should form an integral part of the orientation.

It is important for all managers involved in the process (the third group) to understand the basic program guidelines. This may require that the information be placed in general policy manuals and that discussions of the policies be held in management meetings, particularly in the departments where the program has its highest concentration. Special attention should be given to those involved in the program in an advisory or mentor capacity. They must understand it thoroughly, as their role may require them to explain the program or administer a portion of it.

It may be appropriate for the entire organization (the fourth group) to know about policies involving the education and training program. Employees at all levels may need to understand why the organization recruits college graduates and what it does to make them productive, contributing employees. This is particularly important when many new graduates are recruited each year. General information included in human resource or organization-wide general interest publications may be helpful to enhance the understanding of the program and develop a positive attitude toward it. Finally, the organization may find it useful to communicate policies to colleges or other potential sources of new college graduates (the fifth group). This kind of external communication is important in recruiting and helps build the reputation of the organization by explaining its commitment to developing its human resources.

Some organizations go beyond publishing general, objective information on policy and program guidelines by developing useful tips to help the participants succeed in the program. Under the label of "survival tips," "how to get answers to questions," or "how to get the most out of your training," these guides give frank and candid answers to sensitive questions about how to succeed in the program. Some organizations distribute reprints of articles aimed at providing this advice to new college graduates. One such article, used by several organizations, is found in Phillips (1978b). Too many new college graduates with excellent abilities become victims of organizational politics: they may say the wrong things, act the wrong way, or fail to take proper action. These organizational "no-nos" can get new graduates into much trouble, lower morale, or occasionally result in a turnover statistic. This is an important issue that should be addressed in written form or in frank, open conversations with new graduates. Protocol and politics are a way of life in every organization, and new graduates rarely learn in campus courses how to survive in this setting. They need a dose of realism and the organization should address this important issue when developing program policies and guidelines.

Program Content: Management and Interpersonal Skills

New graduates may need additional education or training in interpersonal skills and in some cases additional supervisory skills. One frequent complaint about technical and business schools is that graduates do not have a chance to develop interpersonal skills. Few college courses teach graduates how to interact productively with groups of people, make presentations before groups, supervise employees, or handle difficult employee situations. Yet, the success or failure of graduates frequently depends on the quality of the interpersonal relationships developed and cultivated over time. It is an important area that should not be neglected in the overall education and training of new graduates. Specific courses in this area vary widely; they usually depend on the individual's job needs and background.

Human Relations/Leadership Skills. Graduates need to understand how people work together effectively and ineffectively. Good interpersonal skills allow graduates to make quality contributions while interacting with others and build cooperation and teamwork among fellow professional employees. Courses in this area provide theories and foundations in human relations or employee relations, including information about human behavior that is essential for maximum productivity. Business and technical graduates may be deficient in human relations skills based on their academic preparation.

Some organizations teach their new graduates leadership skills. This type of program is designed for professional employees, not necessarily those destined to be supervisors. The rationale: These employees will be future leaders—in some cases the leaders within their work area—and this is an excellent time to begin developing leadership skills for future opportunities. For example, in one large aerospace firm, recently recruited, nonsupervisory graduates attend a thirty-hour, professional leadership course that covers such topics as: work motivation basics, leadership styles and models, giving instructions, managing time, selling yourself, performance standards, and improving cooperation and teamwork. This course helps participants develop their capacities to identify situations that prevent desired and defined production goals from being achieved on time, in acceptable quality, quantity, and cost, at the professional employee's level of responsibility.

Communication Skills. Closely related to the human relations skills are the communication skills needed for graduates to be successful on the job. In many cases employers have been disappointed with the quality of communication skills of their new college graduates. Because of the importance of communication and the serious consequences of communication failures, an investment in communication education/training can realize a significant return. The ability to communicate effectively is an asset to anyone's career. Improvement usually centers on five distinct areas: listening, speaking, writing, reading, and body language.

Failure to *listen*, a common communication problem, can be particularly destructive when new graduates fail to listen to management and co-workers. This problem of listening is inherent in our communication structure. Individuals are capable of understanding speech at a rate of about 600 words per minute, yet most people speak at only 100 to 140 words per minute. Thus, the brain enjoys a considerable amount of idle time while someone is talking and so tends to wander (Christenson and others, 1982, p. 108). Listening is sometimes integrated with regular communication skills courses and other times presented as a separate course.

Improving *oral communication* is important because it consumes more time than other types of communication. Most attempts to improve oral communication focus on upgrading the way meetings are conducted. Other organizations concentrate on improving skills in making formal presentations because new graduates are often required to make presentations before peer groups. Courses on improving presentations rely heavily on confidence building to prepare graduates to make presentations. Other programs focus on thorough preparation, establishing an agenda, the mechanics of the presentation, and securing feedback from the audience. Both of these approaches have achieved promising results. Good oral presentation skills can make the difference in career advancement because these skills are highly visible.

Another crucial communication skill for new graduates is *writing*. New graduates write memos, letters, notes, and reports. Although good writing is a skill that seems to come naturally for some people, it is not necessarily an inherent ability; it can be learned. Just as oral presentations are important to success, writing can have considerable impact on a new graduate's advancement. Managers sometimes decide that a new recruit lacks ability on the sole evidence of a poorly written report. Repeatedly, poor writing is linked with lack of ability and intelligence, although this is not necessarily true. Also, effective writing does not necessarily correlate with a certain level of education. Some colleges are turning out graduates who have not mastered the skill of writing clear, concise, grammatically correct sentences and paragraphs. When these people enter an organization, they often continue to turn out reports, letters, and memos that are confusing, ambiguous, and at times meaningless. As a consequence, the recipients of these muddled messages frequently do not know what to do or may follow an incorrect course of action (Macdonald, 1982, p. 140).

Reading habits and practices can also be improved. Although this skill is not as critical as the others discussed, it can be an important skill for new graduates whose jobs require a great deal of reading. Organizations attempt to improve reading skills through rapid-reading or speed-reading courses. A few of these courses have produced impressive increases in reading speed and comprehension. One problem is lack of continued improvement: Unless the skills developed in the courses are practiced and reinforced regularly, reading speed and comprehension can fall back to previous levels.

In recent years, increased attention has been given to *body language* and other forms of nonverbal communication. Body language refers to physical signals that people use to communicate information without words. Subconsciously or consciously people use some body language in their communication process. New graduates need to be aware of the impact of body language and know how to interpret it. A few organizations provide courses on body language to teach new recruits to use it to their advantage.

Supervisory Skills/Management Principles. For those graduates destined to be supervisors, an important part of the education or training program is building supervisory skills and developing management practices. Although supervision depends to a large extent on specific employee situations, generally accepted steps can be used in handling interaction with almost all employees. Because of this, many firms prepare their supervisors to handle difficult job situations. This process, sometimes referred to as behavior modeling, is a very popular approach to prepare new supervisors for their assignments. Table 8 shows the titles for typical behavior modeling modules and illustrates the broad scope of situations this technique addresses.

Table 8. Titles of Typical Modules for Building Supervisory Skills.

Proactive Modules
Orienting the New Employee
Improving Attendance
Reducing Tardiness
Overcoming Resistance to Change
Delegating Responsibility
Motivating the Average Performer
Teaching an Employee a New Job
Gaining Acceptance as a New
  Supervisor
Overcoming Resentment
Terminating an Employee

Reactive Modules
Handling Employee Complaints
Handling Customer (Client)
  Complaints
Handling Emotional Situations
Handling Discrimination
  Complaints
Taking Immediate Corrective
  Action
Handling Grievances
Handling Interdepartmental
  Complaints
Handling Patient Complaints

Performance Management Modules
Improving Employee Performance
Improving Work Habits
Maintaining Improved
  Performance
Utilizing Effective Follow-Up
  Action
Utilizing Effective Disciplinary
  Action

Source: Development Dimensions International, DDI Plaza, Box 13379, Pittsburgh, PA 15243.

Management practices and principles sometimes are an important ingredient in a management education and training program. When graduates have no prior educational experiences in this area, these courses provide a basic knowledge of management and management theories. For example, technical graduates are rarely exposed to management or supervision theories, whereas business majors may have extensive course work in those areas.

Program Content: Technical and Job Specific

The most common education and training topics are job-related, many of them technical in nature, which are necessary for a sufficient understanding of the planned, permanent job. They are unique to the organization but usually focus on policies and procedures, technical processes, product/service indoctrinations, and departmental visitations.

Policies and Procedures. In addition to what is covered in the orientation process, policies and procedures are an important area of program content. New graduates must have an understanding of the policies within which they must function and the procedures through which the work is accomplished, including accounting standards, engineering practices, standard practice instructions, process specifications, and other documents that describe in detail the work and information flows in the organization. This part of the education and training program (1) prepares new graduates for their jobs, (2) improves their understanding of the organization, (3) ensures consistency in the application of the organization's policies, procedures, and practices, and (4) minimizes frustrations and personal problems of new graduates as they struggle to adjust to the organization.

Technical Processes. Almost every organization has unique technical processes for producing a product or providing a service. Depending on the specific job, a thorough understanding of the technology of the organization may be required. Even graduates with technical degrees may need additional technical education or training. Technical content varies considerably, but typical content areas include work flows and processes, manufacturing and production technology, computers and information systems, equipment orientations, automation, chemical and physical processes, and distribution channels. It is important to select only the technical material necessary to function successfully in the permanent job. Too much technical information, too soon, can be counterproductive. In large, technology-oriented organizations, such as DuPont, exosing new graduates to even an overview of all the technical processes used by the company would be difficult and probably fruitless.

Product/Service Indoctrinations. Although the organization's products and services should be discussed in orientation, some graduates need additional information about them, particularly those graduates directly involved in manufacturing or marketing them. For example, sales representatives must have detailed information on all product lines they will be selling, while accounting graduates may need only a brief orientation on the products or services. In another example, new graduates being recruited for social worker jobs in a government agency would need additional education on the services provided by the agency and how they are delivered. Common topics include product/service descriptions, product/service history, product applications, competitive products/services, and competitive history. Providing education and training in this area helps new graduates understand the organization and their role in it. Also, it is an excellent way to build pride in the organization.

Departmental Visitations. Although the orientation program may include a brief visit to specific departments or locations, some jobs may require detailed exposure to the functions, activities, and interactions of several departments. In this case, visits ranging from a day to a month for each department or plant may be necessary. These visits must be conducted effectively with objectives, detailed assignments, and planned activities to keep new graduates involved and their interest and enthusiasm high; otherwise they can easily turn into "stand by and watch" duty, which is boring and generally a waste of time. The departments visited should be carefully selected around the needs of the individual. With each visit, new graduates should learn the basic functions of the department, understand the department's role in producing the product or providing the service, meet the key employees in the department, and learn how the department interfaces with other departments. Some organizations develop questions for new graduates to answer during the visit. Others develop checklists of activities to be completed. Regardless of the type of approach, these visits can be very helpful during the transition process.

Approaches to Education and Training

Several approaches are available to prepare new graduates for their jobs or make them more effective. Although each approach has specific advantages and disadvantages, their effectiveness will depend on the organization, the individual, and the nature of the job.

Internal Classroom Programs. One of the most common types of education and training is the internally presented classroom program. Almost every organization with a formal HRD department offers internal programs with subjects ranging from principles of selling to effective writing. This approach is almost synonymous with education and training, and the "classroom" ranges from outside conference rooms to elaborate education and training centers situated some distance from regular facilities. One such center is IBM's Management Development Center, a campus-like facility located on twenty-six acres at Armonk, New York. The heart of the campus is a multipurpose building that contains administrative offices, the company's archives, separate sets of classrooms, a personnel resources library with video playback rooms, a lounge, and a formal dining room. Other organizations use local hotels, college campuses, or conference centers for their education and training programs.

Specific learning methods used in internal classroom programs include lectures, group discussions, exercises, case studies, films, videotapes, and skill practices. Most programs use several methods that are tailored to the education and training setting. Some methods are more effective than others, depending on the subject matter, previous experience of the learners, and the effectiveness of the program leader. Additional information on approaches to education and training can be found in Nadler (1984).

One particularly effective and relatively new approach to internal classroom training is called behavior modeling, which was discussed briefly in the previous chapter. The HRD field has had its share of new fads with fancy names, but this approach to training seems to be producing significant results. Many companies, including AT&T, General Electric, and IBM, have used behavior modeling with much success. Behavior modeling develops interpersonal skills, and its primary application is to develop supervisors. It is frequently an integral part of management education programs. A typical modeling sequence embraces six stages (Bittel and Ramsey, 1983):

1. presentation of the concept
2. step-by-step demonstration (on cassette or film) of the key steps a learner must take to handle the situation
3. the learner's behavioral rehearsal in a supportive environment
4. supportive feedback from peers and/or trainers
5. an action plan or performance contract to transfer learning to the actual job setting
6. follow-up to assess the problems encountered and to suggest ways to overcome them.

Because they normally deal with employees' common interpersonal problems, both experienced and inexperienced learners can benefit from these types of programs. A complete description of this approach can be found in Robinson (1983).

Outside Seminars. Outside seminars represent another important approach to education and training of new graduates. In smaller organizations, because of their limited budgets and staffs, the total formal education and training effort might rest on what is available in the outside market. In larger organizations, outside seminars are usually integrated into the overall education and training system to complement what is offered internally. It is difficult to develop internal programs to meet *all* the education and training needs of graduates, at least on an economical basis.

The HRD staff should identify a core of proven outside programs that meet the needs of new graduates.

Much care must be exercised in selecting an outside seminar because of the abundance of poorly developed and presented seminars. The HRD staff should carefully evaluate these programs before using them. This may require gathering detailed information, checking references on speakers, and contacting previous participants. In addition, these programs should be monitored and evaluated routinely to make sure their quality is being maintained. Specific techniques for developing an effective approach to using outside seminars are found in Phillips (1983b).

Self-Study. Much of the new graduate's learning is individually focused and, from any point of view, self-directed learning is a growing requirement for professionals. Graduates should be motivated to learn new skills, technology, and methods. Most organizations recognize their obligation to make learning opportunities available and to stimulate interest in those opportunities. At the same time, organizations recognize that most learning is self-directed and, because of this, are placing increased emphasis on self-study as an approach to training and education. Highly motivated graduates, eager to learn more about their jobs, will take advantage of this approach. Others will follow suit if encouraged or required to do so. Because of this, many transition programs require new graduates to read and study on their own.

Organizations have used several approaches to self-study. Some provide a required reading list for graduates. Others develop their own reading material with assignments and follow-up meetings to see if the new recruits have read the material. Programmed instruction (PI) courses are commonly used as a self-teaching technique. This approach requires the active involvement of the learner, who responds to questions that follow the presentation of small amounts of information. It allows the learner to proceed at his or her own pace, mastering one topic before going to the next. It also provides immediate feedback about the quality of the learner's response. Learners can immediately compare their response with the preferred answer. A variety of courses are available in this format from the major publishing companies, though some HRD departments develop their own courses. This approach is suited for situations where only a few graduates are to be trained at any given time at a specific location. Home study courses are another approach to self-study. They help graduates sharpen their skills as well as build expertise in a variety of topics. Courses are available from commercial correspondence schools, industry and trade groups, and local colleges and universities.

Mentors/Advisers/Role Models. An increasingly popular approach to providing training and education experiences for new graduates is the use of mentors, sometimes called advisers, counselors, or role models. In some programs, graduates select mentors on their own as a way to secure help with their development. In other programs it is a step in their development. Even then, it is important for graduates to enter this process on a voluntary basis. It should not be forced on them, as it takes two willing partners to make a successful relationship.

Mentors usually come from the management ranks and have several duties. They provide counseling on career decisions. Career planning is of utmost importance to new graduates, and a seasoned mentor can provide helpful advice in this area. Mentors provide advice on how to succeed in the organization. It takes more than knowledge and ability to make it in many organizations; office politics and cultural norms can have an important impact on the graduate's future, and a mentor can give frank and candid advice on these sensitive issues. Mentors assist new graduates in solving difficult problems either directly or indirectly related to the job. New graduates lack the necessary experience and background to solve some of the more delicate problems, and the advice of an experienced person can be extremely helpful. Finally, mentors provide counseling on substandard performance that may be caused by a variety of factors. A skilled mentor can help improve performance to an acceptable level. For further details on this approach, see Chapter Eight.

On-the-Job Coaching. A practical and somewhat informal approach to training new graduates is on-the-job coaching, usually conducted by the supervisor. This approach is based on the premise that the majority of a new graduate's learning occurs on-the-job as a result of guided experience under the direction of effective supervisors. Coaching is not a one-time effort but rather a continuous process involving discussions between the supervisor and the graduate. The supervisor (coach) observes, gives feedback, and plans specific actions to correct performance deficiencies. Because this process is ongoing, graduates feel less anxiety toward coaching than toward the typical performance appraisal.

Sometimes supervisors confuse coaching with criticism and consequently avoid the process. New graduates need a thorough understanding of their duties and the standards by which they are evaluated. They must know the goals, targets, and mission of their department, division, and organization. Performance feedback must be frank, open, and straightforward so that new graduates know when their performance is good and when it is unacceptable. Coaching should not be confused with cheerleading. Although positive reinforcement and motivation are an important part of coaching, a coach should attempt to raise the morale of graduates only when low morale is an issue.

Organizations sometimes have the mistaken belief that coaching is necessary only for fast-track graduates or marginal performers. In reality, all new graduates need coaching: It helps marginal performers improve their performance to an acceptable standard; it helps average performers identify strengths and weaknesses and develop skills necessary to perform above average; and it helps super performers maintain their outstanding records and advance to other jobs in the organization. Although new graduates may come to view their coach as a role model, the coach is not a leader in the strictest sense of the term. A coach does not carry the ball. The coach may *help* the graduate with a performance problem but does not *solve* the problem. It is best for the graduates to handle problems themselves with some advice from the coach if it is necessary. Coaching works best when supervisors of new graduates are fully prepared for their assignments. Because of this, some organizations provide training programs to improve coaching skills. Additional information on coaching techniques can be found in Kirkpatrick (1982) and Fournies (1978).

Job Rotation. Some organizations use a formal job rotation program to prepare graduates for their future assignments. This approach is appropriate when it is important for the new graduate to become familiar with several parts of the organization or gain experience in other functional areas.

A job rotation plan involves more than just visits to departments for brief periods to observe others. It involves actual job duties in the department, preferably in an existing, permanent position that will have to be filled when the new graduate moves on. Job rotation assignments should represent practical work experiences under the same conditions and constraints as those imposed on regular employees. For example, in Kroger Supermarkets' manager training program, manager trainees (usually new college graduates) are rotated through several major parts of a store so they can gain insight into various functions of the supermarket. Each manager trainee must work in the produce department, meat department, frozen food section, delicatessen and bakery, health and beauty aids, and dairy goods, as well as working with the stock crew and in the checkout area. Trainees actually perform existing jobs in these departments and are expected to perform at the same performance level of employees regularly assigned to these duties.

Job rotation is common to many industries. Some firms want their engineers to have some limited experience in the production function. Others want their sales representatives to be exposed to the manufacturing process of all their product lines. Still others want their production supervisors to have some exposure to all of the support departments with which they must work closely. Graduates should have as much exposure to, and experience in, various departments as the organization can economically provide.

This approach has led some organizations to establish an education/training slot in major departments. For example, in one organization the education/training slot is used to educate new supervisors as part of a formal transition program for new college graduates. New graduates rotate through several production supervisor assignments, allowing the permanent supervisor in that area to take vacation, jury duty, personal leave, military leave, or work on special projects or task forces. While costly, this approach allows the organization flexibility in assignments, ensuring a full complement of supervisors for the department while giving the graduates some valuable exposure and experience.

Job rotation has other advantages. The work performed serves as an excellent measure for evaluating progress, not only in terms of performing the task at hand, but of observing attitudes and reactions to assignments, that is, ratings from supervisors in the selected work areas can be used as input into the evaluation of new graduates. Job rotation allows new graduates an opportunity to gain insight into—and appreciation for—the work of others, particularly in areas where large numbers of employees work. Finally, this approach provides a better understanding of the organization, because the new graduates can see how the different parts of the organization fit together to provide a product or service. This increased understanding can be helpful in future assignments.

A properly designed job rotation program can be cost-effective, since graduates are usually productive in their assignments. Judicious scheduling can regularly fill one or more slots in a department with graduates, thereby reducing the overall costs of the education program while gaining productive work at the same time.

Special Projects and Assignments. Although infrequently used, special projects and assignments can be an effective way of providing education or training for new graduates. Special assignments build skills needed in the current job and prepare graduates for future assignments. Four types of special projects are:

- *Special assistance* on major projects. A new graduate might assist an experienced professional employee on a significant assignment or project. The "assistant" would have limited responsibility and would be expected to learn as much as possible while making a contribution. Examples are engineering design projects, computer program design and implementation, market share analyses, or consumer information surveys.

- *Short-term assignments.* A new graduate might be assigned short-term tasks on a full-time basis. Examples are special investigations, problem analyses, exploring the feasibility of a new method, procedure, or technique, or installing new equipment. In these cases, the new graduates are expected to contribute and provide "limited" expertise.
- *Task forces.* A new graduate might be assigned to a task force assembled to solve an important problem or explore alternative ways to develop or implement a new program. Task forces are usually comprised of members representing different disciplines. They may be used to implement a new management information system in the organization, tackle a serious quality problem, or design a cost reduction program.
- *Audit team.* New graduates might serve on audit teams, primarily in an observer role. These teams primarily check actual practices against predetermined standards or procedures. Common in the financial control area, audit teams are also popular in other functional areas, such as marketing, quality control, production, and human resources.

Special projects come in a wide variety of designs. The finance and accounting area in one firm required new graduates to work on one of these projects: forecasting divisional financial results; designing a forecasting model; analyzing actual overall division performance with specific emphasis on general/administrative expenses; or performing in-depth financial analysis of a major competitor. The projects were designed to strengthen skills in the financial area and enable the new graduates to learn the financial structure of the organization.

Another example, taken from the quality assurance section, involved the development of a quality assurance reporting system, identifying key indicators, significant trends, and establishing relationships for the analysis of the organization's quality performance and reliability. This project enabled the organization to have periodic reporting of progress in the area of quality and reliability, and it established new meaningful quality level indicators and rapid communication of information within operations and in the division.

An engineering department of a heavy equipment manufacturer assigned a new graduate the task of developing a computerized program for a product's five-year plan. This program was needed to coordinate all interfacing information among engineering, marketing, service, and operations. This program allowed the company to have an overall integrated computerized product plan for a particular division.

The examples are almost unlimited. With some imagination and creativity, an organization can custom design projects to meet the needs of both the organization and new graduates.

Professional Societies and Associations. Two types of professional associations, one type expressly for management and supervision and the other for technical or professional specialties, can also be used to train graduates. For managers and supervisors, or graduates aspiring to be managers or supervisors, two organizations offer local chapters. The National Management Association and the Industrial Management Council of the YMCA have chapters throughout the United States, both in cities and in individual companies. A third organization, the Society for the Advancement of Management, has local chapters on college campuses only. These associations,through their regular meetings, seminars, courses, and other involvement programs, can enhance leadership skills and provide members a forum for learning and for exchanging information.

The other types of associations include the numerous technical and professional organizations available for individual memberships. For almost any type of work there is a professional association or society connected with it in one way or another. Common among them are the Purchasing Management Association, American Marketing Association, American Society for Production and Inventory Control, Operations Research Society, Public Relations Society of America, Hospital Personnel Association, American Society for Quality Control, and the National Association of Accountants.

Membership in the appropriate association or society can improve technical expertise and thereby assist in the training of new graduates. It also develops peer contacts that can be useful in solving technical problems. Many organizations support participation in these groups by paying for expenses and encouraging new graduates to become actively involved through regular attendance, pursuing a leadership role, serving on a committee, or working on a special project. Active involvement benefits both the individual and the organization, though more benefits may accrue for graduates' long-term growth than for their initial assignment. Because of this, some organizations may not encourage professional societies and associations until the graduates are situated in their permanent assignments.

Additional Formal Education. A few organizations use additional formal educational programs at local colleges to educate or train new college graduates. They integrate day or evening degree programs into the transition process. These arrangements can work several ways:

1. *Organizations may require new graduates to seek an advanced degree on their own time outside normal working hours.* The First Scholar program at the First National Bank of Chicago is a thirty-month general management training program combining employment at the bank with evening graduate programs in the University of Chicago's MBA program or Northwestern University's Managers' program. Admission to one of these programs is a prerequisite for First Chicago's selection decision. Participants are required to take two courses per quarter, which amounts to six hours of classes all year. In addition to receiving an MBA from a first-rate school (the bank prepays the entire tuition), First Scholars experience a wide range of the bank's departments through rotations.

2. *Organizations offer credit courses in their own facilities or in nearby facilities as part of the employee's regular work time.* Some organizations have developed this approach to recruit engineers when there has been a shortage of engineering graduates. As part of their enticement, engineers are promised an opportunity to pursue a master's degree, which they can begin immediately upon arrival and complete within two

years. In some organizations, these programs are conducted by university faculty on company facilities.

3. *Organizations require the new recruits to take selective courses, either on their own time or in off hours, in areas that represent weaknesses in the new graduates' backgrounds.* For example, new management trainees may be required to take a public speaking course if they did not take one in college. New accounting graduates may be required to take a course in report writing at a local university when they have a deficiency in this skill (Salzman and Sullivan, 1985).

Many organizations *do not require, allow, or even encourage* graduates to seek additional formal education in their first year of employment. The rationale: Pursuing additional degrees on a part-time basis, either undergraduate or graduate, can be distracting to the new graduate's career and demotivating for someone who is tired of school. Unplanned, additional formal education may interfere with work assignments, travel, or other required learning experiences. These organizations generally feel that new college graduates should spend all of their spare time learning the organization and their jobs and that they have all the formal education necessary at this point in their career. Additional formal education requires much energy and effort. Even if it is completed in the evenings outside regular work hours, the extra effort drains the energy of new graduates and may cause performance problems in initial assignments. Later, when settled into their assignments, they may be encouraged to pursue additional education, particularly in the form of a graduate degree such as an MBA.

Although opinions differ on the value of immediate additional formal education, the issue should be addressed in every organization. If additional formal educational courses can enhance the skills of a new graduate and are readily available, they should be considered as part of the education and training effort for the graduates. If they distract the graduates' attention and otherwise prevent them from performing as expected, this activity should be discouraged or even prohibited. Most importantly, organizations must clearly communicate their position in regard to this matter, so that new graduates understand why that position has been adopted.

Selecting the Best Approach. Each approach has its advantages and disadvantages and represents varying degrees of investments in staff time and money. Larger organizations with highly structured and well-established programs might utilize all of the approaches described in this section to educate or train new college graduates. Smaller organizations with limited budgets may use only one or two approaches. Factors that must be examined to decide on the appropriate approach are:

- staff resources available to develop, implement, conduct, schedule, and coordinate education and training programs
- skills and knowledge that must be learned to function satisfactorily on the job
- amount of preparation and experience of the new graduate
- timing for the new graduate to assume the new job
- extent of management involvement and support for the education/training effort
- organizational setting, location, and degree of centralization.

Analyzing these factors, the organization can select the best approach to properly educate or train new college graduates.

Summary

An integral part of a formal transition program is the education and training program. Because most new graduates will participate in some type of initial education or training effort, these programs can have a significant impact on their adjustment to the organization and their jobs. This chapter explored important issues that should be considered in the design and implementation of education and training programs aimed at this target group. It addressed items such as needs analysis, program structure, objectives, individual interests, communicating program information, program content, and the various approaches to providing education and training. The availability of a variety of approaches allows organizations to select the ones that best suit their needs, environment, and resources.

6

Nurturing
Employee Adaptation
to the Job
and the Organization

This chapter describes two important stages of the transition process: adaptation and job assignments. The adaptation phase includes all activities undertaken to enhance the graduate's adaptation to the job, work environment, and organization. The performance review is probably the most important measure of adaptation because performance is a reflection of ability to adapt. Effective approaches to improve the performance review process for new graduates are presented in this chapter. In addition, other adaptation enhancement techniques are presented, such as using the Pygmalion effect, providing recognition, conducting meetings, developing newsletters, coordinating social activities, and ensuring job security. Unfortunately, not all graduates adapt to the organization, and action may be needed to correct substandard performance or to remove them from the job. Specific techniques for accomplishing this, in a diplomatic and humane manner, are presented.

Job assignments are an important aspect of formal transition programs, particularly when temporary assignments are part of the formal education or training efforts. Short-term, rotational assignments or special projects are frequently used to prepare graduates for permanent assignments. After the formal transition efforts are complete, graduates are placed into their initial "permanent" assignments. The design of these assignments is very important and should consider such factors as the level of responsibility, the role of the initial supervisor, the degree of participation, and the perceived status.

Performance Reviews

The performance review process is probably the most important way to minimize culture shock and to enable new college graduates to adjust to the environment and work. When conducted effectively, performance reviews help keep graduates on target with education and training efforts as well as initial assignments. This important process forms an integral part of formal transition efforts for new college graduates.

Basic Concepts. A performance review may be defined as a communication process between a supervisor and an employee that (1) determines how effectively the employee is performing in the job, (2) establishes the appropriate performance-based rewards for the employee, and (3) identifies areas for improvement. Performance reviews go by several names, including *performance evaluations, performance appraisals, performance ratings, merit ratings, job reviews,* and *performance assessments.* The terms *performance review* and *performance appraisal* are most common. Few aspects of the employment relationship are as controversial as the performance review process. Yet it is possibly management's most powerful tool in controlling the productivity and morale of new graduates.

Performance reviews for new college graduates are usually designed to meet one or more of the following objectives:

1. review performance over periodic time intervals during the transition process
2. determine the amount of salary increase and/or other rewards based on performance

3. document performance to satisfy administrative and legal requirements
4. identify graduates' strengths and weaknesses as they bear on job-related performance and potential
5. determine additional or supplemental training and educational needs of new graduates.

Due to this wide range of objectives, performance reviews vary in scope and administration. A formal review process attempts to minimize errors and ensure that information is gathered efficiently and is used to meet the objectives. Even organizations without a formal process render informal judgments that are used to arrive at decisions about new employees' careers. For detailed information on various types of performance reviews, see King (1984), Henderson (1984), and Olson (1981). Important issues related to performance reviews are discussed in the remainder of this section.

Timing. The timing of performance reviews must be addressed early in the planning stage of a transition program. Establishing appropriate intervals between reviews represents a trade-off between the time the staff can devote to the process and the time that is necessary to give adequate feedback to new graduates. Although most formal reviews are conducted annually, some reviews are semiannual while still others are conducted quarterly. A few organizations review graduates at the end of each assignment in the transition program to provide an accurate account of performance and to make improvements in the future. While this is important, the formal performance review is no substitute for the frequent feedback new graduates must receive to perform successfully on their assignments. In a recent survey of organizations recruiting MBA graduates, 50 percent of the respondents had annual performance reviews for their MBA graduates. Twenty-five percent had semiannual reviews, and the remaining 25 percent were split evenly between quarterly reviews and end-of-assignment reviews. In the same study, slightly over 10 percent reviewed their MBA graduates more frequently than other professional and/or supervisory employees.

The timing of the review in relation to pay increases is another issue. If the review's objectives focus on development much more than past performance, it should not be conducted at the time merit increases are initiated. However, if the principal purpose of the performance review is to reward past performance, it should be conducted at salary review time and provide the basis for the amount of increase.

Degree of Involvement. Another issue in performance review is the involvement of new graduates in their own performance review process. In traditional systems, the manager or supervisor completed the appraisal form and reviewed it with new graduates; graduates had little, if any, opportunity to provide input in the discussion. Today, many organizations encourage their new graduates to provide substantial input into the process, in some cases as much as their supervisors. In these settings, graduates evaluate their own performance, prepare for the review, and actively participate in the appraisal discussion. Figure 5 shows one organization's review process for professional and supervisory employees who were primarily recent college graduates. This approach maximizes involvement and essentially puts the efforts of the appraisee and the appraisor on equal footing. In this example, both the supervisor (who is being appraised) and the manager receive the appraisal form at the same time. They are given approximately two weeks to gather information and complete the appraisal form. They are allowed a few more days to prepare for the discussion, and as part of this preparation they gather any additional information to support performance results or to explain a lack of results. An appraisal discussion is held in an atmosphere of open, two-way communication. This particular company reports that the information provided on the two forms is similar and that the separate assessments of supervisor performance closely parallel each other. In some cases, the manager's ratings are higher than the supervisor's. During the appraisal discussion they reach agreement on performance ratings, the results achieved, self-development needs, and other appraisal items. Then they agree on goals for the next period, particularly in areas where improvement is needed. Finally, the manager docu-

Figure 5. Performance Appraisal Process.

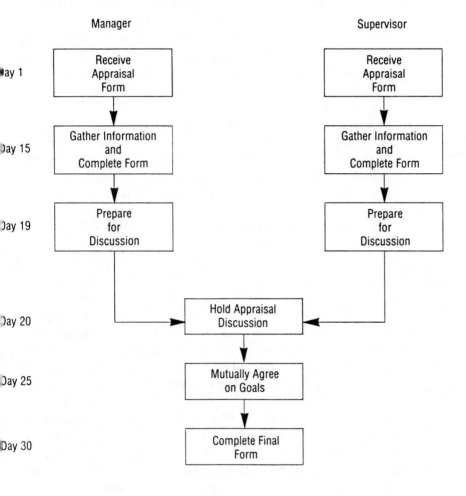

ments the complete appraisal process on a final copy of the form, which is reviewed by upper management and becomes a permanent record of the appraisal discussion.

This process seems to be quite complex, but the extra effort of involving new graduates in the review process can produce at least six distinct advantages:

- A more productive relationship is developed between the supervisor and new graduates. Problems are more likely to be resolved, and solutions will be more readily accepted.
- Clearer boundaries of accountability are established. Each party may present information of which the other was unaware, leading to a more accurate appraisal.
- Self-motivation and initiative on the part of new graduates are encouraged.
- Complaints, charges, and challenges to the appraisal process are minimized because graduates participate in the process.
- Anxieties and frustrations are reduced significantly, since both individuals have an ample opportunity to prepare for the performance discussion. Graduates learn more about themselves.
- It legitimizes a process that most graduates already practice, at least informally.

This approach is not without its share of problems, however. It is time-consuming because both parties must prepare for the appraisal discussion. Up to three forms must be completed, and a lengthy discussion may be required. Some graduates, particularly those from an authoritarian background, prefer to be evaluated by someone else and are comfortable with minimum responsibilities in their own review process. Some managers are also uncomfortable with this approach. They are reluctant to allow new graduates to rate themselves for fear of causing conflicts and disagreements on performance levels. They are also concerned that graduates cannot be objective about their performance. Disagreement is a real possibility, and this could lead to confrontation and conflict, but the advantages of this approach tend to outweigh the problems, as evidenced by the number of organizations moving in this direction.

Critical Incident Files. In a semiannual or annual review process recent events may tend to bias the review. Managers naturally remember recent items, particularly the negative ones. Consistent, positive, overall performance may be overshadowed by a few negative events occurring just before the review discussion.

One way to correct this problem is to have managers keep critical incident files on each new graduate. In practice these files should be kept on all key employee groups. These files contain exceptional items related to job performance—both good and bad. An example of an exceptionally good critical incident might be as follows: "On January 23rd, Susan was particularly effective in resolving a customer complaint that might have led to a cancellation of a large order, had it not been resolved. The net result was a satisfied customer." An example of a negative incident might be as follows: "On July 15th, John failed to complete a project as scheduled. The failure caused delays in a major design effort."

Only exceptional items related to job performance should be placed in the critical incident file. After a few rounds of performance reviews, graduates will come to realize that exceptional incidents are being noticed and documented and work hard at keeping the exceptions in the positive category.

Documentation. Another issue in performance reviews is the documentation required. The critical incident file provides an important part of the documentation of performance. This file may be attached to the review itself or used to supply information for it. In either case, it adds to the accuracy and completeness of the overall review and it is important for four reasons. First, documentation provides a permanent record of performance. Even the best of supervisors and managers may forget details, and the organization cannot rely on their memories for a record of performance. Also, they may leave the organization, taking the mental record of performance with them. Something as important as job performance deserves to be documented thoroughly and accurately.

Second, documentation makes graduates aware of what is on record concerning their performance. This is important both for good and bad performance. Graduates are entitled to have outstanding performance become part of their permanent record, which should enhance future career opportunities and influence their initial job assignments. On the negative side, they should know that an incident of poor performance has become a matter of record. This gives them additional encouragement to overcome deficiencies.

Third, documentation allows managers and supervisors to support personnel actions regarding new graduates, not only job assignments, promotions, and transfers, but discharges as well. New graduates are rarely assigned more responsible jobs unless they have a record of exceptional performance in previous activities or assignments. Also, performance reviews represent one of the best sources of information for evaluating potential for a lateral assignment or transfer. In either case, performance reviews provide the rationale for assignments or transfers and may help support actual moves. Performance reviews are also used to justify the termination of new graduates. It is becoming increasingly difficult for an employer to discharge employees without just cause and ample documentation.

Fourth, documentation will help defend the organization against future discrimination charges. Performance reviews represent one of the areas of the employment relationship that has been challenged by discrimination charges and suits. The law clearly requires objective reviews, and these cannot be accomplished without complete and accurate documentation. Without it employers are defenseless against a discrimination charge where performance is involved.

Effective documentation is time-consuming, and it is difficult to achieve consistency within the organization. If it is not done properly, documentation can be a liability rather than an asset. The organization must define documentation requirements when considering time constraints and the information necessary to support personnel actions.

Sources of Input for Performance Review. Depending on the stage of transition, more than one individual may need to be involved. Graduates working directly for a supervisor in a job assignment should be reviewed by that supervisor. In addition, the transition program coordinator should have input into the review. (This provides two sources of input and two perspectives for the review process; also, it alerts the program coordinator to potential problems as well as successes.) For graduates involved in formal, off-the-job education and training programs, the transition program coordinator should provide input for the performance review. Instructors, other staff members, and supervisors are additional potential sources of input if they have had an opportunity to work with the graduate enough to provide an objective review. Ideally, all individuals who can objectively evaluate new graduates should be considered as potential sources of input.

Communication. Much of the success of the performance review process depends on how well both parties understand it. Communication media range from verbal instructions for a performance review form to elaborate policies, booklets, training sessions, and meetings in which the organization explains the review process in complete detail. Although the extent of communication depends on the organization and the resources available, the system will be understood only to the extent that information about it has been made available both formally and informally. Performance review should never be treated as a secretive process with negative connotations but rather as a positive process beneficial to graduates, supervisors, and the organization.

Enhancing Adaptation

In addition to formal performance reviews, other actions can enhance the adaptation process: the Pygmalion effect, recognition, meetings with new graduates, internal newsletters for graduates, social activities, and job security improvements. Each is designed to help new graduates adjust to the organization, understand their expected roles and behavior, while at the same time ensuring that they become contributing members as soon as possible.

The Pygmalion Effect. Organizations struggling with ways to help new graduates adjust can take lessons from Greek mythology. Pygmalion, sculptor and King of Cypress, carved a statue of the ideal woman and fell in love with his creation. He prayed to the goddess Aphrodite to bring her to life and his prayer was granted. The couple lived happily ever after. The Pygmalion effect, or self-fulfilling prophecy as it is sometimes called, can be a useful tool to enhance the adaptation process for new graduates.

Considerable research has shown that expectations play an important part in actual performance, attitudes, and habits. Managers form expectations about their employees, and particularly new employees, and communicate those expectations with various cues. Employees respond and try to adjust their behavior to meet the expectations, which in turn reinforces the original expectations. The evidence of this effect is very impressive. More than 300 studies involving the impact of expectations on performance have been conducted in a wide range of experimental settings, from the classroom to the military to the work world (Goddard, 1985). The result is one of the most powerful tools for influencing the performance of employees.

Sandler (1986) summarizes this process with eight corollaries.

1. High expectations lead to higher performance; low expectations lead to lower performance.
2. Better employee performance resulting from high expectations leads managers to like employees more; lower employee performance resulting from low expectations leads managers to like employees less.
3. We tend to be comfortable with people who meet our expectations whether they are high or low. We tend not to be comfortable with people who do not meet our expectations whether they are high or low.
4. Forming expectations is natural and unavoidable.
5. Once formed, expectations about ourselves tend to be self-sustaining.
6. Good managers produce employees who perform well and feel good about themselves. Bad managers produce employees who perform poorly and feel badly about themselves.
7. Performance ratings do not just summarize the past, they help determine future performance.
8. The best managers have confidence in themselves and in their ability to hire, develop, and motivate people; largely because

of their self-confidence, they communicate high expectations to others.

The self-fulfilling prophecy challenges organizations to ensure that managers and transition program coordinators develop and communicate high expectations of new college graduates. This is important in setting the climate for the work environment, developing work assignments and projects, and providing feedback to new graduates.

To help ensure success in the early stages of their careers, supervisors and managers of new graduates should observe what managers of high-expectation employees do. According to Sandler (1986), they create a warmer social and emotional mood. They nod their heads approvingly and look into subordinates' eyes more often. They are generally more supportive, friendly, accepting, and encouraging. More assignments and projects, as well as the more difficult ones, are given to the high-expectation employees. Managers give them more opportunities to speak at meetings, afford them high levels of visibility, and give them a chance to offer their opinions or to disagree with the manager's opinions. They pay closer attention to their responses and give them more assistance or encouragement in generating solutions to problems. And finally, managers give more positive reinforcement to high-expectation employees, praising more for good work and criticizing less for making mistakes. Consequently, confidence grows. If this effect is understood and practiced by organizations, the results can be a quicker adaptation, with higher levels of performance achieved by motivated and challenged graduates.

Using Recognition. Another important way to enhance the adaptation process of new graduates is through the use of recognition for their efforts and accomplishments. Positive recognition is appropriate when new graduates have excelled on the job or in an education or training program, or when they have completed tasks that are above and beyond expectations. Recognition focuses on nonmonetary rewards from middle managers, top management, and the organization.

Recognition can take many forms, but in general it is defined as an act or gesture of appreciation to an employee who has reached an important milestone. Recognition is a very powerful motivator. The interesting thing about recognition is that the way recognition is bestowed (style) is just as important as the type of recognition (substance). Some types of recognition may be potentially effective but if given improperly can actually have a negative impact. Five basic factors compose recognition style:

1. *Recognition must be timely.* Outstanding performance should be recognized promptly. Postponing the mention of the achievement a month after it occurred might even be counter-productive. The best time to reward a new graduate is right after the praiseworthy action.

2. *The substance of recognition must be appropriate for the achievement.* The size of the reward must be matched with the accomplishment. A free cup of coffee or a lunch for a new graduate who has broken a significant company record would certainly not be an appropriate reward. A bonus or gift, along with public acknowledgment, might be more fitting.

3. *The substance of recognition must be perceived as being worthwhile.* Although a manager may think a reward is appropriate, the person receiving it may not look at it that way. In one organization, a management trainee was selected to be a United Way campaign representative as a reward for an outstanding accomplishment. The trainee did not perceive it as a reward but instead as punishment. In his eyes it was not a worthwhile form of recognition.

4. *Most recognition should be bestowed in public.* The old cliche "Reward in public, criticize in private" is usually the best rule to follow. In most cases, new graduates should be given praise and recognition in the presence of fellow employees and possibly before an audience of managers. This lets others know what has been accomplished and that management and the organization are both pleased with that accomplishment.

5. *Recognition must show sincerity.* If a manager hands out a reward merely because of policy or past practice, its impact

will be minimized or even negated. Recognition must be given in an honest and sincere manner.

Many types of recognition can be used effectively. Here are a few common ones:

- Initial job assignment
- Promotions
- Shortened education program
- Merit increases
- Bonuses
- Special assignments
- Commendation memos
- Dinners or receptions
- Announcements in meetings
- Weekend trips
- Organizational publications
- Special thanks.

No organizational group is more important to new graduates than top management. Although new graduates strive for recognition from top management, most settle for an occasional acknowledgment that they exist. Top management recognition of graduates can have a lasting effect and a strong motivational impact; management actions can improve the performance, job satisfaction, and organizational commitment of new graduates. Before taking action, top management must know which new recruits are performing at their best, which deserve special recognition, or which just need to be congratulated for joining the organization. This may become a problem in large organizations with several layers of management. Some executives designate someone to remind them of employees who deserve special attention or recognition. The top human resources executive is a logical choice for this assignment.

Three simple, yet effective, approaches are often used to provide top management recognition. A *personal visit* from a top executive who mentions an accomplishment or offers congratulations can provide a powerful stimulation for new graduates.

Personal visits, though time-consuming, can be effective and even rewarding for the executive who has the chance to keep in touch with new talent. A *telephone call* from a top executive can also have a significant impact on new graduates, almost to the same extent as a personal visit. Just realizing that a top executive took the time to phone does much for new recruits. Calls should be planned and executed on a timely basis soon after important accomplishments or special events. If this method is used too often, however, it loses its effectiveness and becomes just another routine way of communicating. Similar to visits and calls, a *personal note* is another effective way to provide recognition. A personal note, highlighting achievement, makes it clear to new graduates that someone in the organization cares and is watching their performance. Executives who take the time to visit, call, or write will be long remembered as effective executives in the organization.

One of the most effective kinds of recognition is public recognition. All of management, including the graduate's peer group, and in some cases the entire organization, can learn about the contributions of new graduates through public recognition. Several effective approaches may be used. Announcing accomplishments in organizational publications is an excellent way to highlight achievements. Almost every organization has some type of in-house publication designed to distribute company news and other information to employees. Providing recognition should be one of the goals of the internal publication and articles about achievements and assignments should be planned regularly. Some organizations have a special publication for the management group—an ideal medium for disseminating information about achievements of new graduates; in fact, providing recognition is usually one of the fundamental purposes for having the management publication. Another excellent opportunity to recognize new graduates is in regular meetings of the management group. Many organizations conduct these meetings on a periodic basis and include recognition of performance of new graduates as one of the items on the agenda. Regular departmental staff meetings also form an excellent setting in which to recognize new graduates in the department.

Although support from top executives and public recognition are important, new graduates are motivated best by recognition from their immediate managers. These managers will have the most impact on career advancement and pay increases (unless graduates are involved in an off-the-job education or training program, in which case the program coordinator should provide reinforcement or recognition). Graduates need frequent feedback on how they are doing, and no kind of formal recognition or reward program can replace it. Yet quite often managers and supervisors do not take the time or know how to give positive reinforcement. To remedy this, some organizations train managers to use positive reinforcement and feedback to keep their new recruits motivated.

Meetings with New Graduates. Two types of meetings can enhance the adaptation process. The first is the periodic update meeting where general information is disseminated to new graduates and problems or concerns are discussed. The second type involves small group discussion meetings with senior management where graduates have an opportunity to air complaints and receive candid information straight from the top of the organization.

Periodic meetings may be held weekly, biweekly, or monthly, depending on the organizational setting and the need for this type of communication. Transition program coordinators meet with new graduates to discuss their progress, work assignments, schedules, policies and procedures, organizational plans, program changes, and the success of previous participants in the program. This meeting molds new graduates into a cohesive group and helps ensure that they all receive the same message and have an opportunity to ask questions. Typically lasting from one hour to a half-day depending on the agenda, this meeting is frequently used to discuss transition problems.

Small group meetings with senior management allow the organization to resolve complaints facing new graduates while keeping lines of communication open with top management. Virtually all new employees have complaints, yet new graduates have few methods available to resolve them. Informal, frank discussions can allow graduates to express their feelings in a nonthreatening environment, usually to a member of top management. These meetings provide the opportunity for contact with top management, which is important to new graduates as they are developing organizational commitment. Meetings with senior management help build loyalty and teamwork and should be conducted in a trusting atmosphere where the graduates feel free to make comments without fear of retaliation. Sometimes, the new graduate's immediate supervisor and in some cases even the program coordinators are not invited because they may be part of the problem. This way new employees feel free to discuss items directly with upper management. This "skip level" technique is successful in developing a feeling among new graduates that someone at the top is willing to listen to them. On the negative side, this approach can create anxiety in supervisors of new graduates, particularly the insecure, nervous ones who may feel that top management is circumventing their authority or spying on their activities. Clear communication, up front, can help alleviate these concerns and keep supervisors from being fearful about the process. Important issues, brought to the attention of top management in these meetings, may need action. If management takes no action on these issues, new graduates should be notified as to the reasons why no action is planned. Otherwise, the entire exercise may be considered a waste of time.

Newsletter for New Graduates. New college graduates need timely information from official sources and through a variety of media. They need information to help them adjust to the organization, learn their profession, and handle pressing job situations. To meet this need, some organizations add an extra dimension to the communication effort by developing a publication specifically for new college graduates in their early months and years of employment. A special publication shows new graduates the importance the organization places on their success and helps build loyalty and commitment.

Although the format and content for this newsletter may vary considerably, certain principles should be followed to produce an effective newsletter. First, it must be factual and newsworthy, largely void of editorials and opinions. Verifiable facts and interesting information is essential. Second, timely information must be presented. Occasionally, important news should be announced in this publication, possibly ahead of other sources, such as the grapevine. This builds interest in the publication and creates a desire for the graduates to read it promptly. Third, information should be provided directly to graduates, rather than through the chain of command. The newsletter may be the only item intended exclusively for new graduates. Fourth, transition issues should be addressed, including tips to help graduates adjust to the organization and minimize culture shock. Success stories, advice, suggestions and recommendations, all aimed at minimizing transition problems, should be an integral part of the publication. It should answer questions often asked by new recruits, provide helpful assistance and advice, and disseminate important news. Realistically, however, this communication channel may be feasible only in organizations with numerous new college graduates.

Social Activities. The social involvement of new graduates is an integral part of the adjustment process. Social activities with four internal groups should be encouraged or initiated. New graduates need social time with *other graduates* during initial work assignments or while they are involved in formal education or training programs. This type of social event enables graduates to exchange views, impressions, and ideas in a relaxed atmosphere, resulting in a camaraderie important to their success. Graduates are more apt to be candid with each other, share concerns, and discuss problems in this atmosphere. Social events, such as dinner meetings and field trips, should be integrated into formal training and education programs. Recreational sports teams, such as golf, tennis, and bowling, can be inexpensive but helpful in building the team spirit necessary for success. A word of caution is in order. This camaraderie could create cliques or subgroups, with a counterproductive result. Careful monitoring of activities and taking corrective action when necessary can help prevent this.

Every type of organization has its unique social atmosphere. New graduates should be encouraged, or possibly required, to participate in *organizational social activities*, such as annual picnics, plant tours, field trips, sports tournaments, art shows, or other special events that attract large numbers of employees. Interaction with the key management team in a relaxed atmosphere is an important part of the adaptation process. *Social activities with key managers* such as in receptions, dinners, or even weekend retreats can encourage interaction, involvement, and information exchange. Inviting new graduates to management group social functions can also be helpful in the adjustment process. *Social activities with former participants* of transition programs may be one of the best sources of information for current participants. Special activities where new graduates have an opportunity to seek advice and counsel from former graduates can be invaluable to the adjustment process. They can learn "survival techniques" and "secrets of success" from those who participated earlier. An annual alumni meeting is an ideal setting to allow current and former participants an opportunity to exchange information.

Together, these four informal approaches provide ample opportunities for graduates to meet others who can help them make the adjustment and adapt to the organization. Unfortunately, not enough organizations aptly plan for new graduates to be involved in social activities, although there are usually ample opportunities for participation.

Improving Job Security. The last thing new college graduates need is to be concerned about losing their job for reasons other than performance. However, because of business fluctuations and sudden changes in market demand, some firms routinely decrease their work force because of these changes, and some graduates find themselves caught up in short-term reductions, layoffs, or reassignments. New graduates should not have to be overly concerned about job security. They have enough problems with meeting responsibilities, understanding the organization, and learning the job. New graduates seek stable employment levels. The employer's stability is a feature that attracted the graduates to the organization in the first place (Levering, Moskowitz and Katz, 1984; and Derr, 1986).

A layoff or transfer, even on a temporary basis, can be a traumatic experience. When a decline in the organization is apparent or when rumors of a potential displacement filter down through the organization, graduates begin to worry about their fate. They reach conclusions based on how the organization has handled these situations in the past—conclusions often based on rumors. Previous unfair or inequitable applications of policies on layoffs heighten the concern over job security. New graduates, being the lowest in seniority, see themselves as powerless and having little or no control over their own destiny; this creates an unproductive environment, and even the best graduates may leave.

College-educated employees are valuable assets that represent a significant investment. They can have a significant impact on an organization's long-term success and should be retained during economic downturns. Such prestigious organizations as IBM, Delta Airlines, and Hewlett-Packard have adopted full-employment policies that do not allow layoffs. They consider retaining professional employees as an investment in the future, not an extra expense. Also, with today's cost of layoffs, keeping professional, technical, and supervisory personnel in downturns is becoming an attractive, cost-saving alternative. Severance pay, higher unemployment compensation taxes, continuation of health and other benefits for a period of time after layoff, administrative costs, and legal fees have staggering financial implications for organizations.

Obviously, some situations require layoffs of professional personnel. An organization facing serious problems and little or no hope of returning to previous employment levels may have to consider layoffs as part of a drastic restructuring necessary to keep the organization healthy. In this situation, survival is the issue. Also, plant closings, which may wipe out an entire work force, leave the organization with few options for its professional, technical, and supervisory employees.

A positive approach is needed to find productive alternatives for these employees during periods of displacement. Some possible actions are:

- move displaced graduates to temporary assignments in other locations
- assign displaced graduates to work duties different from what they would normally be performing
- give displaced graduates special projects to complete
- prepare graduates for other types of jobs through an education program
- place graduates on worthwhile outside community and public service assignments
- relocate displaced graduates to other areas where employment prospects are much better.

Although this issue can be addressed with proper planning and recruitment strategies, it nevertheless occurs in many organizations because of the unpredictability of the business climate. It is important to communicate the organization's intended actions in case of displacement. New professional employees should know what to expect of the organization during a downturn. Providing information about job security is almost as important as the actions taken to relieve job insecurity. Some consideration should be given to developing and publishing a policy on layoffs. Such a policy should be carefully worded so that it does not represent a binding employment contract unless that is the intention. A policy statement can probably do more to boost the morale of those concerned about stability than any other single action regarding job security. Even in good times, with no downturns anticipated in the short-term, this policy should be communicated to new graduates. It reinforces their decision to join the organization and relieves much of their concern about potential job loss in the near future.

Confronting Substandard Performance

Unfortunately, not all new graduates succeed in their education or training programs or initial job assignments. Inevitably, some will perform unacceptably or will be so dissatisfied with their jobs that they become detrimental to employee morale. When faced with this dilemma, organizations have five basic courses of action, the first of which is counseling. The other actions range from reassignment to termination. Before examining these actions, several important points should be reviewed about confronting the problem of substandard performance. First, action should be taken quickly because of the impact that new graduates have on the performance of other employees. Their visibility is high and in some cases they set examples for others. Too often, ineffective new graduates are allowed to founder and sink, damaging themselves and possibly others in the process.

Second, the dignity and self-esteem of the individual should be respected, particularly when the responsibility for failure rests partially with management. The failure may be the result of improper selection, ineffective orientation, or inadequate training, so the individual may not be entirely at fault.

Third, other graduates, as well as potential new recruits, monitor these situations. Substandard performance draws attention, and fellow employees usually want the problem corrected to keep an ineffective co-worker from draining the organization's performance. Conversely, they want fellow employees to be treated fairly and humanely, as they do not want to fear unfair treatment in the future. Potential recruits, who may learn about the situation, will evaluate the outcome and use it in their decision to join the organization. If they learn that the graduate was given every opportunity to perform, they will be satisfied; otherwise, they may perceive the organization as unfair in its treatment of new graduates.

Counseling. Substandard performance should signal a need for counseling from as many as three sources. Graduates should receive immediate counseling from their supervisor or manager. In a formal transition program, the program coordinator should be involved in counseling sessions. And finally, the graduates' mentors, if available, should provide counseling. The most important individual in the counseling process is the one with the best vantage point from which to assess problem areas and to know the strengths and weaknesses of the graduates. Although this number of counselors might appear excessive, the investment in the graduate at this point is significant and all appropriate actions to salvage the new graduate should be attempted. Sometimes a new graduate responds to certain individuals more favorably than others. With up to three individuals providing counseling the chances of success are increased.

The best way to handle performance counseling is to clearly describe the situation in candid, understandable terms. Counseling should be provided as soon as performance deficiencies are detected. Although regular performance reviews uncover substandard performance, problems can develop quickly and become serious before the next scheduled review. Therefore, it is important to monitor performance routinely and take action when problems are encountered. Assuming the other stages of the transition program have been effective, poor performance should not lead to devastating or disastrous outcomes for either the organization or new graduates. Problems should be confronted and solutions sought.

Counseling should take on a positive, progressive approach. Discussions should focus on confidence-building and the use of positive reinforcement to accomplish the job or correct problem areas. Negative comments and threats will do little to help and may actually worsen the situation or cause graduates to seek employment elsewhere. In the progressive approach, supervisors should express the consequences of continued unacceptable performance in sincere diplomatic terms. A follow-up discussion should be planned. If problems continue, each progressive discussion outlines the consequences of continued poor performance until the only alternative left is to remove the graduate from the job or the particular stage of the transition program. These actions are discussed next.

Transfer to Another Assignment. Depending on the reason for the substandard performance, a transfer to another job assignment may be an appropriate action for salvaging ineffective new college graduates. Problems in adjusting to a particular management style, getting along with fellow employees at the workplace, or cooperating with staff support groups could possibly be resolved by a transfer to another job assignment in another department or section. Some supervisory styles are inappropriate for developing college-trained talent. An assignment with a supervisor who resents new graduates or with one who is less than effective in developing people may create problems for new graduates. A move to another location may be the best course of action. This approach needs to be carefully examined to ensure that new graduates succeed in a new location. It should not be considered as a chance to flee from a particularly challenging or difficult job, or from an area in which the graduate does not want to work. It is also important to examine the potential job assignment to ensure that the factors that led to the previous failure will not recur in the new assignment. In many cases a change from a distasteful situation can spark a renewed determination to succeed in the assignment.

Transfer or Demotion to a Nonprofessional Job. Another possible approach is to consider a transfer to a job that demands less ability and skill than the one originally planned for the new graduate. In a few cases, graduates, unable to meet the challenges placed on them in their assignments, will take jobs with less responsibility in order to stay with the organization. For example, an engineering graduate who is unable to perform adequately in an engineer position may be assigned the job of engineering technician, a job requiring fewer skills and less ability than engineer. Although this is not a common approach, it may be a viable one under the right circumstances. In these situations it is important to determine the graduate's reactions to, and attitudes toward, the demotion or reassignment. Otherwise, a potential morale problem may develop, rendering this approach ineffective. It is important to maintain the self-esteem of the individual and minimize the loss of status caused by change in job assignment.

Termination. The least desired outcome of a substandard performance discussion is termination, but this action is still taken far too frequently by organizations faced with a performance problem. New professional, technical, and supervisory employees are terminated even though their performance deficiencies could be corrected through counseling. This solution should be used as a last resort, when other approaches to correct the problem do not work. A few problems are serious enough, however, to justify termination as the only logical course of action. For example, an organization faced with the situation of a new graduate found guilty of dishonesty or illegal activities may view termination as the only alternative. Also, when management fails in the selection process, resulting in a poor match between individual and organization, termination may be the best approach.

Outplacement. Providing outplacement services to professional, technical, and supervisory personnel who cannot function in the job represents a growing trend. Outplacement includes assistance to find another job, counseling and coaching in job-hunting skills, and in some cases providing travel allowances needed to conduct a job search. For new college graduates the extent of outplacement services will probably be limited to assistance in finding a job and making job contacts. Providing assistance to locate another job leaves the graduate and the organization with positive feelings about the way a potentially distasteful situation is handled. In some cases, it may be better to provide outplacement with an external agency rather than to try to do it in house. This places a "neutral" third party in charge of the job outplacement—possibly presenting the terminated employee in a more favorable light.

Temporary Work Assignments During Transition

Most education and training efforts during transition involve one or more temporary work assignments for new graduates, ranging from jobs regularly performed by other employees to special projects developed exclusively for new graduates to prepare them for permanent assignments. The scope of temporary assignments and the conditions under which graduates perform them are important issues that must be addressed in the design of the transition program. The major issues are addressed in this section.

Importance of Productive and Challenging Assignments. Requiring new graduates to perform menial jobs may have some merit, but an assignment with no challenge and little opportunity to make a contribution can be demoralizing and demotivating. Assigning challenging jobs commensurate with abilities can also improve efficiency, although it may be difficult for new graduates to make a contribution early in the assignment.

An example best illustrates the importance of this issue. Outside sales representatives are recruited and prepared for field assignments to sell products for a medium-size manufacturing firm. As part of the transition process, new graduates work in a variety of assignments, all of which are selected to provide insight into how the product is manufactured, sold, and shipped to the customer. In one assignment, in a customer service function, under the direct supervision of the customer service manager, graduates investigate complaints, recommend solutions, and work with the quality assurance department to see that problems are corrected. As a special project, new recruits write reports with recommendations for reducing customer complaints. Although the job level of customer service representative may be lower than that of an outside sales representative, this "hands on" experience represents a challenging assignment that allows new graduates to make a contribution to the organization. In contrast, an assignment on a shipping dock loading railcars for a month would do no more than develop an appreciation for the hard work of those employees in the shipping department. A one- or two-day visit would probably suffice to give some insight into the problems of shipping and handling the product.

Challenging assignments related to future permanent jobs can increase satisfaction as well as motivate graduates to achieve or excel in each assignment. Assignments should be of short duration and fully explained to graduates. Routine and menial tasks, although they have some value in gaining appreciation for the work, may lower morale and self-esteem, prompting new graduates to wonder why they attended college to be employed as a laborer. This approach may have some valid exceptions. For example, new graduates destined to be first-level supervisors may benefit from short-term assignments in one or more of the jobs held by the employees they will be supervising in the future, even though the work involves only general labor.

Routine and menial tasks are sometimes assigned for longer periods as an attitude check. Organizations sometimes want new graduates who are willing to perform these tough assignments with a positive attitude. This is fine as long as it is not carried to an extreme. The judgment of a graduate, who spends six months performing general labor without complaining in a diplomatic way, would have to be questioned by most progressive managers. Only so much can be gained from this type of assignment; in addition, it is a gross misuse of resources.

Developing Work Assignments. Temporary work assignments must be carefully planned and scheduled. The specific types of assignments required are normally determined from a needs analysis, which outlines experiences, skills, and knowledge necessary for new graduates to succeed in the planned permanent job. Once assignments are identified, the scope of the activities and work must be outlined with each participating department. The time required to complete the assignment or a specific measure of job completion should be established. In some organizations new graduates work on assignments until they reach certain performance levels. In others, they successfully complete an examination of the work area or work processes. In still others, they continue on the assignment until they finish a special project.

A variety of assignments may not be practical in every situation, and some care must be taken to sort out necessary assignments. Ideally, new graduates should be exposed to all the jobs and learn about all the work flows and technical processes; organizations are limited, however, in the amount of time and expense they can invest in the training and education of new graduates. Also, there are limits to the amount of "learning" new graduates can feasibly endure on the way to their permanent assignments. Because of this, most organizations generally restrict work assignments to those areas necessary to succeed in the permanent jobs.

The department or section where new graduates temporarily work must have a thorough understanding of the purpose, scope, and duration of work assignments. The attitude and support of temporary supervisors are critical. Supportive and encouraging supervisors can provide help to new graduates as they learn assignments; whereas, supervisors indifferent to the purposes of the program and insensitive to the needs of graduates may devote little attention to them and may even resent their presence in the department. Therefore, some organizations, when faced with a choice, select sections or departments with managers or supervisors supportive of the transition program. The best trainers are identified, based on previous successes, and assigned this special duty.

Finally, the organization should provide a clear explanation of what is expected from new graduates on each assignment, thus avoiding misunderstandings and dissatisfaction resulting from unmet expectations. Self-evaluation questions, by which new graduates can assess their progress through the work assignment, may be appropriate. One organization provides a detailed notebook filled with questions that must be answered for each part of the work assignment. The Marriott Corporation sends its trainees to a location for eight to sixteen weeks armed with a manual of tasks to be completed and signed off by appropriate coaching personnel (Lean, 1985).

Authority and Responsibility. Another important issue to consider for the work assignment is the amount of responsibility and/or authority provided to new graduates. *Responsibility* is usually defined as the accountability for reaching objectives through the proper use of resources and adherence to organizational policy. *Authority* is usually defined as a right to command, expend resources, and influence behavior. Authority is necessary to carry out responsibilities.

Regardless of the type of assignment, some responsibility must go along with it. Because of the new graduates' short duration in the work area and their lack of experience, they may be given only partial responsibility for performing the work. In some cases, they must check with others before making decisions regarding the normal functions on the job. The amount of responsibility provided must balance two concerns: the new graduates' desire for responsibility and the organization's need to ensure that the work is done properly and efficiently. Balancing these concerns appropriately is not easy. Giving graduates little or no responsibility may inhibit motivation and learning and thus hamper the effectiveness of the transition process (see the next section on permanent assignments).

Authority is another important issue with new graduates, particularly for graduates destined to become first-level supervisors, as their initial assignments in the transition program may require limited authority in temporary supervisory duties. New graduates need to understand the various sources of authority. Authority based on position, sometimes called legitimate or legal authority, represents decision-making limits inherent in the job and the control individuals exercise over others in the organization. The assets controlled, the number of employees supervised, or the budget managed help determine the amount of authority. Authority may also be based on performance and expertise. Top performers in the organization, having the ability to get things done and make things happen, command respect and can influence others. Their expert knowledge and high levels of competence make them valuable to the organization, a value that increases their authority. Finally, individuals have authority based on behavior and trust. They have developed certain traits, habits, characteristics, and interpersonal skills over a period of time. Individuals usually earn this kind of authority by working with people in an open and honest way and by projecting a postive image that is attractive to others.

Learning how authority is granted and earned helps new graduates understand how they can acquire more; they should understand early in the transition process that they do have some control over gaining authority. Overzealous new recruits can destroy respect and credibility for themselves and the organization by trying to exercise authority that has not been granted or earned. Conversely, new graduates must have the authority necessary to carry out responsibilities if they are held accountable for the results. As with other items, it is important for all parties involved (graduates, managers, other employees) to understand the extent of authority inherent in new graduates' work assignments. For additional information on specific ways to increase authority, see Phillips (1986).

Permanent Assignments

After new graduates complete the formal transition program, they are transferred or promoted to a permanent assignment. The word *permanent* may be misleading, since graduates usually move on to many other jobs as they gain experience. In this section, the term *permanent assignment* is used to describe the first assignment outside the formal transition program. For some graduates this assignment may materialize soon after employment, following a brief orientation session. For others, it may come after several months or even years of preparation involving rotational assignments and projects. In either case, the initial permanent job is a very important one, for it provides the first real opportunity for new graduates to test their abilities. It is the time new graduates have waited for—an opportunity to make a meaningful contribution. The first permanent assignment also provides graduates with additional opportunity to learn more about their chosen field and the organization through actual work experience. It also gives the organization the opportunity to continue to learn more about individual graduates. Developing the permanent assignment cannot be taken lightly and involves several important considerations.

Timing. The timing of the permanent assignment varies with the organization, but in general the assignment should not be made too early, before graduates are fully prepared, nor should it be delayed too long, as graduates want an opportunity to show what they can do as soon as possible. For some, the transition is very simple, such as when a special project or training assignment is converted to a permanent job. For others, the permanent assignment is accompanied by much fanfare, considerable recognition, and possibly even relocation to another area.

Importance of the Supervisor. As mentioned earlier in this chapter, the graduate's immediate supervisor for the initial assignment plays an important role in the graduate's success. Even though the formal transition program may be over, the supervisor or manager has the responsibility to mold new graduates into long-term contributing members of the organization. On-the-job learning is a continuous process, and no one affects learning more than the immediate supervisor. In their study of socialization practices, McShane and Baal (1984) identified four characteristics of effective first supervisors:

1. *Supportive.* Effective first supervisors must have well-developed helping skills, which include tolerance for errors and patience during the learning stage, friendliness, and generally good interpersonal skills. The supervisor's supportive skills can neutralize new employees' anxiety and convey a positive image of the organization (Porter, Lawler and Hackman, 1975; Van Maanen, 1976).
2. *Communicative.* Supervisors must be able to communicate well to new graduates. Specifically, supervisors should be able to explain how the organization operates and provide relevant and timely feedback in a constructive manner. Another aspect of this attribute is the supervisor's ability to steer the new graduate in the right direction for maximum job performance and greater role clarity. Thus, first supervisors must have directive as well as supportive leadership skills in order to offset the ambiguity of the work environment (Van Maanen, 1976).
3. *Representative.* Because supervisors represent the organization to new employees, it is important that they manifest the values and beliefs of the organization as well as provide a respectable role model to all new graduates. Supervisors should be loyal to the organization and have values that are consistent with policy and management philosophy. They should also be both dynamic and flexible, reflecting the desired characteristics of new graduates.
4. *Motivated.* Lastly, first supervisors must be motivated to develop employees. Similarly, they should appear to be enthusiastic and energetic toward their own work, again providing a model for the new graduate.

The scope of this list does not mean that managers who do not fit all the facets of the above description should not be allowed to supervise new recruits. In many situations, assignments cannot be juggled; however, when there is some flexibility, new graduates should be placed with supervisors who can make the most of the resource.

In addition to selecting the most appropriate supervisor, the attitudes, skills, and abilities of all supervisors of new graduates should be improved to enhance on-the-job learning. To meet this challenge some organizations conduct workshops for all supervisors of new graduates. Specific objectives of one such workshop are:

- to understand why the organization must recruit, train, educate, and ultimately retain college-trained talent, since many supervisors may not have a formal education
- to heighten supervisors' awareness of problems new graduates face on-the-job and the transition issues faced by the organization
- to provide an opportunity for supervisors to share with each other their concerns about college graduates and their attitudes toward them
- to share ideas from the staff and from other supervisors on successful approaches and experiences in effectively working with college graduates
- to create relationships among supervisors that will make it possible to consult with one another as a means of obtaining help with new and unusual problems that may arise with college graduates
- to develop skills necessary to be effective first supervisors of new graduates.

These objectives can be met through short seminars and workshops for supervisors and managers who even occasionally supervise new graduates.

Responsibility Level. As with temporary assignments, giving new graduates too little responsibility in their permanent assignment is almost as serious as giving them too much. Either approach may lead to a turnover statistic. In general, the responsi-

bility level for college graduates should be maximized in their
initial permanent assignment. This simple notion does not emerge
in practice. Many managers and supervisors are reluctant to
challenge new recruits with high responsibility levels because of
three faulty assumptions concerning graduates and their ability to
handle assignments.

The first assumption is that college graduates are immature,
uninformed, and incapable of assuming high-responsibility work.
Managers and supervisors with this perception will be reluctant to
give much responsibility to new graduates. The dilemma, of
course, is that college graduates have no way to disprove this
stereotype as long as they are prevented from doing important and
responsible work. And without a chance to prove themselves,
graduates reinforce their supervisors' perceptions about their
inability to perform. A vicious cycle develops, similar to the self-
fulfilling prophecy discussed earlier in this chapter. Neither the
organization nor the graduate are benefiting from the skills,
knowledge, and ability of the graduates.

The second assumption is that high-responsibility work is
too complicated and complex for new graduates; therefore, they
must have thorough guidance and additional education before
they can assume such roles. Many transition programs operate on
the theory that the permanent assignment is so technical and
difficult that new graduates, no matter how well-educated, cannot
perform it without periods of formal education or training. This
attitude is reinforced by the new graduates' desire for education or
training partly to ensure against failures that might result if they
immediately assume the job. The dilemma here is that the
organization may be unwittingly colluding with new graduates by
putting off certain tests that both need. Although it may be a valid
diagnosis that plunging a new graduate immediately into a work
assignment is too threatening, it does not necessarily follow that
the correct solution is to place the graduate in a prolonged period
of formal education or training in which no real work is involved.
In essence, this overprotection forms the rationale for many formal
education and training programs that may not be necessary.

A third assumption involves a widespread conservative
attitude to avoid risk, an attitude that encourages managers to take

few chances and hold new graduates back until they are absolutely sure they can do the work. To these managers, it makes little sense to give important tasks to newcomers who may fail and thus hurt themselves and the department in the process. "Better safe than sorry" is at the heart of their approach. In many organizations the need to play it safe and avoid failure at all costs may become part of the organization's culture, which may be one reason why very conservative businesses, such as public utilities, have difficulty in attracting and retaining college graduates who have high potential for advancement. New graduates want an opporunity to succeed at the risk of failing.

It is a challenge for organizations to overcome these concerns and place responsibility squarely on new graduates. Although assigning responsibility beyond an individual's capabilities is not prudent, continual searching for the upper limit of capabilities is recommended. This approach not only helps retain graduates and keeps them challenged but also improves their morale and attitudes toward the organization, not to mention the organizational benefits gained from the graduates' extra efforts.

Perceived Job Status. Most college graduates want highly visible jobs with considerable status and freedom. They have visions of an important job where they make significant decisions, are responsible for major tasks, and are highly respected in the organization. They want to enjoy the fruits of their college labors. Unfortunately, not all entry-level professional jobs fit that description; many are rather mundane assignments with little glory. Job tasks are sometimes routine and job titles and work stations are less than exciting. Such an environment may cause some graduates to seek better opportunities.

Although job status may be more related to job design than to the transition process, all factors that can help keep talented people with the organization should be considered. If the perceived job status is suffering, a review of job status might be in order, including such aspects as the job title, level of freedom, work area, and the level of respect in the organization. This is not to suggest that new graduates be retitled vice-president or provided spacious offices with generous perks. However, changing the title, providing privacy, and increasing respect for the job can accomplish a great deal. For example, "field accountant" is a more respectable title than "relief clerk." "Supervisor" or "manager" might be more appropriate than "foreman." Instead of an open area with no privacy, a simple cubicle can help elevate the status of the job and improve performance at the same time. Work layout and job design can reap many important benefits (see Ford, 1979; Kastens, 1980; and Walters, 1975).

Degree of Involvement and Participation. Although the graduates' degree of job involvement and participation is a major factor in job design, it should also be considered in the design of the transition program. Most college graduates are exposed to management theories and behavioral science research showing that participation and involvement in the decision-making process is an important trend in today's organizations. They expect no less from their employer. They want to be involved in decisions affecting their jobs.

Many organizations have turned to participative management techniques to help boost productivity, improve employee relations, and solve a variety of problems. Participative management enables managers and supervisors to utilize more resources, thereby increasing the chances for better decisions. A climate of participation can also help break down the barriers to upward communication that exist in many organizations. The participative process allows the organization to tap the minds of high-potential college graduates. Working together, supervisors and new graduates can come up with innovative decisions. Many important, creative ideas have been the result of group input rather than the independent thoughts of an individual.

Probably the most important advantage of participative management is that it improves acceptance of decisions by the group that must live with them. The responsibility for decision making does not stop when the decision has been made. It must be implemented successfully, and the biggest stumbling block to successful implementation is usually lack of acceptance by employees. Any action that can increase such acceptance will positively affect the outcome of the decision.

Participative management can raise morale and motivate employees. Participation in the various steps of the decision-making process provides an important source of job satisfaction and a new feeling of purpose and meaning in work. New graduates want to think that their ideas are important and are sought by the organization. When they regularly provide input into the problems and decisions of the work unit, they have a much greater feeling of identification with the organization and its goals and objectives. They develop a personal stake in the success of the department, division, and organization as a whole.

Finally, employees can learn and grow through the participative management process. It provides them with an opportunity to utilize new skills and helps them to reach their maximum potential. They can also learn from other employees who are providing input. Participative management, when compared to "just taking orders," helps individuals become more mature and responsible.

With all these advantages, organizations should logically place increased emphasis on participative management, particularly for jobs held by college graduates. Yet many organizations are reluctant to share decision making with any employees, much less new graduates.

As with most other management processes, participative management has some disadvantages. When input is solicited from several people, significantly more time is needed to make decisions. The amount of additional time depends on the type of decision and the group discussion skills of the manager or supervisor. Participative management may also generate more costs than individual decision making. For many organizations lost production or output may occur while the group provides input to help make decisions. This cost factor is important and must be considered before the process is encouraged. Even with these disadvantages, the participative management approach shows great promise for college-educated talent. For more information on participative management see Lawler (1986).

What Next? After starting permanent assignments, many new graduates wonder about their future. Completing a comprehensive transition program is an important milestone that may be followed by post-program depression. Graduates receive much attention and many challenges while in the transition program. In many cases, lines of communication are open all the way to the top. Usually there are extensive discussions about jobs and career opportunities. Once they have completed the program they may be concerned about being ignored and forgotten.

After the transition program is completed, the graduates should be integrated into regular career development programs in the organization. Through performance reviews, human resources planning, and career development efforts, opportunities should be available for, and communicated to, new graduates. They should regularly see signs of upward mobility if that is what they desire. Unfortunately, even in organizations where transition programs are functioning effectively, the developmental programs for regular employees may not be sufficient to meet the needs of these graduates. They will not have frequent career discussions or opportunities to talk with top management or receive the attention they enjoyed during the transition program. When this is the case, organizations need to examine the effectiveness of regular career-planning programs to see if adjustments are in order. Career-planning systems must ensure that the career aspirations of graduates who have completed formal transition programs are consistent with the long-range requirements of the organization. See Chapter Three for discussion of an important study by Derr (1986) that categorizes employees' career aspirations.

Even if career needs were unknown at the time of recruitment, they are usually pinpointed during the transition process. Mismatches in career aspirations with organizational needs can create problems for the organization. The important point here is that the issues must be addressed in the future.

Periodic follow-up activities with new graduates may be necessary to provide both attention and information. Today, young, highly educated, and motivated employees need considerable information about careers; without it they may lose interest, though they may perform successfully on the job, make contributions, and be reasonably satisfied with their work. An investment in a career-planning and development program, particularly for college-educated employees, is an option worth serious consideration in most organizations.

Summary

The adaptation and work assignment stages of the transition process come during or after formal education or training efforts. The most visible and effective action to enhance the adaptation process is the performance review. Although the performance review for new graduates may be no different from that of other employees, more frequent and detailed reviews are recommended to ensure that graduates are on target with performance. When performance is satisfactory, the adaptation process is probably working.

In addition to performance reviews, a variety of other activities can help enhance adaptation, such as utilizing the Pygmalion effect, where employees rise to the expectations of their managers, providing recognition, conducting meetings with graduates, developing newsletters, coordinating social activities, and ensuring job security.

Unfortunately, not all graduates will succeed, no matter how much is done to enhance adaptation and keep performance on track. Problems must be handled quickly, sincerely, and with the highest regard for the esteem of the individual. A variety of alternatives can help make the best of the situation.

The content of the assignment is an important part of the transition program. Many formal education efforts involve special projects, rotational assignments, or short-term job duties where graduates are expected to perform and make a contribution. These assignments should be selected properly and discussed thoroughly with graduates. They should be carefully planned to ensure continuing challenge and performance. For this purpose the organization needs capable supervisors who can develop their employees and provide them with maximum levels of responsibility. Job design factors should be reviewed to see if improvements are in order. The end result is a highly motivated, challenged group of new employees who can make an outstanding contribution to the organization.

7

Monitoring Results
and Improving
the Transition Process

Although evaluation was presented as the last step in the transition model outlined in Chapter One, this is not entirely accurate—evaluation should occur at virtually every stage of transition; only the results should be formally summarized and communicated as a final step. As discussed earlier, no human resources program representing the magnitude of expenditures necessary for a successful transition effort should be allowed to continue without an evaluation effort of some type. Evaluation provides the impetus for program improvements, exhibits the worth of the program to interested observers, and allows the program planners and managers to see the fruits of their labor through tangible results.

This chapter provides the concepts, ideas, and techniques for a comprehensive evaluation of the transition process. It begins with a description of the types of data collected and the levels of evaluation—fundamental concepts in the evaluation process. The most common instruments used to collect data for evaluation are detailed, followed by descriptions of various evaluation designs that provide the overall scheme of data collection. Next, the major techniques for evaluation are presented, ranging from collecting feedback from graduates to tracking performance of individuals.

Another important part of this chapter covers the areas of focus for measurement and evaluation. Five important areas are discussed, ranging from monitoring the progress of graduates to tracking the long-term performance of those who have completed the transition programs. The final section of this chapter focuses on the use of evaluation data. It outlines specific audiences who need to know about the evaluation data and provides some helpful advice on how to communicate this data to them.

Types of Data and Levels of Evaluation

Program evaluation entails collecting and analyzing data— data that show the results of the transition program. Although there are several types of data, a distinction can be made between two general categories: hard data and soft data. Hard data are the primary measurement of improvement or success, presented as rational, indisputable facts, easily accumulated. They are usually the most desired data to collect. Soft data are more subjective and are used when hard data are not available.

Hard Data. Hard data are easy to measure and quantify, relatively easy to assign dollar values, and objectively based. A common measure of organizational performance, hard data are very credible in the eyes of management. Hard data can be grouped into four categories (or subdivisions), as shown in Table 9. These categories—output, quality, costs, and time—are typical performance measures in almost every organization. When they are not available, the desired approach is to convert soft data to one of these four basic measurements.

Distinguishing these four groups of hard data is sometimes difficult because some do overlap. For example, in collecting data on employee accidents, accident costs may be listed under the cost category, the number of accidents listed under quality, and the lost-time days under the time category. As another example, an incentive bonus may be listed as output (because the amount of bonus is usually based directly on the output of an employee or group of employees) or as a cost (since the bonus is usually presented in cash).

Table 9. Examples of Hard Data.

Output	Time
Units produced	Equipment downtime
Tons manufactured	Overtime
Items assembled	On-time shipments
Money collected	Time to project completion
Items sold	Processing time
Forms processed	Supervisory time
Loans approved	Break-in time for new employees
Service calls completed	Training time
Inventory turnover	Meeting schedules
Patients visited	Repair time
Applications processed	Efficiency
Students graduated	Work stoppages
Output per hour	Order response
Productivity	Late reporting
Work backlog	Lost-time days
Incentive bonus	
Shipments	*Quality*
	Scrap
Costs	Waste
Budget variances	Rejects
Unit costs	Error rates
Cost by account	Customer complaints
Variable costs	Rework
Fixed costs	Shortages
Overhead costs	Product defects
Operating costs	Deviation from standard
Number of cost reductions	Product failures
Project cost savings	Inventory adjustments
Accident costs	Time card corrections
Program costs	Percentage of tasks completed promptly
Sales expense	Number of accidents

Soft Data. When hard, rational numbers just do not exist, soft data must be used in evaluating programs. Although soft data are less credible as a performance measurement and are usually behaviorally oriented—relating to a feeling, attitude, or perception, such as a complaint, grievance, or action, they can provide additional evidence of transition program success (Wilkinson and Orth, 1986). Table 10 shows typical kinds of soft data. For convenience, soft data have been categorized into six areas—work habits, new skills, work climate, development/advancement,

Table 10. Examples of Soft Data.

Work Habits	*New Skills*
Absenteeism	Decisions made
Tardiness	Problems solved
Visits to dispensary	Conflicts avoided
First aid treatments	Grievances resolved
Violations of safety rules	Counseling problems solved
Number of communication break- downs	Listening skills Reading speed
Excessive breaks	Intention to use new skills
	Frequency of use of new skills
Work Climate	
Number of grievances	*Development/Advancement*
Number of discrimination charges	Number of promotions
Employee complaints	Number of pay increases
Job satisfaction	Number of training programs at-
Unionization avoidance	tended
Employee turnover	Requests for transfer
	Performance appraisal ratings
Feelings/Attitudes	Increases in job effectiveness
Attitude changes	
Perceptions of job responsibilities	*Initiative*
Perceived changes in performance	Generation of new ideas
Employee loyalty	Successful completion of projects
Role conflict	Implementation of new programs
Role ambiguity	Number of suggestions submitted
Organizational commitment	Number of suggestions imple-
Behavioral intention	mented

feelings/attitudes, and initiative—although other categorization schemes are possible.

Levels of Evaluation. Just as there are different types of data, there are different levels of evaluation. In a sense, the level of evaluation reflects the type of data collected, but it also reflects the timing of data collection, the characteristics of the evaluation instrument, and the setting within which the data are collected. A comprehensive description of several models of the various levels of evaluation are presented in Phillips (1983a). The most common and widely accepted model was developed by Kirkpatrick (1977), who proposes four levels: reaction, learning, behavior, and results.

As they relate to transition programs, these four levels answer four important questions:

Level	Questions
1. Reaction	Were the new graduates satisfied with the transition program?
2. Learning	What did the new graduates learn in the program?
3. Behavior	Did the new graduates change or modify their behavior based on what was learned?
4. Results	Did the learning or change in behavior positively affect the organization?

Reaction refers to the feedback from graduates involved in the various stages of the transition program. It represents attitudes and feelings about all aspects of the program. Reactions almost always involve the collection of soft data and can be conveniently obtained at every transition stage through questionnaires and interviews. Most HRD professionals agree that initial receptivity provides a good atmosphere for learning the material in the program but does not necessarily lead to high levels of learning.

The evaluation of *learning* is important in almost every stage, since transition program objectives usually center on new graduates learning as much as possible about the organization, job, and environment. Measuring learning, which is more difficult than measuring reaction, involves an assessment of the knowledge, skills, and abilities at different stages of transition. Learning is a critical issue in the education and training stage of transition, where it is the principal focus.

Behavior changes in new graduates represent another important level of evaluation. The goal of much of the transition process is to shape the behavior of new graduates so they adapt to the organization's culture and environment. Graduates are expected to exhibit generally accepted job-related behavior.

Behavior change is usually represented by soft data and is frequently measured by observations and interviews.

The ultimate level of evaluation is the *results* obtained from the transition program. Results are usually hard-data performance records expressed in turnover rates and actual job performance of graduates who participated in the transition process.

The Kirkpatrick model is based on several assumptions. First, the value of the information increases as you move from measuring reaction to measuring results. The evaluation of results has the highest value to the organization. Second, the measurement of reaction is the most frequently used evaluation method, while the measurement of results is the least frequently used method. Several studies support these assumptions (Newstrom, 1978). Apparently, not enough HRD professionals are evaluating the results of their efforts. Finally, measuring reactions is easier than measuring results, an assumption that is verified when examining the methods of evaluation, presented later in this chapter. It is a relatively simple process to secure reaction to a training program, but it can be extremely difficult to measure accurately the economic impact of the program on the organization (the results).

These levels of evaluation, coupled with the different types of data, provide an overall framework from which the organization can approach evaluation. They must be carefully considered in designing the evaluation stage of transition programs and in selecting instruments for evaluation.

Evaluation Instrument Design

An evaluation instrument is a data-gathering device administered at the appropriate stages in the transition process. An integral part of evaluation, instruments come in a variety of forms but usually include questionnaires, surveys, tests, interviews, and observations, all of which are discussed in this section. First, a few general comments.

General Principles. Prior to instrument design, several questions should be asked.

1. *How will the data be used?* The basic purpose(s) of evaluation must be reviewed before selecting or designing an instrument. Will the data be used to calculate a return on investment? Will it be used to strengthen the transition process? Will it be used to recruit new graduates? The answers to these questions can have an impact on the type of instrument needed.

2. *How will the data be analyzed?* Data are usually collected to be tabulated, summarized, and reported to others. The types of analyses required, including statistical comparisons, should be considered in the design of the instrument.

3. *Who will use the information?* The target audience is an important issue. Who will be reviewing the information in its raw state and in a summarized manner? This determination can lead to the insertion of specific questions on the instrument.

4. *What facts are needed?* Facts are essential for an effective evaluation. Which ones are best for the evaluation? Costs, output, time, quality, attitudes, reactions, or observations may need to be collected by the instrument.

5. *Should the instrument be tested?* It may be appropriate to test an instrument before using it, particularly when the transition program represents a significant investment and evaluation takes on greater importance. Pilot-testing provides an opportunity to determine if there are any problems with the instrument.

6. *Is there a standard instrument?* In some cases standard instruments can be more effective with less cost than custom-designed instruments. Broad-based areas such as communications, human relations, or leadership may be suitable for standard instruments. Of course, the program content and objectives must be appropriate for the scope of the instrument.

7. *What are the consequences of wrong answers or biased information?* An often overlooked potential problem is the consequence of participants supplying biased or incorrect information on the instrument. Evaluation data are usually supplied on a voluntary basis, sometimes anonymously. The graduate's biases can influence the information and, unless opinions and attitudes are sought, the information will not be

reliable. Purposeful wrong answers can possibly have a significant influence on an individual, a budget, or a group of employees. If so, steps should be taken to prevent it.

Characteristics of Good Instruments. An instrument should be easy to administer. It should not be burdensome nor difficult for the participant or administrator. Simple and straightforward directions increase the likelihood that it will be administered consistently among different individuals. Written instructions, as well as verbal explanations, will help to ensure consistent application.

Two other characteristics of a good instrument are simplicity and brevity. The level of readability should be appropriate for the participant's knowledge, ability, and background. Short objective responses, whenever practical, should be sought. The fewest number of questions necessary to cover a particular topic is recommended. There seems to be a natural tendency to "over-survey," which may frustrate participants.

As with every stage in the transition process, economics must be considered in the design and/or selection of an evaluation instrument. A good instrument will be one that is economical for its planned use. Cost must be considered in the design, development, or purchase of an instrument, as well as the time required to present data in a meaningful format, to administer it, and to analyze the data.

Probably the most important characteristic of an evaluation instrument is validity. A valid instrument measures what the person using the instrument wishes to measure. Relative validity is the degree to which it performs this function satisfactorily. Validity is important when skeptics question the appropriateness of a particular instrument. The economic considerations of design may dictate that little time is spent establishing validity, whereas the evaluation of elaborate programs may demand more attention to validity.

Reliability is a final characteristic of a good evaluation instrument. A reliable instrument is consistent enough that subsequent measurements of an item give approximately the same results. For example, an attitude survey is administered to a new graduate. The same survey is administered to the same graduate two days later. The results should be the same, assuming that nothing in the interim period has changed the attitude. Significant differences in the results indicate an unreliable instrument, since the results fluctuated without additional effort to change the graduate's attitude. For more information on validity and reliability, see Ghiselli, Campbell, and Zedeck (1981).

Questionnaires. Probably the most common form of program evaluation instrument is the questionnaire. Ranging from short reaction forms to detailed follow-up instruments, questionnaires come in all sizes. They can be used to obtain subjective information, such as attitudes, as well as to document measurable results for use in an economic analysis. With this versatility and popularity, it is important that questionnaires be designed properly to satisfy their intended purposes. Five types of questions (or statements) are common. A questionnaire may contain any or all of these types:

- *open-ended question*—the question is followed by an ample blank space for the response
- *checklist*—all important responses are checked
- *two-way question*—alternate responses, "yes"/"no" responses, or other possibilities
- *multiple-choice question*—the correct choice is selected from among several choices
- *ranking scales*—a list of items are ranked.

Questionnaires can be designed following these logical steps.

1. *Determine the information needed.* As a first step in questionnaire design, the subjects, skills, or abilities presented in the transition program are tabulated. It might be appropriate to list this information in outline form so that related questions can be grouped together.
2. *Select the type(s) of questions.* Using the five types of questions listed above as a guide, the type(s) best suited for the

intended purpose are selected, taking into consideration the planned data analysis and the variety of data to be collected.

3. *Develop the questions.* The next step is to develop questions based on the type of questions planned and the information needed. Questions should be simple and straightforward and avoid confusing or leading the participant to a desired response. Terms or expressions unfamiliar to the participant should be avoided. The appropriate number and variety of questions are then developed consistent with validity and reliability concerns.

4. *Test the questions.* Once the questions are developed, they should be tested for understanding. Ideally, questions should be tested on a pilot group. If this is not feasible, they should be tested on a group of employees at approximately the same job level as new graduates. After testing, revisions may be in order.

5. *Develop the completed questionnaire and prepare a data summary.* Questions should be integrated to develop a final questionnaire, including proper instructions so that it can be administered effectively.

Once these steps are completed, the questionnaire is ready to be administered. Smooth administration is a critical element in the data-collecting process. For additional information on questionnaire design see Sudman and Bradburn (1982).

Attitude Surveys. Attitude surveys represent a specific type of questionnaire with several applications for measuring the results of transition programs. A portion of the transition program may be aimed at developing employee attitudes toward work, policies, procedures, the organization, and even the immediate supervisor. Job satisfaction, organizational commitment, role conflict, and role ambiguity are typical measures obtained from attitude surveys. Before-and-after program measurements are used to show changes in attitude.

Measuring attitudes is a complex task. It is impossible to measure an attitude precisely, since the information gathered may not represent the graduate's true feelings. Also, the behavior, beliefs, and feelings of individuals do not always correlate; attitudes tend to change with time. Even with these shortcomings, it is still possible to get a reasonable fix on the new graduates' attitudes and on how education and training programs have changed these attitudes (Kirkpatrick, 1986).

The principles of attitude survey construction are similar to questionnaire design. However, a few guidelines, unique to the design or purchase of an attitude survey, are suggested here. For additional information on attitude surveys, see Henerson (1978).

1. *The attitudes to be measured should be clearly identified.* This advice may appear obvious, but it is easy to stray into areas unrelated to the topic being evaluated. "While we're at it, let's check their attitude on this" is a familiar trap. Although the extra information may be interesting, if it is not related, it should be omitted.

2. *Survey statements should be constructed for simplicity.* New graduates need to understand the meaning of a statement or question, with little room for different interpretations. Also, new graduates should know enough about the subject to provide a response.

3. *Responses should be anonymous.* New graduates must feel free to respond openly to statements or questions. As a result, the confidentiality of responses is of the utmost importance. If the survey does identify respondents, an external party should collect and process the data.

4. *The purpose of the survey should be clearly communicated.* New graduates will gladly cooperate in an activity when they understand its purpose. Explanations should be provided when a survey is administered.

5. *Determine survey comparisons.* Attitudes by themselves are virtually meaningless. They must be compared to attitudes before or after the program or compared with the attitudes of another group from a separate division or department. For purchased surveys, normative information may be available for similar industries. Specific comparisons should be planned before administering the survey.

6. *Data should be collected for easy tabulation.* In an attitude survey, "yes/no" responses or varying degrees of agreement and disagreement are the usual responses. These uniform types of responses make it easier for tabulation and comparisons. On a scale of "strongly agree" to "strongly disagree," numbers are usually assigned to reflect responses. For instance, a one (1) may represent strongly agree and a five (5) strongly disagree. An average response of 2.2 on a pre-program survey followed by a post-program average response of 4.3 shows a significant change in attitude. Some critics argue that this kind of scale merely permits the respondent to select the midpoint and not be forced to make a choice. If this is a concern, an even-numbered scale should be used.

Tests. Testing is important in many program evaluations. Pre- and post-program comparisons using tests are common. An improvement in test scores shows the amount of change in skill, knowledge, or ability that could be attributed to the program. The principles of test development are similar to the design and development of questionnaires and attitude surveys (see Denova, 1979).

Several types of tests are available, including oral examinations, essay tests, objective tests, norm-referenced tests, criterion-referenced tests, and performance tests. Oral examinations and essay tests have limited use in transition program evaluation; they are probably more useful in academic settings. Objective tests have answers which are specific and precise, based on the objectives of a program. Attitudes, feelings, creativity, problem-solving processes, and other intangible skills and abilities cannot be measured accurately with objective tests.

Norm-referenced tests compare participants with each other or to other groups rather than to specific instructional objectives. They are used to compare graduates to the "norm" or average. Although norm-referenced tests have limited use in most transition program evaluations, they may be useful in programs involving large numbers of graduates where average scores and relative rankings are important. In some situations, graduates scoring highest on exams are given special recognition or awards or become eligible for other special activities. For example, in one organization the top 50 percent of the graduates from a transition program are selected for promotion or assignment. The measurement is norm-referenced, since graduates are ranked rather than held to a specific cutoff score. If a minimum passing score is established and graduates are selected on that basis, then the measurement device is a criterion-referenced measurement.

The criterion-referenced test (CRT), an objective test with a predetermined cutoff score, is a measure against carefully written objectives for the transition program. In a CRT the interest lies in whether graduates meet the desired minimum standards, not how one ranks with others. The primary concern is to measure, report, and analyze participant performance as it relates to instructional objectives. Criterion-referenced testing is a popular measurement instrument in education and training. It has the advantage of being objectively based, precise, and relatively easy to administer. It does, however, require transition programs with clearly defined objectives that can be measured.

Performance testing allows graduates to exhibit a skill (and occasionally knowledge or attitudes) which has been learned in an education or training program. The skill can be manual, verbal, or analytical, or a combination of all three. Performance testing is used frequently in job-related training. In supervisory and management training, performance testing takes the form of skill practices or role plays in which graduates demonstrate discussion or problem-solving skills they have acquired. In one example of performance testing, newly recruited industrial engineers are required to attend a course on motion and time study. As a final test of the program, participants are given the assignment to conduct a motion and time study on an actual job in a plant. The new recruits perform the study and are observed by the instructor. The instructor performs the same study and compares the results with those of the new graduate. These comparisons provide an evaluation of the program and reflect the skills learned in the course. In a second example, new college graduates learn how to motivate average performers as part of a formal management education program. Part of the course evaluation requires graduates to document an actual situation involving an average performer. They are then asked to conduct the skill practice on another member of the group using the real situation and applying the principles and steps taught in the program. The skill practice is observed by the instructor, and a written critique is provided at the end of the practice. These critiques provide part of the evaluation of the program.

Interviews. Another useful evaluation instrument is the interview, although it is not used as frequently as other methods. Interviews can be conducted by the HR staff, supervisors, or outside third parties. Interviews can secure data not available in performance records, or data difficult to obtain through written responses or observations. New graduates may be reluctant to volunteer information in a questionnaire but will respond to a skillful interviewer who probes for it. The interview process uncovers changes in behavior, reaction, and results. The same principles involved in designing questions for a questionnaire can also apply to the interview. Interviews are time-consuming, however, and may require the training or preparation of interviewers to ensure that the process is conducted in a consistent and effective manner.

As discussed in Chapter Three, interviews usually fall into two basic types: (1) structured and (2) unstructured. A structured interview is much like a questionnaire. Specific questions are asked with little room to deviate from the desired responses. The primary advantages of the structured interview over the questionnaire are the assurance that all important questions will be answered and that the interviewer understands the responses supplied by the graduate. The unstructured interview allows for deeper probing. This interview contains a few general questions and then allows for collection of more detailed information as responses emerge. For additional information on constructing the evaluation interview, see Kerlinger (1986).

Observations. Observing the graduate either before, during, or after a stage of transition to record changes in behavior is still another evaluation instrument. The observer may be a member of the HR staff, a supervisor, a member of a peer group, or an outside party. The most common observer, and probably the most practical choice, is a member of the HR staff. Four common methods of observation are available depending on the type of information needed. A behavior checklist can be useful for recording the presence, absence, frequency, or duration of a graduate's behavior, as it occurs. A checklist does not usually provide information on the quality, intensity, or possibly the circumstances surrounding the behavior observed. To increase efficiency, the number of behaviors on the checklist should be small and listed in a logical sequence if they normally occur in a sequence. Also, behaviors anticipated to be used more frequently should be placed first so they can be easily checked.

Another, more time-consuming method of observation involves entering a code that identifies a specific behavior. Such a coded record is useful when it is essential to document (as much as possible) what actually happened or when a large number of behaviors precludes use of a checklist system. The disadvantage of this system is that the data are very difficult to summarize and interpret. It may be a time-consuming process, since the observer must memorize special codes or devise codes as the observation is taking place.

The third and least useful method of observation is delayed reporting. In this approach the observer does not use any forms or written materials during the observation but rather records the information after the observation is completed or at particular time intervals during an observation. In other words, the observer tries to reconstruct what he has observed during the observation period. The advantage of this approach is that the observer can be more a participant and so less distracting. An obvious disadvantage is that delayed information may not be as accurate and reliable as the information collected at the time it occurred.

The fourth method is the use of a video camera to record the behavior of the participant. This technique records exactly what happened in every detail—an obvious advantage. However, there are disadvantages. It may be awkward and cumbersome to provide for videotaping of the behavior. Also, when compared to direct observation, participants may be more nervous or self-conscious when they are being videotaped. If the camera is concealed, the

Table 11. Comparison of Common Evaluation Instruments.

INSTRUMENTS	EVALUATION LEVELS				ADVANTAGES	LIMITATIONS
	Reaction	Learning	Behavior	Results		
Questionnaire	✓		✓	✓	Low cost Honesty increased Anonymity optional Respondent sets pace Variety of Options	May not collect accurate inforamtion On-job responding conditions uncontrolled Respondent sets pace Return rate rarely controllable
Attitude Survey	✓		✓	✓	Standardization possible Quickly processed Easy to administer	Predetermined alternatives Response choices Reliance on norms may distort individual performance May not reflect true feelings
Written Test		✓			Low purchase cost Readily scored Quickly processed Easily administered Wide sampling possible	May be threatening to participant Possible low relation to job performance Reliance on norms may distort individual performance Possible cultural bias
Performance Test		✓	✓		Reliability Simulation potential Objective based	Time consuming Simulation often difficult High development costs
Interview	✓		✓	✓	Flexible Opportunity for clarification Depth possible Personal contact	High reactive effects High cost Face-to-face threat potential Labor-intensive Trained interviewers necessary
Observation	✓		✓		Non-threatening to participant Excellent way to measure behavior change	Possibly disruptive Reactive effect Unreliable Trained observers necessary

Source: Adapted in part from a comparison developed by the U.S. Office of Personnel Management.

privacy of the participant may be invaded. Because of this, video-recording of on-the-job behavior is not frequently used.

Table 11 summarizes the various evaluation instruments presented in this section and the most appropriate level of evaluation and the advantages and limitations of each instrument. This table serves as a quick aid to compare the common types of instruments used in evaluation. Additional information on evaluation instrument design is contained in Kerlinger (1986), Phillips (1983a), and Sudman and Bradburn (1982).

Evaluation Design

Evaluation design is primarily concerned with the timing of measurements (or tests). Testing may be performed before the program, during the stages of transition, and at subsequent intervals after the program. The post-test part of a design is never omitted because it directly measures the results of a program. Careful attention needs to be given to determining when and how pre-tests and post-tests are conducted. Selecting the appropriate evaluation design is a key part of the evaluation strategy. Three common designs used in program evaluations are presented in this section.

One-shot program design. One of the most common, and unfortunately least valid, designs is the "one-shot" program, which uses only one measurement after a program or stage is completed. No data are collected prior to the program. Many uncontrolled factors might influence the measurement and invalidate conclusions based on results achieved through this design. However, the information obtained in this one-shot evaluation is better than no evaluation at all. This design may be useful for measuring the performance of an individual or group when there is no way to measure performance beforehand or, possibly, when there is little related knowledge or skill existing before the program is conducted, as is the case with most transition programs.

Pre- and post-test design. This design goes one step beyond the one-shot design by collecting data before and after the program, stage, or segment. The participants' knowledge or skills before the program can be compared to these same abilities after the program to detect improvements. Although many organizations are using this design (Moore, 1984), it does have disadvantages. The pre-test may "tune the graduates in" to the topics and questions they might not ordinarily perceive. Consequently, changes measured by the post-test may result not only from the transition program, but also from the fact that the pre-test alerted the graduates to what would be tested. The effect of external factors should be taken into account in this design. Changes in the organization, environment, the work setting, or other factors may cause changes in the performance of graduates.

Time series design. Another design for evaluating programs, the time series design, uses multiple measurements before and after the program, which allows for comparison with initial results and enables measurement of the long-term effects of the program. This design may not be practical for transition program evaluation, since prior measurements are not always possible.

Which design to choose. The designs outlined above are very basic types of evaluation designs. Many other designs are available, using control groups and a variety of measurement schemes. However, for most transition programs, these three designs will suffice. The question of which design to use depends on several factors. In all probability the nature of the transition program and the practical considerations of the working environment will dictate the appropriate design. The more complex the design, the more costly the evaluation effort. Yet, the results are more valid. There is no way to isolate completely the effects of factors outside the learning situation. If a design is less than optimum, the individuals responsible for evaluation must be prepared to defend its use in terms of trade-offs. Additional information on evaluation designs can be found in Stone (1978), Phillips (1983a), Rutman (1984), and Kerlinger (1986).

Evaluation Methods

This section covers methods of data collection, usually referred to as evaluation methods, which relate directly to the evaluation instruments and evaluation design. The evaluation method is concerned with the practical applications of the follow-up. Additional information on evaluation methods can be found in Patton (1982), Phillips (1983a), Miles and Huberman (1984), and Merwin (1986).

Feedback from Graduates. The most frequently used, though least reliable, method of collecting data for evaluation is feedback from the graduates. The popularity of this form of data collection is astounding. Ratings from reaction questionnaires can be so critical that a person's job may be at stake, as in the case of instructor ratings in school systems. Although the approach is popular, it is also subject to misuse. Sometimes referred to as a "happiness rating," it has been criticized by many HRD professionals because of the questionable value of the subjective data (Dunn and Thomas, 1985). The criticism may not be totally justified: Some research shows a direct correlation between positive comments at the end of a program and the actual improved performance on the job. Elkins (1977) studied the results achieved by ninety government supervisors and managers who completed a basic management course. In all the variables examined, trainee reaction showed the strongest correlation of on-the-job application of the new management principles. Participants who enjoyed the program most were those who achieved the most on the job. Those who did not like it apparently did not bother to do too much of anything with it. Although it is risky to generalize from this study, it appears that if graduates have enjoyed an education and training program and state they plan to use the information and/or skills, they probably will. A carefully designed and properly administered feedback questionnaire at the end of an education or training program might suffice for a more sophisticated evaluation method. Feedback questionnaires have a definite place in transition program evaluation.

The areas of feedback used on reaction forms depend, to a large extent, on the organization and the purpose of evaluation. Some forms are very simple while others are detailed and require a considerable amount of time to complete. In essence, the feedback questionnaire should be designed to supply the information needed by the organization. Common areas for feedback are:

- Program content
- Program duration/timing
- Instructional/educational materials
- On-the-job assignments
- Method of presentation

- Instructors
- Program coordinator
- Facilities
- General evaluation
- Planned improvements.

Objective questions on these and other areas give new graduates an opportunity to provide thorough feedback, which can be very useful in program evaluation. For lengthy programs, an end-of-program evaluation may leave graduates unable to remember what happened at what time. To help improve on this situation, an ongoing evaluation is conducted at different stages of transition or at the end of brief education or training sessions.

Feedback questionnaires obtain a quick reaction from graduates while information is still fresh on their minds. Quite often, at the end of a program or part of a program, graduates have passed judgment on the usefulness of program material. This reaction can be helpful for making adjustments or for providing evidence of the program's effectiveness. Feedback questionnaires are easy to administer, usually taking only a few minutes. If constructed properly, they can be easily analyzed, tabulated, and summarized.

A major disadvantage to feedback questionnaires is that the data are subjective, based on the opinions and feelings of graduates at one point in time. Opinions and feelings change and personal bias may exaggerate ratings. At the end of a program, new graduates are often pleased and may be happy just to be done with it. As a result, they may give positive ratings when they actually feel differently. Also, good ratings at the end of a program are no assurance that new graduates will practice what has been taught in the program.

Feedback from Others. Another useful source of evaluation data is the feedback from other individuals who have worked closely with new graduates in the transition program. Usually, these groups fall into five categories: (1) supervisors of new graduates, (2) subordinates of new graduates, if applicable, (3) peers, (4) members of the HR staff, and (5) specially trained observers.

Feedback from supervisors provides detailed information on performance improvement resulting from the program. An on-the-job supervisor is possibly the best person to evaluate performance. Feedback is usually obtained during a follow-up evaluation using a questionnaire or interview and focusing on tangible change. This approach can develop reliable feedback data.

For new graduates involved in management or supervisory training programs, a useful feedback group is their subordinates, if they have any. Information from this group may not be as reliable as that obtained from superiors, since it may be biased or opinionated, depending on the subordinate's attitude toward the new graduate. Nevertheless, it can be useful in the evaluation process. With this type of data collection, subordinates are usually asked about changes or improvements in their supervisors' (new graduates) behavior since their involvement in an education or training program.

Probably the least-used feedback group is the peer group. This approach involves securing input, through questionnaires or interviews, directly from peers on how graduates have performed after a program or program segment. Soliciting feedback from peers is rare, since it is highly subjective and may be unreliable because of the loose ties between the evaluator and the graduate. A word of caution is in order for collecting information from all of these groups. Any information collected from another group may tend to put new graduates "on trial." Group members are watching unusually closely to see if the graduates perform in a particular manner. This close scrutiny, while it may be important to evaluation, may not be appropriate for the acceptance and endorsement of the overall transition program.

Another group used for feedback purposes is the HR staff. In these situations, staff members, properly trained in observation techniques, observe new graduates and provide feedback on their performance. The specific methods of observation used to collect feedback on performance were outlined earlier in this chapter. Staff evaluation can be very helpful and can represent a professional and unbiased method of data collection.

The assessment center method was briefly discussed in Chapter Three. The feedback is provided by a group of specially trained observers (called assessors), not usually HR staff members. For years the assessment center approach has been an effective tool for employee selection. Recently, it has shown great promise as a tool for evaluating the effectiveness of an education or training program (Byham, 1982). Graduates are placed in a high-risk situation where they are asked to exhibit new and untried behaviors. (This is not the case when the center is used for selection, since those being assessed will produce lower-risk behavior to second guess the assessors' desired outcomes.) Although the popularity of this method seems to be growing, it still may not be feasible in some organizations, as it is quite involved and time-consuming for the participants and the assessors. The latter group must be carefully trained to be objective and reliable. However, for programs spending a great deal to make improvements in the soft-data area, the assessment center approach may be the most promising way to measure the impact of the program. This is particularly true for an organization where the assessment center process is already in use for selection.

Follow-Up Evaluation. An important extension of the end-of-program evaluation is a follow-up at a predetermined time after program completion. In many situations, the follow-up evaluation relates to a previous evaluation and normally involves the use of a feedback questionnaire, although interviews and observations may also be used as instruments. The primary purposes of the follow-up are (1) to help measure the lasting results of the program, (2) to isolate the areas where graduates show the most improvement, and (3) to compare the responses at follow-up time with those provided at the end of the program. This evaluation technique is necessary to measure the long-term success of a formal transition program. In addition to the questionnaire design principles presented earlier in this chapter, several useful guidelines can enhance the effectiveness of a follow-up evaluation.

1. *Determine progress made since the program was conducted.* The follow-up is an excellent time to determine the graduate's accomplishments since completing the transition program. Additional data reflecting the success of the program should be available. Each item requiring an action at the end of the program should be monitored during the follow-up to measure accomplishment.
2. *Ask many of the same or similar questions.* To provide the continuity for data comparison, the same questions asked on the end-of-program questionnaire should be repeated on the

follow-up, if appropriate. For example, a question at the end of a program concerning organizational commitment should be asked again on the follow-up. Different responses to the same question could reveal a problem in program content or in the lasting effect of the program.

3. *Solicit reasons for lack of results.* Not all follow-up evaluations will generate positive results. Some will indicate no improvement or will contain negative comments. A good follow-up will try to determine why the new graduates do not achieve desired results. Many obstacles can impede performance improvement, such as lack of support from the supervisor, restricting policies and procedures, or lack of interest on the part of graduates. Identifying these obstacles can be as valuable as identifying the reasons for success.

4. *Participants should expect a follow-up.* There should be no surprises at follow-up time. The intention to administer a follow-up instrument should be clearly communicated during the program, preferably at the end of a stage of transition or at the end of the overall program. The time period for the follow-up is critical, allowing enough time to achieve the desired improvement, yet short enough so that information is still relatively fresh.

5. *Consider a follow-up assignment.* In some cases follow-up assignments can enhance the evaluation process. In a typical follow-up assignment, graduates are required to achieve a goal or complete a task by the follow-up date. A summary of completed assignments provides further evidence of the impact of the transition program.

6. *Follow-up information should be shared with the graduate's supervisor.* Ideally, the new graduate's immediate on-the-job supervisor should be involved in the application of what was learned in the transition program. The supervisor should know what results have been achieved.

7. *Graduates should be required to complete the follow-up.* The follow-up evaluation should not be optional. Participants are expecting it and management must see that it is completed. This input is essential to determine the impact of the program and good responses on follow-up evaluations are not difficult

to obtain. Some organizations boast of a 100 percent response on follow-up evaluation after the first reminder.

Action Plan Audit. An action plan audit is an extension of the follow-up assignment described above. In this approach, new graduates are required to develop action plans as part of the transition program. These action plans contain detailed steps to accomplish specific objectives related to the program. The plan is typically prepared on a printed form, showing what is to be done, by whom, and at what time to accomplish the objectives. The action plan approach is a straightforward, easy-to-use method for determining how participants will perform on the job. The approach produces data that answer such questions as:

- What job performance resulted from the transition program?
- Are the improvements the ones expected by the program designers?
- What may have prevented new graduates from accomplishing specific action items?

With this information, management can decide if a program should be modified and in what ways, while assessing the findings to evaluate the worth of the program.

Developing the action plan entails two steps: (1) determining the areas for action and (2) writing the action items. Both tasks should be completed during the transition program. The areas for action should evolve from the material presented in the program and, at the same time, be related to on-the-job activities. A list of potential areas for action can be developed in a group discussion, or possibly a new graduate may identify a particular area needing attention in the future. The following questions should be asked when developing the areas:

- How much time will this action take?
- Are the skills for accomplishing this action item available?
- Who has the authority to implement the action plan?
- Will this action have an effect on other individuals?

- Are there any organizational constraints for accomplishing this action item?

The specific action items are usually more difficult to write than the identification of the action areas. Most importantly, an action item should be written so that everyone involved will know when it occurs. If appropriate, each item should have a date for completion and indicate other individuals or resources required for completion. Also, planned behavior changes should be observable, making it obvious to new graduates and others when it happens.

Action plans, as used in this context, do not require the prior approval or input from the participant's supervisor, although it may be helpful. New recruits may not have prior knowledge of the action plan requirement for the program. Frequently, an introduction to, and a description of, the process is an integral part of the transition program. Action plans should be reviewed before the end of the transition program to check for accuracy, feasibility, and completeness. At that time, it should be made clear that the plan will be audited.

To tabulate the results achieved from the action plans, an audit (or follow-up) is conducted—usually four to six months after the program is completed. This audit investigates and documents the progress that has been made toward planned objectives. It can be accomplished through either questionnaires or interviews. In the first approach, questionnaires are mailed to graduates at the specified follow-up time, accompanied by a cover letter and a detailed list of questions about the plans, much like any other audit. Questionnaires have ample space to describe, for each action item, what was done, how it was done, who was involved, and how often it was tried. The detailed results are documented. If the items were not accomplished, information is gathered to explain why they were not accomplished. Problems encountered or obstacles to success are listed. Although questionnaires are usually gathered directly from graduates, other options, just as effective, are:

- contacting only a sample of the graduates for a follow-up
- reconvening a group of graduates to complete the follow-up questionnaires

• obtaining input from both the graduates and their supervisors.

The interview approach to an action plan audit begins with a letter reminding participants about the follow-up audit and focusing attention on the action items before the interviews take place. Graduates are contacted for an appointment and should be interviewed at their convenience to minimize distractions on the job. The same type of information on the questionnaire is obtained in the interview, the difference being the way it is collected (face-to-face versus over the telephone).

The action plan approach is flexible and has many inherent advantages. It is simple, understandable, and easy to administer. It is useful when collecting a variety of information and can measure reaction, learning, and results. It can be used independently as the only method of evaluation or in conjunction with other evaluation methods. Youker (1985) cites ten important benefits of the action plan approach.

While there are advantages, there are also disadvantages. The method relies on direct input from individuals, and, as such, the information can be biased and unreliable. The data collected are usually subjective, in the soft-data category, and if more concrete information is available through another method, then it should be used. It can be time-consuming for graduates, and if their supervisors are not involved in the process, graduates have a tendency not to complete the assignment.

Job Simulations. A somewhat versatile evaluation method is the use of job simulations. This method involves the construction and application of a procedure or task that simulates or models the activity for which the program is being conducted. Simulations are designed to represent, as closely as possible, actual job situations. They may be used as an integral part of an education or training program or in the evaluation stage. In evaluation, graduates are provided an opportunity to try out their performance in a simulated activity and have it evaluated based on how well the task was accomplished. The assessment center method discussed earlier is actually a simulation in which each exercise is designed to reproduce a work situation where graduates exhibit behavior related to one or more job dimensions. Simulations may be used during the program, at the end of the program, or as part of the follow-up evaluation.

Job simulations offer several advantages. They can reproduce a job or part of a job in a manner almost identical to the real setting. Through careful planning and design, the simulation can have all of the central characteristics of the real situation. Sometimes expensive to construct, simulations can be cost-effective in the long run, however, through repeated applications. In some situations the cost of learning on the job becomes prohibitive to the point where simulation becomes attractive as an alternative. Safety is another advantage, particularly where equipment operation is involved. The nature of many jobs requires participants to be trained or evaluated in simulated conditions instead of real situations.

A variety of simulation techniques are used to evaluate program results. Some common techniques are:

1. *Electrical/mechanical simulation* uses a combination of electronic and mechanical devices, such as a flight simulator, to simulate the real-life situations. These simulations are used in conjunction with programs to develop operational and diagnostic skills and are not common in transition programs.

2. *Task simulation* involves the performance of a simulated task as part of an evaluation. These are usually job-related, manual tasks, usually a part of standard procedures. This type of simulation is not common in evaluating transition programs.

3. *Business games* are simulations of a part or all of a business enterprise. Graduates change the variables of the business and observe the effect of those changes. Given specific objectives, graduates play the game while their output is monitored. Their performance can usually be documented and measured. Typical objectives are to maximize profit, sales, market share, or return on investment.

4. *In-basket exercises* are particularly useful in supervisory and management programs. Portions of a supervisor's job are simulated through a series of items that normally appear in the in-basket. Memos, notes, letters, and reports create realistic

conditions facing the supervisor. The graduate must decide what to do with each item while taking into consideration the principles taught in an education or training program.

5. *Case studies* represent a detailed description of a problem, usually followed by a list of several questions. Graduates are asked to analyze the case and determine the best course of action. The problem should reflect the conditions in the real world setting and the content in the transition program. The difficulty with case studies lies in objectively evaluating the graduates' performance. Frequently, solutions to a case study include several possible courses of action, some equally as effective as others, making it extremely difficult to evaluate objectively performance for the analysis and interpretation of the case.

6. *Role plays,* sometimes referred to as skill practices, allow graduates to practice newly learned skills while they are being observed. Although several types of role plays are designed for different purposes, in the context of evaluation graduates are provided roles with specific instructions, which sometimes include an ultimate course of action. The graduates then practice the skill with other individuals to accomplish the desired objectives.

In summary, simulations can provide extremely accurate evaluations if the performance in the simulation is objective and can be clearly measured.

Job Performance. Organizational performance records, which enable management to determine and document job performance in terms of output, quality, costs, and time, are necessary for an accurate evaluation system. Table 9 lists common performance records (or hard-data measurements) for an employee or group of employees. In determining the use of performance measures in evaluation, the first consideration should be the use of existing performance records. In most organizations, records are readily available for measuring improvement resulting from the transition program. The following guidelines are recommended to ensure that the system for measuring job performance is effective:

1. *Identify appropriate records.* The performance records of the organization should be thoroughly researched to identify those that are related to the objectives of the specific stage(s) of transition. Frequently, the organization has several performance measures related to the same item.

2. *Determine if a sampling plan is necessary.* When a large number of graduates are involved in a program, total figures may not be available; in this case a sampling of records is adequate to supply the information needed. If sampling is required, the sampling plan should be structured to provide an adequate sample size and one that is selected on a random basis.

3. *Convert current records to usable ones.* Occasionally, existing performance records are integrated with other related data. In this situation all existing data records to be used in the measurement should be extracted and retabulated to be more appropriate for comparison. Conversion factors may be necessary. For example, the average number of new sales orders per month may be presented regularly in the performance measures for the sales department. The sales costs per salesman are also presented. However, in the evaluation of a transition program, the average cost per new sale may be needed. The two existing performance records are thus combined to provide the data necessary for comparison.

4. *Develop a data collection plan.* A data collection plan defines when the data are collected, who will collect them and where they will be collected. This plan should contain provisions for the evaluator to secure copies of performance records in a timely manner so that the items can be recorded and prepared for analysis.

In some cases records are not available for the information needed to measure the effectiveness of a transition program. The program administrator must work with the appropriate managers to develop record-keeping systems, if they are economically feasible. For example, in evaluating the orientation stage of transition, several types of data were needed in a service organization. One of these involved comparisons of the survival rates of new employees after six months. The survival rate is the percentage of new employees who remain with the company more than six months. At the time the new orientation program was implemented, these records were not available. The organization began collecting data for comparison, and this new record provided a basis for evaluation of the effectiveness of the orientation.

In creating new records several questions are relevant:

- Which department will develop the record-keeping system?
- Who will record the data?
- Where will it be recorded?
- Will forms be used?
- Over what time period will the records be kept?

These questions will usually involve other departments or a management decision extending past the scope of human resources. The administration, accounting, or industrial engineering departments may be instrumental in determining if new records are needed and, if so, how they will be collected.

Tests. A final and very popular evaluation method involves administering tests before and after a program segment. This method measures changes in skills, knowledge, and attitudes (see the discussion earlier in this chapter). Tests are easy to administer and improvement can be easily tabulated. However, improvement measured during the program does not ensure that it will occur on the job. Also, the effects of testing may have an impact on the post-program score, that is, the first test might influence the score on the second. Nevertheless, pre-course and post-course measurements are used frequently and represent a significant method of evaluation, particularly in the education and training stage of transition.

Areas of Measurement and Evaluation

An important consideration in program evaluation are the specific areas on which to focus data collection efforts. Five major areas of measurement and evaluation are common, ranging from progress of new graduates to the long-term performance of graduates who complete the transition program.

Monitoring Progress of New Graduates. Monitoring the progress of new graduates in transition programs enables program coordinators to take corrective action when problems emerge and to alter assignments or activities to assure that the program operates smoothly. In far too many cases new graduates become disenchanted with an organization and ultimately leave because of perceived unfair treatment, unmet expectations, lack of communication, or other problems that could have been avoided during the transition program. Unfortunately, in most cases the organization may never learn the real reasons why a recent graduate leaves. Even the best exit interview process does not always uncover true feelings. Departing professionals are reluctant to speak with frankness and candor about how they have been treated for fear of "burning bridges": Many graduates want to keep their options open for using the organization as a reference or for a potential return to the organization. The only way an organization may know the feelings and attitudes is to monitor progress, request feedback, and take corrective action when necessary.

An observant management team, and particularly the program coordinator, can identify danger signals that indicate problems with new graduates—problems that may not surface in formal comments during planned progress reports and feedback sessions. Examples of danger signals are:

1. A graduate expresses statements of displeasure about the program and the way it is handled.
2. An otherwise talkative graduate suddenly becomes very quiet in the presence of managers or coordinators.
3. Enthusiasm has suddenly disappeared.
4. A graduate fails to attend the program's extracurricular activities and social events.
5. A graduate relentlessly pursues a hobby or part-time employment after hours, or devotes an unusual amount of time to personal projects.

6. Absenteeism suddenly increases (possibly for outside interviews with other organizations).
7. A graduate enters night school to pursue an advanced degree without any discussion with or approval by program coordinators.
8. A graduate frequently asks for clarification of program goals, missions, and purposes.

Any of the above situations could spell problems with graduates—problems that could lead to unnecessary terminations if left unresolved.

Probably the most formal approach for monitoring progress and spotting problem areas is through the use of progress reports completed by each new graduate. Progress reports provide an opportunity to recap what has been learned, problems and obstacles encountered, and reactions to the program. They can range from simple forms that only require checking boxes to detailed questions requiring essay-type responses. Written responses are sometimes preferred because they provide new graduates an opportunity to demonstrate writing skills as well as provide information on their progress. Progress reports can be completed at any interval desired by the organization. Some organizations require monthly reports, while others require them quarterly. It may be appropriate to wait until the end of an education/training program, a rotational visit, or a job assignment before completing the progress report. These reports can provide valuable insight into how the program is working and, most importantly, how new graduates are adjusting to the program and organization. Also, they can be an important part of the evaluation of new graduates. For example, in one organization, department heads select new graduates from the transition program to enter permanent employment. The department head reviews all of the progress report forms to determine how much the individual has learned as well as evaluate written communication skills in reports.

When formal mentors are assigned to graduates, their input can be extremely valuable. Input can be secured in feedback meetings between mentors and program coordinators, or it can be obtained through written progress reports. However, it is important not to burden mentors with unnecessary paperwork and frequent reports, which can diminish the attractiveness of mentor assignments. Questionnaires usually suffice. The same types of questions asked of the graduates are asked of the mentor, providing program coordinators an opportunity to learn about problems and successes of the graduates as well as needed changes or adjustments.

Supervisors and managers who have contact with new graduates are in an excellent position to provide input on their progress. Immediate supervisors of graduates working on job assignments can easily spot performance and attitude problems and keep the program coordinators apprised of the situation. Other managers with limited involvement should also be encouraged to report progress. The extent of their formal reporting and the weight placed on their input will depend on their degree of involvement with the participants in the program.

In some programs, particularly formal programs lasting several months or more, periodic meetings with new graduates are helpful for discussing important program information and monitoring progress. These meetings provide an excellent opportunity to assess the progress of individuals. Excessive complaints or lack of participation could signal a problem with a participant.

Finally, routine visits to job sites or to education or training locations can provide additional insight into the progress of new graduates. These visits are particularly helpful when programs are conducted at multisite facilities or when assignments rotate from one department or section to another. Face-to-face visits by the program coordinator provide another opportunity for graduates to discuss problems or concerns with the program coordinator.

Evaluating the Program Design. Through questionnaires, interviews and observations, data is collected to help program designers improve the efffectiveness of the transition process. Among the areas to consider for feedback on program design are the following:

- objectives
- program structure
- activities
- special events
- timing
- formality
- flexibility

- pre-employment education
- recruitment
- orientation
- education and training segments
- performance feedback
- job assignments
- mentor relationships.

These and other items need to be examined regularly for possible change.

Probably the most important group from whom to obtain feedback on the program design is the new graduates. From their unique vantage point they can provide important insight into the changes needed to make the program more effective. Most graduates will offer constructive criticism regarding the program design, particularly on some part of the program that they disliked or perceived to be useless in their development.

Some aspects of the program may be more helpful in later years, and they fail to recognize this at the time; feedback on these activities should be minimized or avoided altogether. For example, one manufacturing firm requires all of its new graduates to spend a small part of their formal transition program at a customer's facilities examining the customer's problems and concerns with its product. At the end of a formal transition program some new graduates perceive the assignment to be a waste of time, but in their later years of employment, when they are more concerned about product applications, sales, or quality control techniques, customer satisfaction has more meaning because of that experience. Asking the graduates for input on the usefulness of this assignment might produce suggestions to shorten it or eliminate it altogether, an action that would not be received well by top management.

Input from former participants can also provide helpful comments about program design. In a follow-up evaluation that collects several different types of data, additional input may be desired on program design. A few months or even a year after completing the transition program, graduates have had ample time to reflect on whether aspects of the program design listed above should be lengthened, shortened, added, deleted, or modified.

The management group is another important source of input on the program design. Of this group, probably the most important for input on program design are the immediate supervisors of new graduates. Whether supervising new graduates during transition or in their first permanent assignments, supervisors can observe flaws that should be communicated to program designers. Supervisory input can pinpoint motivational problems, inflated expectations, or other danger signals that indicate a less-than-effective transition process. Not all feedback, of course, will be negative. Supervisors often reinforce what has been accomplished and are pleased with the results of the transition program. Other managers with varying degrees of involvement in transition could provide input on the program design. Mentors, if available, can provide input on their aspect of the program design, as well as other areas uncovered in discussion with graduates. They have an important vantage point since they listen to the concerns and problems of graduates. They may obtain information unavailable from other sources. Together these three groups—current participants, former participants and management—provide useful information to help program designers make improvements in the transition process.

Program Results—Subjective Measures. The results achieved by graduates in a transition program are the ultimate level of evaluation and a true measure of the program's success. For convenience, program results are divided into two categories, subjective and objective. Subjective results are usually based on soft data; objective measures are usually based on hard data, although the distinction between these two forms of data is sometimes vague.

Evaluation based on program results are usually directly linked to the objectives of the transition program. For example, an objective to improve organizational commitment requires measures of organizational commitment in the evaluation process.

Several subjective measures of transition program success are discussed below; others are covered in Chapter One.

Job satisfaction (or in some cases satisfaction with the transition program) is one of the most important variables to monitor. Input obtained through surveys or questionnaires indicates degree of satisfaction with the various elements of the transition program as well as temporary and permanent job assignments. The relationship between job satisfaction and job performance appears to be significant (Petty, McGee, and Cavender 1984), and the relationship between job satisfaction and turnover is even stronger (Cotton and Tuttle, 1986). Job satisfaction may be measured by a number of commercially available instruments such as the job descriptive index (JDI), which measures five components of satisfaction: satisfaction with supervision, satisfaction with pay, satisfaction with co-workers, satisfaction with the work itself, and satisfaction with promotion/ advancement.

Another important subjective area to measure is the degree of motivation. Most organizations want their new college graduates to be highly motivated: to have a desire to achieve and succeed on the job. Research has shown that a high degree of motivation leads to high performance levels (Miner, 1980). Measures of motivation can be taken during the program or at the end of the program through surveys and questionnaires.

Measuring the degree of organizational commitment or attachment of new graduates is also important. Organizations desire high degrees of commitment to the goals and philosophy of the organization. They want loyal, dedicated employees who will remain with them for significant time periods, at least until their contributions exceed their investment. Research has shown that organizational commitment is related to turnover (Mobley, 1982). A high degree of commitment leads to lower turnover. Organizational commitment can be measured through surveys, questionnaires and even interviews.

A transition program sometimes focuses on role ambiguity. New graduates need to have a clear understanding of their jobs, duties, and roles in the organization. A measure of this item can indicate success with the transition program assuming that one of the objectives is to accomplish improvements in role ambiguity. Research has shown a positive correlation between role ambiguity and intention to quit, implying that when graduates are unclear of their role in the organization, they are more likely to leave (Jones, 1986).

Stress tolerance is another focus for some transition programs. In some occupations the work is extremely stressful, and an effective transition program enables new graduates to cope with and tolerate the stresses inherent in the occupation. Research has shown that high levels of stress lead to higher levels of turnover (Mobley, 1982). Stress tolerance can be measured using a variety of instruments.

A final area of subjective measure is that of organizational image. Transition programs are sometimes undertaken to provide graduates with an improved image of the organization, hoping that a better image may lead to other measures of commitment and success. In addition, positive images can stimulate other college students to pursue the organization for future employment. The image of an organization can be measured through questionnaires, surveys and interviews.

Program Results—Objective Measures. The most important measures of results are those based on objective data which are usually indisputable and credible in the eyes of management. Probably the most important measure of the success of a transition program is turnover, particularly in the early months and years of employment. As discussed in Chapter One, considerable evidence shows that the ease of adjustment correlates with turnover. The greater the problems in adjustment and transition, the more likely an individual is to leave the organization. Ideally, turnover should be measured in transition program groups and then compared to a control group who did not experience the program. However, in most organizations all new graduates participate in the formal transition program. Program and control groups are feasible only during trial periods when a new or revised segment of transition is developed.

Turnover in a specific occupation can be compared with turnover data in the same occupation in other organizations. For example, the turnover of accountants may be compared with the turnover of accountants on a national or regional basis if data is readily available for comparison. Also, turnover data in one organization can be compared with turnover data in similar industries. For example, turnover of a hospital's professional personnel can be compared with other hospitals to judge if it is excessive. This comparison would not necessarily pinpoint the effectiveness of the transition program but merely be one of the factors that needs consideration in evaluation.

The performance of graduates who participated in the transition process is another important measure of the success of transition. Their job performance can be compared with those who did not participate in the transition program and to the performance of others in similar occupations or industries. Performance measures are readily available in some occupations. For instance, the measure of performance of new sales representatives in an insurance firm may be the new policies written or the premiums sold in a certain time period. A stockbroker's performance may be measured in total commissions. The performance of a first-line supervisor, responsible for a production group, may be measured in terms of output of the production team. However, for other graduates, such as engineers, accountants, and public relations specialists, objective measures of output are difficult to establish. In those cases, performance ratings obtained from the performance review process may provide the best measure of performance. Items such as merit-based salary increases and promotions may also be used as measures, assuming that pay and promotions are based on performance.

The ultimate objective measurement of program results is the return on the investment in the transition program. This item may be reported as a return on assets, a cost/benefit analysis, or an increase in human capital based on human resources accounting principles. This concept involves calculating the dollar value of all of the improvements resulting from the formal transition program and comparing it with the investment in resources for the program. This is difficult to calculate precisely but has been estimated for some programs and organizations. For additional information on these approaches, see Phillips (1983a) and Flamholtz (1985).

Long-Term Performance of Graduates. The ultimate long-term payoff is the success of graduates in the years following their formal transition program. New college graduates, when properly recruited and prepared for their new assignments, should quickly learn the organization, make a contribution, and succeed. An effective transition program provides a head start on the career track when compared to graduates without an effective formal transition program. Therefore, it is important to monitor the progress made after program completion, at least for the first few years. Obviously, after a few years on the job, the effect of the transition would be minimal. This approach to evaluation may involve tracking a variety of performance measures, including salary increases, promotions, performance ratings, performance output, turnover, special awards and commendations for a period of time after program completion. Ideally, this performance data should be compared with that of other employees who did not participate in a formal transition program. Short of that, comparisons could be made with other industries or with the same occupation in other organizations.

An important part of performance monitoring after program completion is to identify those individuals who represent a success in the eyes of other graduates or even potential graduates. Key managers, experts, specialists, high performers or other individuals who have demonstrated outstanding achievement in the organization are likely targets if their performance in some way is linked to the formal transition process. It is not unusual for organizations to track performance of key employees and try to relate their accomplishments to earlier experiences. A word of caution is in order in using these success stories. If the transition program is given all the credit for an individual's success, it will possibly bring criticism and ridicule. There may be little evidence to link the success with the formal transition program. The connection should be subtle, hinting that the formal transition program may have been one of the factors in the individual's exceptional achievements. This information is best communicated directly to potential graduates in recruiting brochures and to current graduates through direct involvement with the transition program. Previous graduates with outstanding accomplishments make ideal guest speakers, lecturers, or even discussion leaders in education and training programs for new graduates. Also, it can be helpful for them to be involved in either recruiting or orientation, since their presence and subtle connection with the program provides an important incentive for graduates to participate in the formal transition program.

Although, at best, the connection between superior performance and a formal transition program ten years earlier is weak, the organization should take advantage of the successes of individuals who have participated in them. These programs have produced outstanding candidates who have become leaders in organizations. Why shouldn't some of the credit for this success go to the initial entry process in the organization?

Communicating and Using Evaluation Data

Collecting data is a meaningless exercise unless the data are analyzed, evaluated, and communicated to those individuals or groups who will use the data properly. Table 12 shows six common uses of evaluation data and the target groups for communication, ranging from future prospects for the transition program to top management who must approve additional expenditures for transition program efforts. Each of these six uses is briefly described below.

Making Program Adjustments. The most important use of evaluation data is to make adjustments or changes in the transition program. The rationale for collecting data at different stages of the transition is to make adjustments for weaknesses in each stage. Evaluation data must be quickly communicated to those who are responsible for making adjustments in the various segments of the transition process. Target groups are program coordinators, employment managers, HRD managers, and HR executives responsible for the overall effort. Ideally, this information would identify exactly what changes are necessary for the desired

Table 12. Target Groups for Using Evaluation Data.

Use of Evaluation Data	Target Group
Make program adjustments	Key managers responsible for the transition program
Justify future program investments	Top management
Increase management support for transition	Middle-management
Reinforce importance of transition program	Current program participants
Recruit future program participants	Future candidates
Show necessity for measuring results	Staff involved in transition efforts

improvement. Also, positive results at different stages would reinforce current efforts to make the program successful.

Justifying Future Program Investments. The second most important reason for collecting evaluation data is to justify future investments in transition efforts. Formal transition programs or stages, ranging from recruiting to training and development, are very expensive and represent a substantial investment. Top management need convincing evidence that the program is working and achieving the desired results. This can only be achieved through a comprehensive evaluation program that monitors and tabulates the overall results. Few executives will fund programs based on gut feelings and hunches. They need hard data usually presented as turnover statistics and in improved performance. Provided with such data, executives will usually approve additional resources to continue or increase transition efforts. Failure to monitor results and report them to top management can place the entire transition program in jeopardy, leaving it as the first program to be curtailed in an economic downturn. Too many organizations have built excellent programs only to have their budgets slashed drastically in tough times because of their failure to show results.

Increasing Management Support for Transition Efforts. The third most important use of evaluation data is to enhance or increase the level of support from the middle-management group. Although using evaluation data is not the only way to secure or increase management support, it is one of the most genuine and realistic approaches. As mentioned earlier, no HR program designed to develop employees on-the-job can be effective without the enthusiastic endorsement of the middle-management group. To a certain degree they are involved in the effort and must assist or reinforce the learning in most of the stages. Either way, their support is essential to success, and evaluation data showing the success of the program can convince even the most reluctant managers to participate in and support the transition effort. Middle managers are usually results oriented. When they see results from a program, they do not mind participating in activities that created those results.

Reinforcing the Importance of Transition Efforts. Another important use of evaluation data is to reinforce the importance of the program to those who are involved in the effort. Current graduates have a keen interest in the success of those who preceded them and particularly in their success after program completion. Evaluation data, collected at various stages, as well as overall results can provide useful feedback to these graduates, reassuring them that they have made the right decision and that they, too, can succeed in the organization. Evaluation data can also be helpful in counseling sessions with current graduates. For example, data showing that a larger number of graduates leave during a job rotation phase of a formal education/training program act as a signal that the phase is a particularly difficult part of the transition program. As another example, data showing low turnover in the first three years of employment may encourage other graduates to stick it out, even if they are having frustrations during a particular part of the program. This information could be presented to graduates in group meetings or individually in performance review sessions. Chapter Six outlined the various types of interactions with graduates, most of which are appropriate settings for this type of feedback.

Recruiting New Candidates for Transition Programs.
Evaluation data can be used in the recruiting stage of transition.
When deciding among several career opportunities, new college
graduates want to join an organization that has the highest
probability for success and a long-term relationship. Tangible
evidence of previous success can be very convincing information to
help graduates decide on joining the organization. Success stories
and the present job level achieved by previous graduates provide
convincing evidence that a program works. Although transition
programs, particularly those with formal training and education
programs, are sometimes described in recruiting brochures, this
approach is not used often because organizations are sometimes
reluctant to discuss the details of their program. If the program is
not working well, the organization would be reluctant to use data
to attract new graduates, though almost any program has a few
success stories. Even when programs are successful, firms tend to
be reluctant to make this "internal data" known to the public—or
to the competition. Although presenting data, such as turnover
rates in the first five years of employment, is a risky proposition, it
can be very convincing to a graduate seeking facts to make career
choices.

Showing Importance of Measuring Results. A final use of
evaluation data is to show the staff involved in the transition
program the importance of measuring the results of their efforts.
As part of an important trend, more organizations are evaluating
their HR programs and are challenged to communicate the results
of their efforts (Fitz-enz, 1985). Each time a staff member is
required to evaluate programs and show results it reinforces the
importance of this action. It is not unusual for HR staff members
to resist measurement of their efforts. They often live in an
intangible world perceived to be unmeasurable. Challenging or
even requiring them to measure results legitimizes the process and
increases the importance of the activity as part of their overall
duties. In addition, creative approaches to measurement and
evaluation applied to one HR program, such as a formal transition effort, might stimulate similar applications with other
programs. Sharing evaluation approaches is an important way of

disseminating information about evaluation and measurement. Results, communicated directly to staff members, adds credibility to what they have done and provides recognition for their efforts.

Summary

This chapter presented the final stage of transition—evaluation of the entire process. Evaluation is important because the rationale for expanding or improving the transition program lies with the quality of evaluation. Although evaluation is listed as the final stage in our model (see Chapter One), evaluation occurs throughout the various stages and must provide interactive feedback for making changes in the transition program when necessary. The chapter explored the types of data, levels of evaluation, evaluation instruments, evaluation designs, and evaluation methods. Together, these techniques allow an organization to develop an overall strategy for evaluating the transition process at various stages and intervals. A discussion of the principal areas of focus for evaluation, as well as tips on how to use evaluation data with various targets, completed the coverage of evaluation.

8

Coordinating
and Supporting
Employee Transition
Programs

Efficient coordination and control of the transition process can make the difference between success and failure. This chapter explores administrative issues, such as reporting relationships, staffing requirements, costs, pay considerations, as well as the requirements for successful coordinators and mentors. It also explores ways to secure and enhance management commitment, support, and involvement in the transition process.

Reporting Relationships and Staffing Needs

What appears to be a relatively simple issue, reporting relationships, can be quite complex and important to success in a transition program. Reporting relationships concern new graduates, program coordinators, trainers, and recruiters. An important consideration in establishing the reporting relationship is to move the control of the program closest to those who are responsible for the final product (that is, the new graduates) while taking into account potential efficiencies gained in a centralized education, training, and recruiting effort.

Recruiters. College recruiters usually report to human resource executives either at a corporate or division level. Recruiting can best be accomplished by the HR department, as long as the recruiting requirements are clearly defined and the department is staffed with capable and competent individuals. The efficiencies gained through centralized recruiting usually outweigh the advantages of decentralized recruiting (see Chapter Three).

Program Coordinator. The reporting relationship of the coordinator is another important issue. In some organizations, particularly in smaller ones, coordination may be a part-time duty assigned to the HR executive closest to the area where graduates will be permanently employed. Decentralization is the key to good program coordination and control. It is difficult for an individual to administer a transition program effectively from a corporate office when all the graduates are working in remote facilities. Ideally, the coordinator should report to a top executive responsible for the areas where new graduates work in their permanent assignments. Several examples illustrate the various approaches to successful reporting relationships. In a manufacturing facility, where most of its 2,000 employees are in one facility along with the corporate office, the program coordinator is on the corporate human resources staff. Because of the close proximity of the graduates to the HR staff and the close working relationship between human resources and line management, this reporting relationship works best.

In a large Fortune 500 firm, which is decentralized into ten major operating divisions, program coordination is delegated to division human resources executives who report to a division president. In this case, the graduates are rotated through several plants within a division's region. The division coordinator makes routine visits with the individuals involved in the program. This arrangement is more effective than trying to have a part-time coordinator at each plant location.

In a health care delivery company with hospitals scattered throughout the world, program coordinators are located at each individual hospital and report to the hospital administrator. Here, because of the relative size of each facility, and the importance of having the proper transition control at the local area, the chief executive (hospital administrator) at each location has the responsibility for the program. If program administration and control is too far removed from the graduates, problems usually surface.

Graduates. The reporting relationship of graduates is not usually given enough attention. Too often the final arrangements are based on convenience and budgetary concerns rather than on the effectiveness of the transition program. Three approaches are common. Graduates report to (1) the program coordinator, (2) the manager or supervisor over the area in which they have temporary work assignments or education and training activities, or (3) the manager of the department where they will eventually work in permanent assignments. Each approach has distinct advantages.

The advantages of the first approach usually center around efficiency and consistency in program administration. The coordinator can work with each participant on the same basis, ensuring fair and consistent treatment. The coordinator can ensure that each graduate has an opportunity to take advantage of all of the planned activities. This arrangement also allows for easy cost-monitoring of all program activities. A disadvantage of this approach is that coordinators are sometimes removed from graduates' daily activities and as a result may not be aware of day-to-day performance nor be available to take corrective action should it be necessary. Also, coordinators may not feel responsible for graduates and thus not provide the supervision and leadership necessary for new graduates to succeed.

The second approach—having graduates report to the individuals responsible for different stages of transition—has the advantage of providing immediate supervision of work progress, transfering responsibility for success to those who can best make it happen. Some program control may be lost, since coordinators may not have enough contact with graduates to ensure that they receive all of the required education, training, and temporary work assignments. In addition, some managers or specialists may be reluctant to supervise new graduates, feeling uncomfortable with the supervisory role or fearing that their evaluation may weigh too heavily on a graduate's future success. As a result, graduates may be unsupervised or undeservedly rated average in performance.

The third approach has the advantage of placing responsibility of new graduates' success in the different stages of transition in the hands of those who will use the end product. Graduates may respond more readily to this reporting relationship than the others, since they may be eager to please their permanent supervisors. (With the other two approaches, the supervisors are only temporary, and graduates may not be as eager to please and perform their best.) This approach works best when each major section has a new graduate recruited to participate in a variety of transition activities prior to being permanently assigned. The section or department manager can assume responsibility for graduates early and help guide and direct them during the process.

Classroom Trainers. Individuals responsible for providing classroom education or training usually report to a corporate or division HRD manager. This approach is usually more effective, since classroom training can be provided more efficiently when centralized, as long as the trainers are familiar with the jobs new graduates will assume. Also, since classroom instruction usually represents a small part of the transition process, there is little need to have trainers report directly to the transition program coordinators or the managers responsible for the graduates' success on the job. However, for programs where formal education or training represents a large part of the transition process, classroom trainers may need to be under the direction of the person responsible for transition. This helps ensure that education and training is relevant and job-related.

On-the-Job Trainers. When large numbers of graduates are assigned to work areas to learn their jobs or prepare for future jobs, on-the-job (OJT) trainers (or educators) usually provide the proper assistance, guidance, and learning activities. In this case, these trainers should probably report to those who are responsible for the success of the graduates—usually a department, plant, or division manager. The alternative of having them report to a centralized HRD department may not be desired. The advantages of job-related education/training provided under the direction of a local executive may outweigh the efficiencies gained in a centralized HRD function. An example illustrates this concept. A large electronics firm recruits new graduate engineers to perform design work on a major defense contract. New graduates participate in a variety of training and education activities prior to being assigned to an engineering design department. There, in groups of three of four engineers, they work under the direction of an experienced design engineer who functions as an OJT trainer. As a full-time trainer, the senior engineer ensures that new engineers learn their jobs and are provided the necessary assistance to function effectively. The OJT trainers report to the department head for that area, thus ensuring proper control over training and the program's success. Having them report to a centralized training facility would probably be a mistake, since the department head would lose some control over the training.

Staffing Requirements. This issue involves staffing for the coordination and administrative functions as well as extra staff that may be necessary to handle large numbers of graduates. (For discussion on optimum number of graduates for transition programs, see Chapter Three.) Additional staff may also be necessary to handle the coordination and administrative duties as well as clerical support. In small-scale programs coordination may be a part-time duty, and additional staffing specifically for this program may be unnecessary. However, as the number of graduates in the program increases, so do the administrative requirements. Some organizations use the rule-of-thumb that for every ten new graduates involved in a formal transition program, an additional coordinator is necessary. This rule, however, can vary significantly with the extent of formal efforts, the nature of the permanent jobs, the duration of the transition program, and the specific duties of the coordinator.

Additional HRD staffing may be necessary to conduct formal classroom education and training programs as well as on-the-job learning activities. It is difficult to pinpoint exactly how many HRD staff are needed, since this can vary widely with individual programs, the ability of the graduates, the organizational setting, and the target jobs. It is, however, an important issue that must be addressed early in the program implementation so that the organization is properly staffed to handle both classroom and on-the-job efforts.

Program Costs

As with virtually every human resources program, the cost of the transition program should be monitored and analyzed. This not only reveals how much is being expended on the program but can also be useful in cost-benefit comparisons. To be meaningful, cost data must be developed for all significant stages and/or parts of the process.

Reasons for Monitoring Costs. The first and most important reason is to determine the overall expenditures for the transition program. Every organization should know approximately how much is spent on its efforts to recruit, educate, and train new graduates to make them productive employees. A few organizations try to calculate these expenditures and make comparisons with others, although such comparisons are difficult because of the different bases for cost calculations and the reluctance of some organizations to disclose their costs. The costs associated with transition go beyond those in the budget for the HR department or other sections assigned the responsibility for transition: participants' salaries, travel expenses, relocation costs, on-the-job training, and general overhead, all of which may not appear in the HR budget. An effective system for cost data collection enables an organization to calculate total transition program expenditures. Ultimately, this information not only helps top management determine how much they *are* spending on transition programs but also how much they *should* spend on these efforts.

A second important reason for monitoring costs is to predict future program costs. Cost data from an existing program help develop standardized data to use in estimating the cost of future programs. This is helpful when revitalizing, expanding, or developing new components for the transition process. In addition, HR departments need a detailed estimate of program costs to determine operating and administrative budgets for the coming year. In recent years the budgeting process has become more scrutinized and more sophisticated. The days of adding a percentage increase to last year's budget are, for the most part, gone. HR departments are asked to examine their activities and programs carefully when preparing a new budget. A few HR departments follow a zero-base budgeting process where each activity must be justified during budget reviews. This assumes no carryover expenses in next year's budget based on the previous year's activity.

A third reason for cost-monitoring is to enable the organization to compare the cost/benefit ratio for the overall transition effort or various stages of the process (see Chapter Seven). Tabulating the benefits derived from HR programs has little meaning unless the benefits are compared with the total cost for the effort. This fact elevates cost data to the same level as evaluation data.

A final reason for monitoring costs is to improve the efficiency of the various stages of the transition efforts. Controlling cost is an important management function, and transition personnel are not exempted from this responsibility. They must be able to monitor and control the cost for developing and delivering programs or program segments. Most HR monthly budgets project costs by various accounts and in some cases by stage or segment of transition. The HR department provides cost reports to show how the department, section, program, or unit is performing against a predetermined budget. Cost reports become tools used to spot problem areas and to take corrective actions when necessary. Therefore, from a practical management viewpoint, the accumulation of cost data is necessary to manage the function effectively.

Who Pays the Salaries? Realistically, some parts of the organization benefit from the formal transition effort more than others. Departments with higher turnover require more new graduates than others with a lower turnover rate. Still others, because of the nature of their work, may not need employees with college degrees. Theoretically, the departments that benefit most from the transition program should bear most of the expense of the program. In practice, however, normal accounting methods may not achieve this goal. One approach is to charge all the salaries to an overhead account, such as Sales, Administrative, and General (SAG), which, in effect, charges the entire organization for the program. This approach not only is unfair to certain parts of the organization but also increases the overhead of the organization—a situation that most organizations constantly try to avoid. A more logical approach is to move participants' salaries to the functional units or divisions using the transition process. Salaries are charged to those parts of the organization in proportion to their need for new graduates. For example, in one organization two-thirds of the transition program benefits the engineering section; as a result, two-thirds of the salaries are charged to engineering as general overhead. In another case, half of the participants in a transition program are prepared for first-line supervisor positions in the production branch. Half of the salaries are charged to general production overhead, ensuring that the production branch pays for its share of the program. However, this approach does not penalize an individual production department that may experience unusually high turnover and require new graduates.

A final approach is to charge participants' salaries directly to the department or section benefiting from the contribution of the new graduates. Although this approach is difficult in situations where new graduates are involved in extensive education programs and their permanent assignments are unknown at the time of employment, in many programs the ultimate assignments are known, or at least the departments are identified. Direct charges to departments directly benefiting places the financial responsibility where it should be. It does, however, penalize a department which may be experiencing unusually high turnover through no fault of its own. For example, some departments are considered "feeder groups" to other parts of the organization; their work is more appropriate for entry-level graduates. With this approach, those departments would bear most of the expense for educating and training new graduates, even though they will not become productive members of the department.

Cost Classification Systems. Transition costs can be classified in two basic ways. One is by a description of the expenditure, such as "labor," "materials," "supplies," "travel," and so on—expense account classifications. The other is by categories or stages of the transition process, such as orientation, program development, delivery, and evaluation. An effective system monitors costs by account categories and also includes a method for accumulating costs by the process/functional category. Many systems do not include this second step. Although the first system is sufficient to give the total cost of the program, it does not allow for a useful comparison with other programs or indicate areas where costs might be excessive by relative comparisons. Therefore, both classification systems are recommended to develop a complete costing system.

An important part of developing a cost system is defining and classifying the various transition expenses. Most of the expense accounts, such as office supplies and travel expenses, are already a part of the existing accounting system. However, certain expenses unique to the transition program must be added to the system. The system design will depend on the organization, the type of programs developed and conducted, and the limits imposed on the current cost-accounting system, if any.

Classifying costs by process or functional category is more difficult to achieve. One approach is to classify costs according to the stage of transition—that is, cost categories for pre-employment education, recruiting, orientation, education/training, adaptation, job assignments, and evaluation. Some organizations, which may not desire to track costs in all these stages, may monitor major categories, such as pre-employment costs, education and training costs, and other costs. Another way to divide costs is through a combination of the functional and expense account classifications. For example, education and training costs related to transition can be further divided into four cost components:

- needs analysis
- program development
- delivery
- evaluation.

In organizations where costs are developed in greater detail, each stage of transition may be subdivided into a variety of other functional areas. For example, transition costs can be placed into one of five cost components:

- program development and revision
- recruiting
- program coordination
- travel expense
- clerical and office expense.

These various approaches to cost classification allow an organization to develop a cost monitoring system to meet its specific needs. Exhibit 1 in Chapter One shows the transition costs monitored in one organization. For additional information on cost systems, see Phillips (1983a) and Spencer (1986).

Pay Considerations

Few aspects of the transition program are more important to new college graduates than their pay, and few things can cause more problems than an improperly administered pay system. Competitive and internally equitable salaries are essential to attract and retain new college graduates. In addition, merit increases, bonuses, incentives, and salary communication are all important issues that must be addressed in the design of the transition program.

Establishing a Compensation Strategy. Developing a compensation system to attract, motivate, and retain new graduates may require the organization to develop a specific strategy for this target group. Although in practice the compensation plans and policies for new graduates may not differ from those of other salaried employees, several compensation issues are unique and require the attention of top management. Some organizations develop general statements to provide direction to management. If they are not written, they are at least understood by the key managers. They outline basic principles the organization uses to guide its compensation plans and programs, addressing such issues as pay for performance, cost-of-living increases, internal equity, and external competitiveness.

The objectives of the compensation system for new college graduates should be specific statements that define the purposes of the compensation plan for these new recruits. They vary considerably with the type of organization and the organization's overall compensation philosophy. Typical compensation objectives for new college graduates are to:

- attract new graduates to professional positions
- keep new graduates from leaving the organization because of perceived unfairness or inequities in compensation
- reward new graduates for their performance and contribution to the organization
- maintain a competitive market position for salaries and benefits of new college graduates
- ensure that new graduates are paid in proportion to the difficulty and worth of their jobs.

These objectives relate directly to important transition program issues. Other objectives may focus on salary costs, legal obligations, compensation flexibility, and overall control of compensation.

Additional factors that must be considered when establishing a competitive compensation system include job evaluation techniques, methods for measuring performance, actual pay structures and salary levels, use of incentives and bonuses, and salary communication. In most organizations these items are no different for new graduates than for other salaried employees. For additional information on compensation policies for new graduates, see Northrup and Malin (1985).

External Competitiveness. A compensation system must have mechanisms for keeping it externally competitive. This is particularly important for new graduates, since an uncompetitive pay system can result in an unfortunate number of turnovers or fail to attract new graduates to the organization. In most cases the initial starting pay for new graduates is based on survey data available from college placement offices. In addition, pay scales may need to be compared with those for other graduates in the local labor market. Although not a factor in every situation, many organizations do compete with others in their locality in attracting graduates. Another potential group for comparison are the organizations engaged in the same type of business or service. This will pinpoint pay differences among graduates involved in similar work. For example, aerospace engineers are compared with other aerospace engineers, construction supervisors are compared with other construction supervisors, and bank loan officers are compared with other bank loan officers. These surveys are usually available through industry, trade, or professional associations and can help ensure that competitive salaries are paid for similar work. Finally, new graduate salaries may need to be compared with regional and national survey data. Usually available from professional services or compensation consultants, national salary data are usually presented regionally and expose geographical differences and even differences in rural and urban areas. National surveys are excellent for companies that operate on a broad, national scale and have professional, technical, and supervisory personnel in many parts of the country. Also, national survey data, when selected in a reliable and valid way, can be very helpful in communicating the competitive position to new graduates.

Internal Equity. Pay for new graduates should be examined for internal equity to ensure that their pay levels are consistent with comparable jobs in the organization and are kept at a proper differential with other groups of employees. The first group to consider is other professional, technical, and supervisory personnel. This becomes important when large numbers of new graduates are recruited and the organization desires to maintain equitable salaries between the various groups. It may be necessary to pay some groups of new graduates more than others, depending on the nature of the work and scope of the jobs. Initial differentials, which are based primarily on the college major, are usually reflected in the starting salaries. However, it may be desired to keep the salaries close to those of other groups. For example, accountants in a large financial services organization may require salaries similar to the data-processing programmers.

Another group to consider is composed of the experienced college graduates who have been on the job a few years more than those currently in the transition program. Some organizations have experienced difficulty in keeping salaries of experienced employees at a reasonable amount above those of new recruits, a particularly difficult task in high inflationary times or when occupations are experiencing a shortage. Competitive salaries drive up the starting rates, and it becomes difficult to keep experienced employees at a proper distance. When this problem surfaces, the existing compensation system should be examined to see if it provides enough movement for experienced people. Many organizations provide benefits that become significantly more valuable with longer service, thereby diminishing the concern about salary differentials. In many cases the job environment and level of responsibility can compensate for the differences in salaries. Experienced graduates usually have more opportunities to participate in challenging and rewarding jobs compared to new recruits.

A third and final comparison group are the supervisors and managers of the new graduates. If market-based job evaluation is used, salaries for supervisors and managers are based on competitive external rates. And because of this, starting salaries for new college graduates, which may be based on a different competitive environment, are sometimes unusually high, thereby causing a "compression" problem with immediate supervisors. When this happens, management must establish minimum differentials between the groups. The approach an organization takes depends on its philosophy and on whether differentials are creating a significant problem. For more information on approaches to maintain salary differentials, see Rock (1984).

Pay for Performance. Some experts differentiate among the motivating aspects of various types of compensation. Ellig (1984) presents a comparison of how various compensation elements rate in attracting, motivating, and retaining employees—three important issues in the transition process. Table 13 presents a summary

Table 13. Impact of Various Compensation Elements on Employees.

Compensation Element	Importance Rating		
	In Attracting	In Motivating	In Retaining
Salary	High	Moderate	High
Employee benefits	Low	Low	Moderate
Short-term incentives	High	High	Moderate
Long-term incentives	Moderate	Moderate	High
Perquisites	Low	Low	Moderate

Source: Ellig, 1984.

of his results. According to Ellig, short-term incentives have the most potential for motivating employees, and perquisites and employee benefits provide relatively low levels of motivation. Salary has only moderate value in motivating employees because, according to Ellig, "Salary adjustments for outstanding performers are tempered by the lack of a downside risk in pay levels" (p. 26). It is also interesting to note that short-term incentives have a high value in attracting employees and a moderate value in retaining them.

From this analysis it appears that the best approach in designing compensation programs to attract, motivate, and retain new college graduates is to place emphasis on pay for performance in the salary plan. It becomes quite clear that pay for performance produces results, and thus it is understandable why many organizations are shifting from cost-of-living and across the board increases to more sophisticated plans that link compensation with performance.

Implementing a pay for performance program involves more than just establishing a merit system and developing bonus plans. It requires implementation of a comprehensive philosophy on rewarding new graduates for their direct contribution and performance. This philosophy should focus on the major elements of a compensation system and the following actions:

- tying current cash compensation directly to the performance and/or contributions of new graduates
- designing performance appraisal systems so that they pinpoint the amount of salary increase
- developing objective measurable criteria to determine the amount of bonus incentive or cash award
- keeping the time lag between pay and performance as short as possible
- simplifying the pay system as much as possible so it can be understood by all involved.

Although a variety of incentives or bonus plans can be developed for new graduates, it may be difficult to tie pay to performance in the early stages of a transition program, as new graduates do not always have an opportunity to make a contribution during this period. Work unit performance bonuses, profit-sharing plans, gainsharing programs, year-end bonuses, and cost reduction programs are examples of incentive and bonus plans that may be appropriate for new graduates. During the transition program, plans that reward new college graduates for their performance in permanent assignments should be developed and implemented. As stated earlier, this can help attract new graduates and motivate them to high levels of achievement while enticing them to stay with the organization. For more discussion on designing incentive plans for new graduates, see Sibson (1981).

Communicating the Compensation Program. Probably no aspect of compensation is mishandled more frequently than communication. New graduates, as well as other employees, are usually left uninformed about pay practices. Sometimes, organizations even do a poor job of communicating the small amount of information they want employees to have. Developing a trusting environment is an important task. New graduates are quick to compare their compensation system, or at least what they know about the system, with what they hear about other systems. They develop an opinion as to whether the system is fair, equitable, and motivational. It is important that they have accurate and reliable information from which to form opinions. This helps build credibility while building a trusting relationship between top management and graduates.

Establishing a communication plan for compensation involves three general considerations. First, the organization must determine the degree of openness of the pay plan. This involves identifying how much information can be efficiently communicated and what information is appropriate to release to graduates. Second, communication objectives must be developed. Third, communication methods must be established, including a variety of effective communication media.

The extent of compensation information provided to employees is sometimes a controversial issue. Some organizations communicate everything about the pay system—individual salaries, salary ranges, pay grades, and policies and procedures. Nothing is kept secret. This does not work in most organizations but is common in government agencies and educational institutions. At the other extreme, some organizations reveal only the employee's own salary. No information is provided about the policies, procedures, ranges, or the basis for pay increases. A completely open policy would spell disaster for some organizations while a completely closed system would mean disaster for others. An organization must establish a position between these two extremes, one that meets the needs of new graduates and fits the culture of the organization.

New graduates usually want as much information about the compensation system as they can secure. If the system is too secretive, it breeds distrust and discontent, leaving new graduates thinking that the organization has something to hide. Positive reactions can be generated from effective compensation communication, unless the system is unfair or uncompetitive.

New graduates want information about performance requirements and expectations. They want to know who measures them, how their performance compares to standards, or how they stack up with others in the department or division. In addition, they want to know the importance the organization places on extra efforts and how they will be rewarded for such efforts. They want to know about future job opportunities, including the possibility of promotions and transfers and the salary growth they can expect with those opportunities. Usually they do not ask for specifics but rather for a general indication of what levels of compensation can be achieved if they are willing to pay the price for those opportunities.

Changing to a more open system should be accomplished at a gradual, calculated pace. Communicating a pay system is a sensitive and difficult task for an organization, and successful implementation may depend on the timing and cautions observed. The process is virtually irreversible. Once a pay system is opened up, it is difficult, if not impossible, to return to a closed system. Employees become accustomed to receiving certain information about pay; and, if it is suddenly stopped, they will have more distrust for the organization than if they had received no information at all. This point must be considered before any decision is made to release additional information.

The types of information communicated can vary considerably. The most common items are:

- philosophy of the compensation system
- objectives of the compensation system
- compensation policies
- how the organization maintains internal equity
- how the organization maintains external competitiveness
- basis for job evaluation
- salary structures (positions and ranges)
- pay range and position in the range
- salary grade
- basis for merit increases and pay actions
- potential for salary growth.

Although the last item is usually optional, communicating the other items would be consistent with the practices of most business and industrial organizations. They tend to be more conservative in their approach to compensation communication than government agencies, educational institutions, and nonprofit organizations.

The Program Coordinator

The importance of having an effective transition program coordinator cannot be overemphasized. Quite often the coordinator can make the difference between success and failure of an otherwise well-designed program. The coordinator influences the recruitment process, the quality of education or training efforts, and the ultimate success of the graduates in the program.

Selection Criteria and Preparation. Program coordinators must be carefully selected to match job requirements. Although selection criteria depend on the type of industry and transition program as well as the jobs the program is designed to fill, a few general requirements should be considered for the coordinator of any type of transition program. First, the prospective coordinator must thoroughly understand the organization, work flows, departmental functions, technical processes, products, services, facilities, and locations. Quite often, the coordinator is the primary source of information during certain stages in the program. He or she must earn the respect of the participants and this can only occur when the individual is knowledgeable and informed.

Second, the coordinator should have a better than casual knowledge of college recruiting, career planning, vocational trends, and the preparation needed for different types of jobs. Experience as a college recruiter or as a career counselor are helpful to provide insight into the college relations and career development field, enabling the coordinator to deal effectively with the problems of recent graduates and to discuss career opportunities with them.

Third, the coordinator should understand the problems of today's youth, particularly career-minded graduates whose problems are sometimes quite different from those of older employees. This does not necessarily mean that the program coordinator has to be young; sometimes, young coordinators do not relate well to young employees, while older individuals relate very effectively to this younger group. It is the ability to understand and relate to the twenty-one to thirty age group that is important.

Fourth, the coordinator must earn the respect of key managers in the organization and have credibility at virtually all levels. This requires an individual who knows organizational politics, has a successful track record in the organization, can speak with authority, can implement innovative policies, and can influence others. This criterion is essential to develop appropriate job assignments and learning experiences.

Fifth, the coordinator must be a college graduate, preferably in one of the disciplines for which the program is designed. For example, a formal transition program for new engineering graduates might be best coordinated by an individual with an engineering degree. This helps build credibility with present and potential graduates. An advanced degree is preferred to keep the coordinator above the others in educational achievement. In addition, some transition programs are designed for graduate students, such as MBA graduates. In this setting, it is essential that the program coordinator have an advanced degree.

Sixth, the coordinator must be results oriented, an attitude necessary for a successful program. The program coordinator must have a strong determination to reach goals set for the program and make necessary adjustments to improve results. The program coordinator must see the need for a strong evaluation effort and have a burning desire to achieve the ultimate results—successful graduates contributing to the organization in the shortest time possible.

Finally, the coordinator must have good communication and interpersonal skills. Both written and oral presentations are often required and the individual must be able to develop and present ideas effectively. Group presentations and documents, reports, and memos are necessary to keep the program on track and to report results. The coordinator needs effective interpersonal skills and one-to-one communication to resolve conflicts and personality problems arising in the program's administration.

In addition to these general background qualifications, the program coordinator should have additional preparation before assuming job duties. For example, the individual may not be knowledgeable about the HRD process: how to conduct a needs assessment, design an education or training program, conduct learning sessions, and monitor progress. Or the coordinator may not be skilled in counseling. Workshops or seminars may help to overcome weaknesses in these areas. The coordinator must be knowledgeable in the professional areas for which the program is designed. For example, in a program designed to develop loan officers, the program coordinator should have an opportunity to observe the job of a loan officer. This may involve brief on-the-job training sessions where the coordinator experiences the job duties and observes the skills needed for job success.

Duties/Responsibilities. The specific duties and responsibilities of the program coordinator vary with the scope and duration of the transition program. A few specific duties or responsibilities common to most formal transition program coordinators are to:

- provide input into the recruiting process, recommending changes and adjustments in recruiting practices
- develop a profile of ideal candidates for the program around the requirements for success on the job
- coordinate pre-employment activities for new graduates
- conduct (or coordinate) orientation for new graduates
- develop, implement, and/or coordinate formal education and training sessions for new graduates
- develop specific education and training projects and assignments that help prepare graduates to perform the planned permanent job successfully
- monitor progress of participants in the program and make adjustments as necessary
- conduct performance review sessions or provide input into performance reviews to ensure that new graduates are performing satisfactorily
- evaluate the program at different stages and report the results to a variety of target audiences.

The degree of responsibility in the above areas, as well as the scope of additional responsibilities, depend on the organization. For example, in some organizations, the program coordinator is entirely responsible for recruiting new graduates. In others, the coordinator supervises the graduates for the duration of the transition program.

Management Commitment and Support for Transition

Several factors relating to the actions and attitudes of the management group have a significant impact on the overall success of transition programs. Managers make decisions to allocate resources, participate in program development, allow graduates to work in their departments, and reinforce what has been taught in the transition program, all of which can affect the program.

Differences in Commitment, Support, and Involvement. Several terms used in the remainder of this chapter need additional explanation. First, *management commitment* primarily refers to the top management group and includes their willingness to allocate resources and lend support to the transition effort in the organization. *Management support* for programs refers to a variety of supportive actions of the entire management group, with emphasis on middle- and first-level management. *Reinforcement* refers to actions that reward or encourage a desired behavior with the goal of increasing the probability of the behavior after a graduate completes the transition program. *Management involvement* refers to the extent to which management, outside the HR department, are actively engaged in the transition process in a productive way.

The HR function is not solely responsible for individual learning and growth in the organization. The function only serves as the coordinating agency or facilitator for learning and growth. The management of the organization is ultimately responsible through their commitment, support, reinforcement, and involvement. The extent of their influence ultimately determines the success of any transition effort.

Assessing and Increasing Commitment. Each chief executive officer (CEO) has some degree of commitment to transition.

The extent of commitment usually varies with the CEO's style, attitude, and philosophy. As a first step in examining top management commitment, it is sometimes helpful to review the extent of commitment currently prevailing in the organization. A checklist or series of review questions can be helpful to gather evidence of commitment. For strong top management commitment, the CEO should:

- allocate the necessary funds for successful transition programs
- allow new graduates adequate time to participate in transition programs
- get actively involved in transition programs and require others to do so
- support the transition effort and ask other managers to do the same
- insist that transition programs be cost-effective and require data to support it
- create an atmosphere of open communication between the CEO and the individual responsible for transition efforts.

How can top management commitment be increased? That represents a puzzling question for many HR professionals. Quite often the extent of commitment has been fixed in the organization for years. Commitment does not necessarily vary with the size or nature of the organization. It usually depends on how the function evolved, the attitude and philosophy of the top management group toward transition, and how the HR function is administered. The actions of the HR department can have a significant impact on future top management commitment. Briefly, here are five actions that can help increase commitment for transition efforts:

- obtaining the results desired from transition programs
- increasing the involvement of all levels of management in the transition process
- developing a very competent and highly professional team to manage the transition process
- communicating development needs to top management so they realize that transition is a necessary, integral process

- utilizing a practical approach when solving transition problems and implementing transition programs.

For more information on ways to increase management commitment for HR programs, see Phillips (1983a).

Management Support. Support from management usually focuses on the supervisors of the new graduates—the middle- and first-line management group. Ideally, management support means:

- Endorsing and approving transition programs for new graduates
- volunteering services or resources to assist in the transition effort
- reinforcing behavior changes resulting from the transition program
- conducting a follow-up of the results achieved from the program
- giving rewards for graduates who have achieved outstanding accomplishments as a result of the transition program.

HR departments can explore several ways to approach this ideal supportive environment. Many important actions are available prior to the transition program. One effective technique is to secure a formal pre-program commitment agreement. For example, an agreement between the HR department and the new graduate's permanent supervisor outlines what the supervisor agrees to do and in turn what the HR department will do. This is essentially a contract that briefly describes the transition program and the various requirements of each party. It is usually secured in a meeting with the supervisors of participants prior to beginning the transition program.

Another pre-program activity involves defining and distributing the responsibilities of both the graduates and the supervisors of graduates. Some organizations develop pamphlets, brochures, or other documents that outline the specific duties of each party. Other organizations define these responsibilities in policy statements and procedure manuals. The responsibilities of graduates are sometimes defined prior to the beginning of the transition program. This way, they are fully aware of expectations, particularly those related to achieving desired results.

In organizations where extensive education and training programs are part of the transition process, it may be important for supervisors of new graduates to attend the programs. This way, supervisors have an opportunity to review the course material and experience the program in the same way as graduates. They usually attend separate sessions but cover essentially the same material. For some situations, a scaled-down version may be more appropriate. It is difficult for a supervisor or manager to have a clear understanding of the program without experiencing it.

Reinforcement. The necessity of getting the graduate's supervisor involved as an integral part of the transition process cannot be understated. Too often graduates complete a formal transition program only to find many obstacles to success in the job environment. Faced with these obstacles, even some of the best participants forget most of what was learned in the program unless there is strong reinforcement. Supervisors of graduates can exert a significant influence on behavior by providing reinforcement in the following ways:

- helping graduates diagnose problems to determine the best course of action
- discussing possible alternatives for handling specific situations
- acting as a coach to help the graduates apply skills and become successful on the job
- serving as a role model for the proper use of the material discussed in the transition program and encouraging graduates to use the material
- giving rewards to graduates when they are successful in using the material in the program.

Each of these activities will serve to reinforce what has been taught and, if handled effectively, can have a tremendous impact on the success of new graduates.

Reinforcement can come from sources other than the supervisor. Graduates receive reinforcement when they practice job skills and achieve success. This self-reinforcement helps some graduates do well after completing a transition program despite obstacles on the job. Graduates may try new skills when they have an obligation to give them a try or when they are curious to see if the skills actually work in a real setting. Sometimes reinforcement can come from a peer group, such as co-workers at the same job level, engaged in similar activities. When some graduates are successful with the application of newly learned job skills, this success can stimulate others to give them a try. Also, it can spawn intergroup coaching among the peer group. In a cooperative environment graduates who are most successful will sometimes show others how to utilize the skills to get the desired results.

Improving the Supportive Relationship. The degree to which management supports the transition process is based on how they perceive the worth of the activity, the function and role of the HR department, and in some cases, the actions of members of the HR staff. To improve management support, the HR department (or other department responsible for transition) should carefully analyze each situation and work on improving the relationship with an individual manager or management group. This improvement requires a series of critical steps:

1. *Identify the key managers whose support is necessary.* Key managers may be the key decision makers, the entire middle-management group, or all of senior management. Individuals selected will probably be strong leaders, either formally or informally.
2. *Analyze the degree of support.* Managers should be grouped according to their degree of support for transition. Support may range from highly supportive to very nonsupportive. Input from the entire HR staff may be helpful to classify all key managers.
3. *Analyze reasons for support or nonsupport.* Managers will usually show support (or nonsupport) based on a series of facts, beliefs, and values related to the transition process.

4. *Select the best approach.* The strategy for dealing with a particular manager depends on the manager's degree of support. Supportive managers are a welcome sight to the HR department. There is little need for any concentrated effort other than to show appreciation for the support they now give. Possibly they should be involved in the transition program in the capacities described in the next two sections. This involvement will usually help maintain their support. Managers who are not strong supporters should be sold on the results of the transition so they will become strong supporters. They may see it as their responsibility and look for a return on investment, whether their investment is in time or money. Nonsupportive managers represent challenges to the HR department. In reality, their number can be large in an organization. The analysis in step 3 should reveal the basis for the nonsupport, either facts, beliefs, or values. Depending on the basis, the problem can be tackled by providing additional information, getting them involved in the transition effort, exhibiting the results of programs, or showing the extent of top management commitment to transition. The strategy used will depend on the individual manager.

Management Involvement

Management involvement in the transition process has been practiced successfully for many years, although it does not appear as often as it should. There are almost as many opportunities for management's involvement in the transition process as there are steps in the design of a transition program. Realistically, however, management provides input and actively participates only in the most significant parts of the process.

Discussion Leaders. The key area of involvement is the use of managers as occasional discussion leaders for orientation, education, or training. Discussion leaders must be carefully chosen based on the following criteria: knowledge and expertise in the subject area, presentation skills, reputation in the organization, and availability. The requirement of knowledge and expertise is usually the largest single reason for soliciting outside assistance. The HR staff cannot be experts in all professional areas, so it is often more meaningful for graduates to have a leader knowledgeable in the subject area.

Good presentation skills are critical. Even the most respected and knowledgeable managers will be ineffective if they cannot make effective presentations. Although it is possible to assist a manager in developing presentation skills, it may not be feasible, from a time standpoint, to prepare outside leaders to this extent.

A good reputation in the organization is another must. Managers, respected because of their ability or position, add credibility to the program. Likewise, managers who are considered poor performers or improper role models will have a negative impact on the program.

Finally, availability is important. Key managers are usually busy individuals who may not have the time to assist in conducting programs. On the other hand, some equally effective managers who are not as challenged may be more likely candidates for discussion leader assignments.

After discussion leaders are selected, they must be prepared for their assignments. This process takes time to be done properly. In some cases the time required to prepare others to conduct a program will be greater than the time required for the HR staff to prepare for the program. Detailed plans, objectives, scripts, visual aids, handouts, and other items must be developed for each discussion leader. If feasible, discussion leaders should have a chance to practice a session before presenting it to a group of new recruits, with the HR staff critiquing the session and offering constructive suggestions.

Program Advisory Committees. Many organizations have developed committees to enhance management involvement in the transition process. Committees, acting in an advisory capacity to the HR department, can be formed for the overall transition program or specific parts or stages of transition. They can be established as one-time committees or standing committees, depending on the duration of the program and their function. The transition program not only benefits from the quality of the combined inputs of committee members but also from the commitment or support obtained when they "buy into" the program. It is difficult for managers to criticize a process of which they are a part.

Typical duties of a committee are to:

- review program needs
- approve the proposed content of the program
- review the methods of presentation and delivery
- review implementation schedules and issues
- recommend potential discussion leaders for the program
- review the program results.

Committees can meet periodically or on an as-needed basis. Needless to say, committee business should be conducted in a professional manner, including precise agendas and brief meetings. Otherwise, members may lose interest and not attend. The selection of the members of the committee is also important. Members should be key managers and influential executives who are knowledgeable and well-respected within the organization. A committee composed of ineffective managers commanding little respect in the organization has little effectiveness, causing it to get bogged down in irrelevant matters and to lose the clout and credibility it could otherwise have. Before deciding to use the committee approach, the HR department should review the potential benefits and determine whether they outweigh the difficulties. Some organizations have a committee for every stage of transition while others manage to survive without them.

Program Design. Another potential area for management involvement is through the use of a program design task force. The task force consists of a group of employees, usually managers, who are charged with the responsibility for developing the transition program or some part of it. This approach is useful when the development task is beyond the capability of the HR staff or when time requirements to develop a program need to be reduced considerably. A major difference between a task force and a committee is that the task force is required to produce a tangible product. They must devote considerable effort to the task, varying from a two-week assignment to a six-month, full-time project. This time span, of course, depends on the nature of the program being developed and the availability of task force members. The selection of members for a task force is even more critical than for a committee. A typical task force may include management or nonmanagement personnel who possess the particular expertise needed for the project. Including management on the task force can add additional credibility and gain additional influence that might help the program succeed once it is completed. One limitation of management personnel is that they may not be available to contribute the time needed for project completion.

The task force design approach is economical. It relieves the HR staff from the time-consuming activity of program development, which may be impossible for a professional area unfamiliar to the staff. In some cases it is not only an effective approach, but it is absolutely necessary to achieve the desired results.

Program Evaluation. Management involvement in program evaluation can affect the quality of evaluation data as well as the acceptance of the transition process. Three primary areas of management involvement in evaluation are common. The first concerns the design of the evaluation system. Management input is helpful to determine what data are important, what data are feasible to collect, and who should collect it. Assistance in evaluation design may come in the form of a permanent committee assignment, as discussed earlier, or in an ad hoc committee formed to focus specifically on the evaluation process. A second important area involves supplying data used in the evaluation process. As discussed earlier, data may be collected in the form of feedback on the program design or through evaluation of graduates during and after the program. Managers, particularly those with direct responsibility over graduates, are in a unique position to provide meaningful evaluation data. The third area for manager involvement is in analyzing the results achieved in the program. In this role, managers become the target audience for communication of evaluation data, passing judgment on what has been achieved. A variety of management groups should be targeted for potential information on evaluation (see Chapter Seven). Although this phase of involvement may not be active, it can be an important part of the managerial influence on the transition program.

Meetings with Upper Management. The final area for management involvement focuses on meetings with the top management group. Although upper management has many opportunities to be involved in different phases of transition, their active involvement should be encouraged in four distinct meetings. The first occurs in the initial phases of the program, usually at orientation, when senior executives are assigned the task of introducing the new graduates to the organization. As an alternative, a casual meeting with the new recruits on the first day of the program may suffice. The visibility of top management early in the transition process is important to most new college graduates. A second opportunity, informal rap sessions with top executives, allows small groups of new graduates to meet with the key executives to discuss their concerns, suggestions, and ideas while at the same time giving them an opportunity to learn about the philosophy and advice from key executives. This exercise can be of tremendous importance to new graduates and can also be a refreshing experience for executives. It provides them an opportunity to observe the attitude, ideas, and philosophy of new graduates who will probably advance to become future leaders of the organization. The nature and scope of these rap sessions were discussed earlier in this chapter. A third opportunity is for upper management to be involved in ceremonial events at the completion of a program, "graduation time" as it is called in some transition programs. Top executives should be encouraged to make end-of-program presentations and issue challenges to new graduates as they embark on their career advancement in the organization. A final type of meeting with top management is during follow-up sessions with graduates, as part of the evaluation process discussed in Chapter Seven. Having top executives participate in, or even conduct, interviews with a group of former participants can be an enlightening experience, not only for the executive but for the former graduates who will realize that their suggestions and ideas are still desired by the organization.

Benefits of Management Involvement. In summary, management involvement in the transition process results in five major benefits:

1. It adds more credibility to the program than it might otherwise have.
2. The program belongs to the management group, since they have been involved in the process of developing, conducting, or evaluating it.
3. Graduates and the HR staff have more interaction with management, which develops a stronger working relationship.
4. It sharpens the skills of managers involved in the process.
5. It is sometimes more economical to use other managers than to add staff to the HR department.

Using Mentors in Transition Programs

Mentors provide an opportunity for significant management involvement in many transition programs. A mentor is a very special person in a graduate's career development. In the context of a formal transition program, a mentor is usually a manager or executive who serves as a counselor, teacher, and friend to a new college graduate. Other labels such as "role model," "adviser," "career counselor," or "coach" are sometimes used to describe this individual. A mentor relationship can reap benefits for the organization, but only if certain conditions are met and mentors are properly selected and prepared for their assignments.

Benefits of Mentoring. The benefits derived from mentoring are shared by the graduates, mentors, and the organization. New graduates, eager to learn the organization, can progress more rapidly and gain more experience with mentors than without them. Graduates are provided exposure to problems and opportunities that they may not otherwise encounter. They receive help on personal development problems and learn how to cope with difficult situations and confront career development issues. Graduates are sometimes inspired by their mentors to achieve or go beyond desired levels of performance.

Mentors benefit from this special relationship. They have an opportunity to contribute to the development of new talent. The experience in working with new graduates often improves their skills and provides them the opportunity to utilize and shape their own experiences. In some cases, outstanding new graduates can even challenge mentors by stretching their imagination.

The organization benefits in two important ways. First, the output of the transition program can be enhanced through the use of mentors if the relationship is effective and productive. Transition problems, particularly culture shock, can be minimized through a productive mentor relationship. Second, the use of several mentors builds support for the transition process and increases commitment to the overall transition effort. Mentors have positive feelings about a process in which they participate.

Selection Criteria and Duties. To help ensure that the process works effectively, mentors need to be carefully selected and prepared for their assignments. Several criteria are important to the success of mentors. First, mentors should have a desire to participate in the mentor relationship and volunteer for the assignment. They must have an interest in encouraging and helping new graduates. Second, mentors must have an excellent reputation in the organization, with a successful track record, or they will not be perceived as important role models. Third, mentors must know the organization's products, processes, and services. They should know how the organization functions and how it relates to others in the industry. Fourth, mentors must understand organizational politics and be able to provide advice and assistance for new graduates as they confront political issues. Understanding and adjusting to organizational politics is one of the important areas where new graduates experience difficulty in adjusting to the organization. Fifth, mentors must know what it takes to succeed on the job. They do not have to be in senior executive positions to know this. In some cases, managers know what it takes to move up but are unwilling to pay the price for these movements. Sixth, mentors must be able to relate to young talent, since most of the participants in the transition program will be young college graduates whose values, beliefs, and philosophies may differ considerably from their own.

The selection criteria helps to define the basic duties and responsibilities of mentors. Typical duties include:

- providing guidance to help new graduates make important decisions
- discussing alternative choices and opportunities as new graduates develop careers
- teaching new graduates the skills, knowledge, and attitudes necessary for success on the job
- inspiring new graduates to perform at their best on job assignments and during education and training efforts
- giving visibility and recognition to new graduates as they adjust to the organization and perform on the job
- helping new graduates resolve political and social dilemmas
- coaching the new graduates to help them build on strengths and overcome weaknesses
- counseling graduates on performance problems and sensitive issues that may impede success on the job.

Other duties and responsibilities may be added as necessary to meet the specific needs of the transition program. For additional information on mentor duties and responsibilities, see Kram (1985a).

Preparing for a Formal Program. Informal mentoring usually occurs in every transition program, whether it is designed as a part of the process or not. The issue becomes the degree to which the process should be formalized as an integral component of the transition program. Recent evidence suggests that organizations can facilitate effective mentoring by creating certain conditions around which a relationship can evolve (Kram, 1985b). The following conditions or guidelines can help ensure that a formal mentor program meets the needs of graduates and mentors. First, the role of mentors needs to be clearly defined. They must understand their responsibilities to the new graduate, to the transition program, and to the organization. Second, if necessary, special training should be provided to help mentors develop coaching and counseling skills. Not all successful managers or specialists have grasped the needed skills, at least to the level that may be required in a formal mentoring relationship. Third, expectations should be outlined indicating what is required from each party. This may come in the form of specific objectives developed for the mentoring component of transition. For example, at Merrill-Lynch, a formal mentoring effort, as part of the firm's Management Readiness Program, included the following objectives:

1. help generate high-level management support and visibility
2. build bridges between high-level managers and new employees
3. help participants learn about the firm's culture
4. increase networking
5. provide opportunities for talented people developers to be seen.

These objectives help new graduates as well as mentors (Farren, Gray, and Kaye, 1984).

Fourth, the rules, regulations, and procedures governing the mentor relationship should be kept to a minimum. Mentors and graduates should feel free to meet whenever necessary and discuss whatever items are important to new graduates. Written feedback should be kept to a minimum, possibly limited to feedback data for evaluation purposes. This approach can help ensure that excessive rules and regulations do not stifle an otherwise effective process. Fifth, mentors should be rewarded for their efforts and given visibility for these assignments. Naturally, they will gain the self-satisfaction of knowing that they assisted and guided new graduates, but more tangible rewards are recommended. Some organizations feature mentors in their internal communications and others provide plaques and gifts for mentors. Still others recognize them during special occasions or provide bonuses and larger pay increases.

Sixth, the new graduate's immediate supervisor, who may be threatened by the mentor relationship, should be involved. In some organizations mentors are encouraged to meet with the graduate's immediate supervisor to discuss problems and achievements.

Last, but not least, mentor relationships should be allowed to die a natural death when they are no longer needed, even if the new graduate has not completed the transition program. In some cases, after the formal transition program is over, mentor relationships may continue and this should be allowed, as long as it does not place a heavy burden on mentors.

Dangers in the Relationship. In some cases mentor relationships can create problems. New graduates may identify too much with the mentor, which may stifle other opportunities. An overprotective mentor may shield new graduates from the results of their mistakes. There can be competition between mentors supporting different candidates. Each mentor may want to promote or advance his or her candidate over others. Also, in situations involving male/female relationships, particularly with male mentors and female new graduates, the relationship can lead to unwanted and unproductive sexual intimidation. This can lower morale or lead to a sexual harrassment charge against the mentor and organization. However, even with these dangers, mentor relationships, particularly when used as part of the transition program, can be an effective approach to help new college graduates succeed on the job.

Summary

This final chapter has explored a variety of administrative issues concerning the smooth and efficient coordination of a formal transition effort. It explored important and sensitive concerns such as reporting relationships, budget and cost considerations, compensation arrangements for graduates, the role and duties of the program coordinator, the influence of the management group, and a variety of ways in which management can be involved in the transition effort. A concluding section on the use of mentors highlighted the importance of mentor relationships, which are becoming an integral part of transition programs. All of these administrative and coordination issues are extremely important to the effective functioning of a transition program, and proper attention must be devoted to each area to ensure success for the transition process.

References

Alderfer, C. P. *Existence, Relatedness, and Growth: Human Needs in Organizational Settings.* New York: Free Press, 1972.

Arthur, D. *Recruiting, Interviewing, Selecting and Orienting New Employees.* New York: AMACOM, 1986.

Babbush, H. E., and Bormann, A. G. *College Relations and Recruiting.* Bethlehem, Pa.: The College Placement Council, 1982.

Barocci, T. A., and Cournoyer, P. E. "Make or Buy: Computer Professionals in a Demand Driven Environment." Sloan School of Management, MIT, Working Paper #1342-82, Sept. 1982, pp. 4-6.

Behrman, J. N., and Levin, R. I. "Are Business Schools Doing Their Jobs?" *Harvard Business Review,* Jan.-Feb. 1984, pp. 140-147.

Bennett, R. L. *Careers Through Cooperative Work Experience.* New York: Wiley, 1977.

Bergmann, T., and Taylor, S. M. "College Recruitment: What Attracts Students to Organizations?" *Personnel,* 1984, *61,* 34-46.

Berlew, D., and Hall, D. "The Socialization of Managers: Effects of Expectations on Performance." *Administrative Science Quarterly,* 1966, *2,* 207-233.

Bewayo, E. D. "What Employees Look for in First and Subsequent Employers." *Personnel,* Apr. 1986, pp. 49-54.

Bittel, L. R., and Ramsey, J. E. "What to Do About Misfit Supervisors." *Management Review,* Mar. 1983, pp. 37-43.

Blakeslee, G. S., Suntrup, E. L., and Kernaghan, J. A. "How Much

Is Turnover Costing You?" *Personnel Journal,* Nov. 1985, pp. 98-103.

Breaugh, J. A. "Realistic Job Previews: A Critical Appraisal and Future Research Directions." *Academy of Management Review,* 1983, *8* (4), 612-619.

Brief, A. P. "Undoing the Educational Process of the Newly-Hired Professional." *Personnel Administrator,* Sept. 1982, pp. 55-58.

Brush, D. H. "Technical Knowledge or Managerial Skills? (Recruiting Graduates Who Have Both)." *Personnel Journal,* Nov. 1979, pp. 771-804.

Buchanan, B. "Building Organizational Commitment: The Socialization of Managers in Work Organizations." *Administrative Science Quarterly,* 1974, *19,* 533-546.

Buss, D. D. "Job Tryouts Without Pay Get More Testing in U.S. Auto Plants." *The Wall Street Journal,* Jan. 10, 1985, p. 29.

Byham, W. C. "How Assessment Centers Are Used to Evaluate Training's Effectiveness." *Training,* Feb. 1982, p. 32.

Byham, W. C. "Screening and Selection." In W. R. Tracey (ed.), *Human Resources Management and Development Handbook.* New York: AMACOM, 1985.

Campbell, L. B., and others. "Unlikely Partners: Company, Town and Gown." *Harvard Business Review,* Nov.-Dec. 1985, pp. 20-28.

Cascio, W. F. *Costing Human Resources.* New York: Van Nostrand Reinhold, 1982.

Cheit, E. F. "Business Schools and Their Critics." *California Management Review,* 1985, *27* (3), 43-62.

Christenson, C., and others. *Supervising.* Reading, Mass.: Addison-Wesley, 1982.

Cotton, J. L., and Tuttle, J. M. "Employee Turnover: A Meta-Analysis and Review with Implications for Research." *Academy of Management Review,* 1986, *2* (1), 55-70.

Cox, A. *The Cox Report on the American Corporation.* New York: Delacorte Press, 1982.

Dean, R. A., Ferris, K. R., and Konstans, C. "Reality Shock: Reducing the Organizational Commitment of Professionals." *Personnel Administrator,* June 1985, pp. 139-148.

Denova, C. C. *Test Construction for Training Evaluation.* New York: Van Nostrand Reinhold, 1979.

Derr, C. B. *Managing the New Careerists: The Diverse Career Success Orientations of Today's Workers.* San Francisco: Jossey-Bass, 1986.

Dobandi, B., and Schattle, A. "Internships: The Mutually Beneficial Relationship." *Personnel Administrator,* May 1984, pp. 101-115.

Dugoni, B. L., and Ilgen, D. R. "Realistic Job Previews and the Adjustment of New Employees." *Academy of Management Journal,* 1981, *24,* 579-591.

Dunn, S., and Thomas, K. "Surpassing the 'Smile Sheet' Approach to Evaluation." *Training,* Apr. 1985, pp. 65-71.

Edwards, C. "Aggressive Recruitment: The Lessons of High-Tech Hiring." *Personnel Journal,* Jan. 1986, pp. 40-48.

Elkins, A. "Some Views on Management Training." *Personnel Journal,* June 1977, 305-311.

Ellig, B. R. "Total Compensation Design: Elements and Issues." *Personnel,* Jan.-Feb. 1984, pp. 22-30.

Farren, C., Gray, J. D., and Kaye, B. "Mentoring: A Boon to Career Development." *Personnel,* Nov.-Dec. 1984, 20-24.

Feldman, D. C. "A Contingency Theory of Socialization." *Administrative Science Quarterly,* 1976a, *21,* 433-454.

Feldman, D. C. "A Practical Program for Employee Socialization." *Organizational Dynamics,* 1976b, *57* (2), 64-80.

Feldman, D. C. "A Socialization Process that Helps New Recruits Succeed." *Personnel,* 1980, *53,* 11-23.

Feldman, D. C. "The Multiple Socialization of Organization Members." *Academy of Management Review,* 1981, *6,* 309-318.

Filoroma, T., and Ziff, D. *Nurse Recruitment Strategies for Success.* Baltimore, Md.: Aspen Systems Corporation, 1980.

Fisher, C. D. "Social Support and Adjustment to Work: A Longitudinal Study." *Journal of Management,* 1986, *11* (3), 39-53.

Fitz-enz, J. *How to Measure Human Resources Management.* New York: McGraw-Hill, 1984.

Fitz-enz, J. "HR Measurement: Formulas for Success." *Personnel Journal,* Oct. 1985, pp. 53-60.

Flamholtz, E. G. *Human Resource Accounting: Advances in Concepts, Methods, and Applications.* (2nd ed.) San Francisco: Jossey-Bass, 1985.

Ford, R. N. *Why Jobs Die and What to Do About It: Job Redesign and Future Productivity.* New York: AMACOM, 1979.

Fournies, F. L. *Coaching for Improved Work Performance.* New York: Van Nostrand Reinhold, 1978.

Gael, S. *Job Analysis: A Guide to Assessing Work Activities.* San Francisco: Jossey-Bass, 1983.

Ghiselli, E. C., Campbell, J. P., and Zedeck, S. *Management Theory for the Behavioral Sciences.* San Francisco: Freeman, 1981.

"Give the Full Recruiting Picture." *Industry Week,* Aug. 5, 1985, p. 5.

Goddard, R. W. "The Pygmalion Effect." *Personnel Journal,* June 1985, pp. 10-16.

Goddard, R. W. "Why Hire Humanities Graduates?" *Personnel Journal,* Feb. 1986, pp. 22-26.

Gomersall, E. R., and Myers, M. S. "Breakthrough in On-the-Job Training." *Harvard Business Review,* 1966, *44,* 62-72.

Hacker, A. "The Shame of Professional Schools." *Harper's,* Oct. 1981, pp. 22-28.

Hall, D. T. *Careers in Organizations.* Pacific Palisades, Calif.: Goodyear, 1976.

Hall, T. "How to Estimate Employee Turnover Cost." *Personnel,* July-Aug. 1981, pp. 43-52.

Henderson, R. I. *Performance Appraisal.* (2nd ed.) Reston, Va.: Reston Publishing, 1984.

Henerson, M. E., Morris, L. L., and Fitz-Gibbon, C. T. *How to Measure Attitudes.* Beverly Hills, Calif.: Sage Publications, 1978.

Hite, R. E. "How to Hire Using College Internship Programs." *Personnel Journal,* Feb. 1986, pp. 110-112.

Hollman, R. W. "Let's Not Forget About New Employee Orientation." *Personnel Journal,* 1976, *55,* 244-250.

Jarrell, D. W. "Professional Development: Get Them Early." *Training in Business and Industry,* Feb. 1974, pp. 23-26.

Jenkins, R. L., Reizenstein, R. C., and Rodgers, F. G. "Report Cards on the MBA." *Harvard Business Review,* Sept.-Oct. 1984, pp. 20-30.

Johnston, J. S., Jr., and Associates. *Educating Managers: Executive Effectiveness Through Liberal Learning.* San Francisco: Jossey-Bass, 1986.

Jones, G. R. "Socialization Tactics, Self-Efficiency, and Newcomers' Adjustment to Organizations." *Academy of Management Journal,* 1986, *29* (2), 262-279.

Kaible, N. "Recruitment and Socialization at Procter & Gamble." Stanford Graduate School of Business, Case II S-BP-236, May 1984.

Kaplan, E. "College Recruitment: The View from Both Sides." *Personnel,* Nov. 1985, pp. 44-48.

Kastens, M. L. *Redefining the Manager's Job.* New York: AMACOM, 1980.

Kearsley, G. *Costs, Benefits and Productivity in Training Systems.* Reading, Mass.: Addison-Wesley, 1982.

Kenney, R. M. "Open House Complements Recruitment Strategies." *Personnel Administrator,* Mar. 1982, pp. 27-32.

Kerlinger, F. N. *Foundations of Behavioral Research.* (3rd ed.) New York: Holt, Rinehart & Winston, 1986.

King, P. *Performance Planning and Appraisal: A How-To Book for Managers.* New York: McGraw-Hill, 1984.

Kirkpatrick, D. L. "Evaluating Training Programs: Evidence vs. Proof." *Training and Development Journal,* Nov. 1977, pp. 9-12.

Kirkpatrick, D. L. *How to Improve Performance Through Appraisal and Coaching.* New York: AMACOM, 1982.

Kirkpatrick, D. L. *A Practical Guide for Supervisory Training and Development.* (2nd ed.) Reading, Mass.: Addison-Wesley, 1983.

Kirkpatrick, D. L. "Do Training Classes Change Attitudes?" *Personnel,* July 1986, pp. 11-15.

Kleinman, C. "Earn While You Learn Concept of Co-Op Education Gaining Favor." *The Birmingham News,* Aug. 24, 1986, p. 6D.

Koeth, B. "The Making of Merchandising Executives: Macy's,

Retailing's Harvard." *Management Review*, June 1985, pp. 28-34.

Kotter, J. P. "Managing the Joining-Up Process." *Personnel*, 1972, *49*, 46-52.

Kram, K. E. *Mentoring at Work: Development Relationships in Organizational Life.* Glenview, Ill.: Scott, Foresman, 1985a.

Kram, K. E. "Improving the Mentoring Process." *Training and Development Journal*, Apr. 1985b, pp. 40-43.

Lawler, E. E., III. *High-Involvement Management: Participative Strategies for Improving Organizational Performance.* San Francisco: Jossey-Bass, 1986.

Lean, E. "No More Pencils, No More Books." *Training and Development Journal*, Apr. 1985, pp. 62-67.

Levering, R., Moskowitz, M., and Katz, M. *The 100 Best Companies to Work for in America.* Reading, Mass.: Addison-Wesley, 1984.

Lindquist, V. R. *Northwestern Endicott Report 1985.* Evanston, Ill.: The Placement Center, Northwestern University, 1985.

Louis, M. R. "Surprise and Sense-Making: What Newcomers Experience in Entering Unfamiliar Organizational Settings." *Administrative Science Quarterly*, 1980, *25*, 226-251.

McBurney, W. J., Jr. *College Recruitment: Effective Programs and Policies.* New York: AMACOM, 1982.

McCormick, E. J. *Job Analysis: Methods and Applications.* New York: AMACOM, 1979.

Macdonald, C. R. *Performance-Based Supervisory Development: Adapted from a Major AT&T Study.* Amherst, Mass.: Human Resource Development Press, 1982.

McGarrell, E. J., Jr. "An Orientation System that Builds Productivity." *Personnel Administrator.* Oct. 1984, pp. 75-85.

McShane, S. L., and Baal, T. *Employee Socialization Practices on Canada's West Coast: A Management Report.* Burnaby, Br. Col.: Simon Fraser University, 1984.

Manley, M. J., and Barile, L. A. "The Bilateral Job Interview." *American Journal of Nursing*, 1984, *84*, 1237.

Mason, R. E., Haines, P. G., and Furtado, L. T. *Cooperative Occupational Education and Work Experience in the Curricu-*

lum. (3rd ed.) Danville, Ill.: Interstate Printers and Publishers, 1981.

"MBA Interns: Finding the Right Stuff." *Training,* Feb. 1985, p. 82.

Merwin, S. *Effective Evaluation Strategies and Techniques: A Key to Successful Training.* San Diego, Calif.: University Associates, 1986.

Miles, M. B., and Huberman, A. M. *Qualitative Data Analysis: A Sourcebook of New Methods.* Beverly Hills, Calif.: Sage Publications, 1984.

Miles, R. E. "The Future of Business Education." *California Management Review,* 1985, 27 (3), 63–73.

Miner, J. B. *Theories of Organizational Behavior.* Hinsdale, Ill.: Dryden Press, 1980.

Mitchell, E. F. *Cooperative Vocational Education: Principles, Methods and Problems.* Boston: Allyn and Bacon, 1977.

Mobley, W. H. *Employee Turnover: Causes, Consequences, and Control.* Reading, Mass.: Addison-Wesley, 1982.

Mobley, W. H., Griffeth, R. W., Hand, H. H., and Meglino, B. M. "Review and Conceptual Analysis of the Employee Turnover Process." *Psychological Bulletin,* 1979, 86, 493–522.

Moore, E. R. "Competency-Based Evaluation." *Training and Development Journal,* Nov. 1984, pp. 92–94.

Moses, J. L., and Byham, W. C. (eds.). *Applying the Assessment Center Method.* Elmsford, N.Y.: Pergamon Press, 1977.

Mowday, R. T., Porter, L. W., and Steers, R. M. *Employee-Organization Linkages: The Psychology of Commitment, Absenteeism, and Turnover.* New York: Academic Press, 1982.

Nadler, L. *Corporate Human Resources Development: A Management Tool.* New York: Van Nostrand Reinhold, 1980.

Nadler, L. *Design Training Programs: A Critical Events Model.* Reading, Mass.: Addison-Wesley, 1982.

Nadler, L. (ed.). *The Handbook of Human Resource Development.* New York: Wiley, 1984.

Newstrom, J. W. "Catch-22: The Problems of Incomplete Evaluation of Training." *Training and Development Journal,* Nov. 1978, pp. 22–23.

Northrup, H. R., and Malin, M. E. *Personnel Policies for Engineers and Scientists.* Manpower and Human Resources Studies No. 11. Philadelphia: The Wharton School, University of Pennsylvania, 1985.

Odiorne, G. S. *Strategic Management of Human Resources: A Portfolio Approach.* San Francisco: Jossey-Bass, 1984.

Olson, R. F. *Performance Appraisal: A Guide to Greater Productivity.* New York: Wiley, 1981.

Pascale, R. "The Paradox of Corporate Culture: Reconciling Ourselves to Socialization." *California Management Review,* 1985, *27* (2), 26-41.

Patton, M. Q. *Practical Evaluation.* Beverly Hills, Calif.: Sage, 1982.

Pavloff, G. "Career Anchoring Pattern." *HRD Quarterly,* Fall 1986, p. 24. (Published by Organization Design and Development, Suite 310, 101 Bryn Mawr Ave., Bryn Mawr, PA 19010.)

Pearson, J. M. "The Transition Into a New Job: Tasks, Problems and Outcomes." *Personnel Journal,* 1982, *61,* 286-290.

Petty, M. M., McGee, G. W., and Cavender, J. W. "A Meta-Analysis of the Relationships Between Individual Job Satisfaction and Individual Performance." *Academy of Management Review,* 1984, *9* (4), 712-721.

Phillips, J. J. "An Employer Evaluation of a Cooperative Education Program." *Journal of Cooperative Education,* Spring 1978a, pp. 104-120.

Phillips, J. J. "How to Survive a Management Training Program." *Advanced Management Journal,* Spring 1978b, pp. 48-57.

Phillips, J. J. "Effective Orientation Cuts New Employee Turnover." *Foundry Management and Technology,* Dec. 1981, pp. 50-57.

Phillips, J. J. *Handbook of Training Evaluation and Measurement Methods.* Houston: Gulf, 1983a.

Phillips, J. J. "How to Keep from Getting Burned on an Outside Seminar." *Supervision,* Nov. 1983b, pp. 7-10.

Phillips, J. J. *Improving Supervisors' Effectiveness: How Organizations Can Raise the Performance of Their First-Level Managers.* San Francisco: Jossey-Bass, 1985.

Phillips, J. J. "The First Steps Toward Increasing Supervisory Authority." *Management Solutions,* Sept. 1986, pp. 37–39.

Porter, L. W., Lawler, E. E., III, and Hackman, J. R. *Behavior in Organizations.* New York: McGraw-Hill, 1975.

Porter, L. W., and Steers, R. M. "Organizational, Work, and Personal Factors in Employee Turnover and Absenteeism." *Psychological Bulletin,* 1973, *80,* 151–176.

"Practical College Relations." *Personnel Administrator,* June 1985, p. 16.

Price, J. L. *The Study of Turnover.* Ames: Iowa State University Press, 1977.

Reilly, R. R., and others. "The Effects of Realistic Job Previews: A Study and Discussion of the Literature." *Personnel Psychology,* 1981, *34,* 823–834.

Robinson, J. C. *Developing Managers Through Behavior Modeling.* Austin, Texas: Learning Concepts, 1983.

Rock, M. L. *Handbook of Wage and Salary Information.* (2nd ed.) New York: McGraw-Hill, 1984.

Rutman, L. (ed.). *Evaluation Research Methods: A Basic Guide.* (2nd ed.) Beverly Hills, Calif.: Sage, 1984.

Rynes, S. L., Heneman, H. G., and Schwab, D. P. "Individual Reactions to Organizational Recruiting: A Review." *Personnel Psychology,* 1980, *33,* 529–541.

St. John, W. D. "The Complete Employee Orientation Program." *Personnel Journal,* 1980, *60,* 373–378.

Salzman, M. L., and Sullivan, D. A. *Inside Management Training: The Career Guide to Training Programs for College Graduates.* New York: New American Library, 1985.

Sandler, L. "Self-Fulfilling Prophecy: Better Management by Magic." *Training,* Feb. 1986, pp. 60–64.

Schein, E. H. "How to Break in the College Graduate." *Harvard Business Review,* 1964, *42* (6), 68–76.

Schein, E. H. "Organizational Socialization and the Profession of Management." *Industrial Management Review,* 1968, *9,* 1–16.

Schein, E. H. *Career Dynamics: Matching Individual and Organizational Needs.* Reading, Mass.: Addison-Wesley, 1978.

Schein, E. H. *Organizational Culture and Leadership: A Dynamic View.* San Francisco: Jossey-Bass, 1985.

Seidel, R. P., and Powell, G. N. "On the Campus: Matching Graduates with Jobs." *Personnel*, 1983, *60*, 66–72.

Shea, G. F. "Induction and Orientation." In W. R. Tracey (ed.), *Human Resources Management and Development Handbook.* New York: AMACOM, 1985.

Sibson, R. E. *Compensation.* (Rev. ed.) New York: AMACOM, 1981.

Solomon, B. A. "For Carfare and Lunch: An Internship Success." *Personnel*, Mar. 1985, pp. 4–7.

Spencer, L. M., Jr. "Calculating Costs and Benefits." In W. R. Tracey (ed.), *Human Resources Management and Development Handbook.* New York: AMACOM, 1985.

Spencer, L. M., Jr. *Calculating Human Resource Costs and Benefits.* New York: Wiley, 1986.

Stantial, L., and others. "Recruiting Literature: Is It Adequate?" *Journal of College Placement*, Summer 1979, pp. 56–60.

Stone, E. F. *Research Methods in Organizational Behavior.* Santa Monica, Calif.: Goodyear, 1978.

Stoops, R. "The Supply and Demand of College Recruiting." *Personnel Journal*, Apr. 1985, pp. 84–86.

Sudman, S., and Bradburn, N. M. *Asking Questions: A Practical Guide to Questionnaire Design.* San Francisco: Jossey-Bass, 1982.

Swartz, S. "Business Schools Revise Programs to Meet Firms' Changing Needs." *The Wall Street Journal*, Mar. 28, 1985, p. 35.

Tanaka, H. "The Japanese Method of Preparing Today's Graduate to Become Tomorrow's Manager." *Personnel Journal*, Feb. 1980, 109–112.

Thain, R. J., Yoxall, G. J., and Stewart, R. A. *The Campus Connection: Effective College Relations and Recruiting.* New York: Brecker and Merryman, 1979.

Thornton, G., III, and Byham, W. *Assessment Centers and Managerial Performance.* Orlando, Fla.: Academic Press, 1982.

"Those Who Can't, Consult." *Harper's*, Nov. 1982, pp. 8–17.

Tracey, W. R. *Human Resource Development Standards.* New York: AMACOM, 1983.

Tracey, W. R. (ed.). *Human Resources Management and Development Handbook.* New York: AMACOM, 1985.

Van Maanen, J. "Breaking In: Socialization to Work." In R. Dubin (ed.), *Handbook of Work, Organization, and Society.* Chicago: Rand McNally, 1976.

Van Maanen, J. "People Processing: Strategies of Organizational Socialization." *Organizational Dynamics,* Summer 1978, pp. 19-36.

Wahba, M., and Bridwell, N. "Maslow Reconsidered: A Review of Research on the Need Hierarchy Theory." *Organizational Behavior and Human Performance,* 1976, *15,* 212-240.

Walsh, W. B., and Betz, N. E. *Tests and Assessment.* Englewood Cliffs, N.J.: Prentice-Hall, 1985.

Walters, R. W. *Job Enrichment for Results: Strategies for Successful Implementation.* Reading, Mass.: Addison-Wesley, 1975.

Wanous, J. P. *Organizational Entry: Recruitment, Selection and Socialization of Newcomers.* Reading, Mass.: Addison-Wesley, 1980.

Wanous, J. P., and Zwany, A. "A Cross Sectional Test of Need Hierarchy Theory." *Organizational Behavior and Human Performance,* 1977, *18,* 78-97.

Wexley, K. N., and Latham, G. P. *Developing and Training Human Resources in Organizations.* Glenview, Ill.: Scott, Foresman, 1981.

Wilkinson, H. E., and Orth, C. D. "Toning the Soft Side." *Training and Development Journal,* Mar. 1986, pp. 34-36.

Wilson, J. W., and Lyons, E. H. *Work-Study College Programs: Appraisal and Report of the Study of Cooperative Education.* Westport, Conn.: Greenwood Press, 1977.

Winter, D. G., and McClelland, D. C., and Stewart, A. J. *A New Case for the Liberal Arts: Assessing Institutional Goals and Student Development.* San Francisco: Jossey-Bass, 1981.

Yoder, D., and Heneman, H. G., Jr. (eds.). *ASPA Handbook of Personnel and Industrial Relations.* Washington, D.C.: Bureau of National Affairs, 1979.

Youker, R. B. "Ten Benefits of Participant Action Planning." *Training,* June 1985, pp. 52-56.

Index

A

Action plan audit, for evaluation, 243-245

Adaptation: actions in model for, 39-40; analysis of, 183-219; background on, 183; enhancing, 191-202; and job security, 200-202; meetings for, 197-198; newsletter for, 198-199; and performance reviews, 184-191; and Pygmalion effect, 191-193; recognition for, 193-197; social activities for, 199-200; and substandard performance, 202-206; summary on, 219

Administration: costs of, and turnover, 21-22; issues of, 264-299

Advisory committees, involvement of, 290-291

AeroJet-General, teleconferenced recruitment by, 112

Affirmative action: and cooperative education, 48-49; and recruitment, 75, 90, 99; and walk-in applicants, 90

Alabama, University of, in partnership, 60-61

Alderfer, C. P., 107

Ambiguity, role, evaluation of, 255-256

American Marketing Association, 179

American Society for Production and Inventory Control, 179

American Society for Quality Control, 179

American Stock Exchange Conference, 7

American Telephone and Telegraph (AT&T): behavior modeling at, 172; and liberal arts majors, 78; recruitment teleconferencing by, 112

Analysis exercises, in job simulations, 100

Apprenticeship, strategy of, 31-32

Arthur, D., 72

Assessment center method: for evaluation, 240-241, 245; for recruitment, 101-104

Assignments: actions in model for, 40-41; authority in, 209-210; background on, 183-184; for cooperative education, 49-51; developing, 208-209; follow-up, 242; and future, 217-219; for internships, 55-57; involvement in, 216-217; permanent, 211-219; productive and challenging, 206-208; responsibility in, 209-210, 213-215; short-term, 178; status of, 215-216; summary on, 219; for summer employment, 66; supervisor important to, 211-213; temporary, 206-210;